Regional Distribution of Soviet Industrial Manpower: 1940-60

Regional Distribution of Soviet Industrial Manpower: 1940-60

Emilo J. Stanley

FREDERICK A. PRAEGER, Publishers
New York · Washington · London

The purpose of the Praeger Special Studies is to make specialized research monographs in U.S. and international economics and politics available to the academic, business, and government communities. For further information, write to the Special Projects Division, Frederick A. Praeger, Publishers, 111 Fourth Avenue, New York, N.Y. 10003.

FREDERICK A. PRAEGER, PUBLISHERS
111 Fourth Avenue, New York, N.Y. 10003, U.S.A.
77-79 Charlotte Street, London W.1, England

Published in the United States of America in 1968
by Frederick A. Praeger, Inc., Publishers

Library of Congress Catalog Card Number: 67-22284

Printed in the United States of America

To Joan,

Kent, Kim,

Karen, and Kristin

ACKNOWLEDGMENTS

The topic of this study was suggested to me by Professor George Kish and my interest in it was prompted by a desire to fill a gap in our knowledge of the geographic distribution of the Soviet industry. The Soviet policy of revealing only selective statistical data on their industrial development has been a serious obstacle for most researchers. My modest hope is that this study might prove of value in other studies of the Soviet industry that will be developed when the additional detailed data (e. g., gross industrial output) become available for all the major economic regions and their subdivisions.

An earlier version of this study was submitted as a doctoral dissertation to the Department of Geography at the University of Michigan and I should like to thank Professor George Kish, under whose supervision the original work was undertaken, for his advice and counsel.

I would like to express my gratitude for the financial support for the original work obtained from the Ford Foundation through the Public Affairs Research Committee of Beloit College, Beloit, Wisconsin, and also to Pitzer College, Claremont, California, for a publication grant. Finally, I owe a great debt to Miss Elizabeth Moses who prepared all the maps and charts for this study.

The responsibility for any errors and misjudgments which may be found in this study is, of course, wholly that of the author.

E. J. S.

Claremont, California

CONTENTS

Chapter | Page

APPENDIXES Page

LIST OF TABLES

Table		Page

LIST OF FIGURES

LIST OF MAPS

Map		Page

GLOSSARY

A. S. S. R.	Autonomous Soviet Socialist Republic, an administrative subdivision similar to an oblast
Kray	Administrative subdivision (usually very large) of the R. S. F. S. R. or a S. S. R.
Oblast	Basic administrative subdivision of the R. S. F. S. R. or a S. S. R.
R. S. F. S. R.	Russian Soviet Federated Socialist Republic
Sovnarkhoz (plural: sovnarkhozy)	Council of the National Economy (in Russian: Soviet narodnogo khozyaystva)
S. S. R.	Soviet Socialist Republic (one of the 15 union republics)

Regional Distribution of Soviet Industrial Manpower: 1940-60

CHAPTER 1 INTRODUCTION

This study is concerned mainly with the problem of graphically presenting the geographic distribution of Soviet industrial manpower. Therefore, it is necessary first to describe briefly the territorial extent of the Soviet Union since 1940 and its political and economic subdivisions.

As the year 1940 drew to a close, the Soviet Union experienced the end of a period of brief but significant territorial growth. Most of the territories that were part of the Russian Empire in 1914, and had to be given up temporarily after the Revolution in 1917 due to the weakness of the fledgling Soviet state, were again within the fold of the U. S. S. R. Finland was a major exception, and although it was defeated in the Winter War of 1939-40, the Soviet Union did not force that country to rejoin her former master but was satisfied with rather minor boundary corrections that indicated Soviet awareness of a potential threat to Leningrad. On the other hand, the Baltic countries (Estonia, Latvia, and Lithuania) ceased to exist as sovereign states and were quickly incorporated into the U. S. S. R. in 1940. The eastern part of Poland was occupied by Soviet troops as part of a secret agreement under the Stalin-Ribbentrop pact of August, 1939, and most of that area was absorbed into the Belorussian S. S. R. and the Ukrainian S. S. R. Bessarabia and Northern Bukovina taken from Romania completed the Soviet acquisitions in Europe in 1940. Thus, by the end of that year, the Soviet Union achieved approximately the territorial extent of the present state. Further gains were made in Europe (the Ruthenian part of Czechoslovakia, and the northern half of former German East Prussia) and in Asia (the southern half of Sakhalin Island, the Kuriles, and Tannu Tuva) by 1945.

In terms of the organizational structure of political administrative units, the territory of the Soviet Union is divided first into fifteen union republics (Soviet Socialist Republics or S. S. R. 's).[1] The boundaries of these republics enclose the fifteen largest and most advanced ethnic groups in the U. S. S. R. as the whole system of political administrative units is based on the principle of nationalities.[2] The largest and most important is the Russian Soviet Federated Socialist Republic (R. S. F. S. R.), occupying about three-fourths of the area and over one-half of the population of the U. S. S. R. The other union republics are the Ukrainian, Moldavian, Belorussian, Lithuanian, Latvian, and Estonian S. S. R. , in the western U. S. S. R. ; Azerbaydzhan, Armenian, and Georgian S. S. R. , in the Trans-Caucasus; and Kazakh, Uzbek, Turkmen, Kirgiz, and Tadzhik S. S. R. , in Soviet Central Asia.

Except for the five smaller republics (Estonian, Latvian, Lithuanian, Moldavian, and Armenian S. S. R.), the union republics and the R. S. F. S. R. are divided into oblasts, krays, and Autonomous Soviet Socialist Republics (A. S. S. R. 's). The oblast is the basic administrative subdivision, roughly comparable to a county in the United States; the A. S. S. R. is similar to an oblast, except that it incorporates an important minority ethnic group, while the kray is usually a very large and sparsely settled territory, mostly in Siberia and in Kazakhstan.[3] While all the three subdivisions (oblast, kray, and A. S. S. R.) are at the same level in the Soviet administrative hierarchy--all three being directly responsible to the R. S. F. S. R. or the union republic--the only subdivision found in all the S. S. R. 's (except the five smaller republics mentioned above) and in the R. S. F. S. R. is the oblast. On the other hand, only three S. S. R. 's and the R. S. F. S. R. contain Autonomous Republics (A. S. S. R. 's), while krays are found only in the R. S. F. S. R. and in one S. S. R. (Kazakh).

Superimposed on the structure of political administrative units in the Soviet Union are fourteen major economic regions which are mainly used for economic planning and also for statistical purposes. The R. S. F. S. R. is divided into nine major economic regions: Center, Northwest, North, North Caucasus, Volga, Ural, West Siberia, East Siberia, and the Far East. The other fourteen union republics are grouped into five major economic regions: South (Ukrainian and Moldavian S. S. R.), West (Belorussian, Lithuanian,

Latvian, and Estonian S. S. R.), Trans-Caucasus (Armenian, Georgian, and Azerbaydzhan S. S. R.), Central Asia (Uzbek, Kirgiz, Turkmen, and Tadzhik S. S. R.), and Kazakh S. S. R. representing a separate major economic region (Kazakhstan). Although the number of the major economic regions and their boundaries have been changing during the Soviet era, during most of the period covered by this study (1940-60) their number (fourteen) and their boundaries have remained stable and are shown on all the maps in this study.

Following the reorganization of Soviet industrial administration in 1957, a system of 104 economic administrative regions or _sovnarkhozy_ was established.[4] The purpose of the _sovnarkhozy_ was to coordinate the control of industries on a regional basis and thus to replace the industrial ministries that exercised a centralized control from Moscow over all the branches of the Soviet industry.[5] In most cases an _oblast_, _kray_, or A. S. S. R. became a _sovnarkhoz_, while in a few cases a _sovnarkhoz_ contained two or more _oblasts_. Also eleven of the S. S. R. 's consisted of one _sovnarkhoz_ each, while the Ukrainian, Uzbek and Kazakh S. S. R. were each divided into several _sovnarkhozy_. The appendixes contain the list of all the 104 _sovnarkhozy_, within the major economic regions to which they belong, and a map showing their boundaries as of 1958.

One of the inspirations for this study was the realization that there was a definite need for such a regional approach, a suggestion made during the conference on the Study of the Soviet Economy held in February, 1961, at Indiana University. As Professor Campbell pointed out, "since past research has been aggregative, we know very little just in descriptive terms about regional differences . . . , the variety of development (or stagnation) patterns that different regions have experienced."[6] Adding that "some might recommend that this kind of work be left to geographers," he emphasized that "such regional studies would be interesting in themselves, but in addition they are one of the ingredients required for interpreting the total system."[7] The author of this study, who participated at the 1961 conference, became interested in a regional study and over a period of several years gathered the material from Soviet regional statistical handbooks which were being published in profusion providing much of the material that was not available before. The decision to attempt this study was made after it became clear that a serious gap existed in our knowledge of the regional distribution of Soviet industrial manpower but also the author could agree with the statement that the time for such an attempt was propitious since "we can now hope realistically to tackle some of the problems--left undone before--because of better data availability."[8]

Once the study was defined as a regional approach to the analysis of the pattern of distribution of Soviet industry, the decision had to be made regarding what quantitative data should be used. This does not imply that we have a wealth of information and thus can choose one set of data as against another; rather the question is posed in order to indicate the alternatives that any study of economic geography, regardless of the country, might present. The alternative is the choice of a particular criterion to be used in the study. If the data for gross industrial output, the number of industrial workers, or the number of industrial establishments were available for the Soviet Union, we would have to decide which of the criteria would best show an accurate pattern of distribution of Soviet industry. A study of American industry has indicated that most of the criteria had a very high coefficient of correlation (.99), and thus it seems that it does not matter which particular criterion is used.[9] Certainly the number of industrial workers, which had a coefficient of correlation of .99 with value added in the study of American industry, could be assumed to have the same degree of accuracy in a study of Soviet industry.[10] However, the main reason that the employment data are used throughout this study is that Soviet data on industrial employment are easier to obtain and are more accurate than the data for value of industrial output.

The main sources of detailed data on Soviet industrial employment are not conveniently available in one volume, such as the Statistical Abstract of the United States. To obtain the detailed regional data, a total of fifty-one _oblast_, six _kray_, fifteen A. S. S. R., and fourteen S. S. R. statistical handbooks are used. The Central Statistical Administration of the Council of Ministers of the U. S. S. R. has published since 1957 the statistical abstracts of all _oblasts_, _krays_, and A. S. S. R. 's of the R. S. F. S. R. except two: Kamchatka _oblast_ and Kaliningrad _oblast_.[11] All other union republics have published their abstracts and most now have also an annual yearbook (yezhegodnik). Unfortunately, very few oblast statistical handbooks have appeared for the union republics. For example, six of the twenty-five oblasts in the Ukraine, fourteen of the sixteen oblasts in the Kazakh S. S. R., nine out of ten in the Uzbek S. S. R., are still not accounted for in detail.[12]

Although the statistical handbooks used in this study represent the whole administrative hierarchy from oblast and kray to A. S. S. R. and union republic (S. S. R.), the basic statistical unit that will be used in the analysis is an economic administrative region or sovnarkhoz with the boundaries as of September 1, 1958. This will not appreciably change the use of most of the abstracts but will rather simplify it.

Another reason for using sovnarkhozy as the basis for this study (when greater detail is required and the breakdown by major economic regions is not quite sufficient) is the fact that some data for 1955 are available for all sovnarkhozy of the Ukraine and Kazakh S. S. R. (but not for all their oblasts). Thus, whenever possible, the analysis will proceed on the basis of 104 sovnarkhozy of the U. S. S. R., and for summarizing the distribution and changes in the pattern of Soviet industry, the discussion will be conducted on the level of major economic regions.

The goal during the research for this study has been to obtain the fullest possible data on the number and the distribution of industrial workers in the Soviet Union for the selected years between 1940 and 1960. When all the available statistical handbooks had been carefully examined, it was evident that the only years for which data were available for all the sovnarkhozy were 1940 and 1955. However, at the level of major economic regions, as explained at the end of this chapter, additional data for 1960 were obtained, making it possible to compare the years 1940 and 1960; at the level of sovnarkhozy, the latest year for which sufficient data are available is 1955. Many sovnarkhozy included also data for 1945 and 1950.

The actual procedure used to obtain or calculate the number of workers consisted of two steps. Here again, the information was almost never available in one table. Usually, first the part of a handbook devoted to "Labor" had to be consulted to obtain the number of industrial-production personnel. This term refers to workers and employees (engineering-technical personnel, salaried employees, and others). Next, another table under "Industry" might give the breakdown of workers by major industrial branches. This breakdown usually was given in the following order: energy and fuel industries, ferrous and nonferrous metallurgy (heavy industry), machine-building and metal-working industries, chemical industries, building materials industry, forest industries, light industry, and food industry.

The data for all S. S. R.'s were complete except that the Lithuanian S. S. R. lacked the breakdown by industries for 1940. At the level of *sovnarkhozy* the data for S. S. R.'s were less complete: eleven S. S. R.'s which consist of one *sovnarkhoz* each, had complete data (except Lithuania--see above), while the Ukrainian, Kazakh and Uzbek S. S. R.'s had data at the level of the republic only (except that the total number of workers in all industries was available by *sovnarkhozy* for the year 1955). On the other hand, the gaps in statistical data for the sixty-eight *sovnarkhozy* of the R. S. F. S. R. were substantial (especially for 1940) as Table 1 illustrates.

Although the latest year for which sufficient data are available at the level of *sovnarkhozy* is 1955, at the level of major economic regions it was possible to obtain the data for 1960. Basically, three sources were used to calculate the 1960 data: (1) the total number of Soviet industrial-production personnel for the eight major branches of industry was obtained from the *U. S. S. R. Statistical Handbook* for 1964;[13] (2) the breakdown of industrial workers by industrial branches for all the major economic regions from a book by L. N. Telepko;[14] and (3) the total number of industrial-production personnel by major economic regions from the *U. S. S. R. Statistical Handbook* for 1960.[15]

The Soviet statistical handbooks for the U. S. S. R. and the R. S. F. S. R. since 1961 have not included the data for the geographic distribution of industrial workers by major economic regions and their breakdowns by industrial branches. We can only hope that the future editions of the Soviet handbooks will be more informative and more complete to make possible some meaningful comparisons in terms of

TABLE 1

Statistical Data Available for the 68 Sovnarkhozy of the R. S. F. S. R.
(Published in Separate Statistical Handbooks)

Data Available	Number of sovnarkhozy for which data are available: 1940	Number of sovnarkhozy for which data are available: 1955
Number of workers and breakdown by industries given	38	55
Number of workers given but no breakdown by industry	19	3
Number of workers missing but breakdown by industry given	2	3
No data in handbook for either workers or the breakdown	6	4
No handbooks published yet[a]	2	3
Total number of sovnarkhozy of the R. S. F. S. R.	67[b]	68

Notes: [a]See Note 11 to Chapter 1.
[b]Kaliningrad sovnarkhoz was not part of the U. S. S. R. in 1940.

chronological changes and geographical distribution of Soviet industrial employment. As long as such data are not available, this study might help to overcome that deficiency, at least temporarily.

Notes to Chapter 1

1. The Karelo-Finnish S. S. R. was established as the 16th union republic in 1940 and was abolished in 1956. It is now known as the Karelian A. S. S. R.

2. Paul E. Lydolph, *Geography of the U. S. S. R.* (New York: John Wiley and Sons, 1964), p. 21.

3. *Ibid.*, pp. 21-22.

4. *Sovnarkhozy* is the plural form of *sovnarkhoz*, an abbreviation for *Soviet narodnogo khozyaystva* or council of the national economy. *Sovnarkhoz* is the term used both for the council of the national economy (an administrative body) and for the territory (economic administrative region) under its control. The latter meaning of the term is the one used throughout this study.

5. For a brief bibliography of literature on the topic of the Soviet industrial reorganization (also called "decentralization") of 1957, see William B. Ballis, "Political Implications of Recent Soviet Economic Reorganizations," *The Review of Politics*, Vol. XXIII, No. 2 (April, 1961), p. 153.

6. Robert W. Campbell, "Research on the Soviet Economy--Achievements and Prospects," *Study of the Soviet Economy* ("Indiana University Publications: Russian and East European Series," Volume 25; Bloomington, Indiana: Indiana University, 1961), p. 141.

7. *Ibid.*, p. 142.

8. *Ibid.*

9. John W. Alexander, Economic Geography (Englewood Cliffs, New Jersey: Prentice-Hall, 1963), pp. 289-90.

For a complete discussion of the meaning and the uses of coefficient of correlation see Ibid., pp. 604-6. Briefly, coefficient of correlation is, according to Alexander, one of many methods for measuring the relationship between two phenomena--if they vary similarly from place to place they have a coefficient that is a positive number and if the correlation is complete the coefficient would be +1.00.

10. Value added is "the differential between the value of a product as it leaves the factory and the value of raw materials, including purchased parts" (Ibid., p. 289). In the U.S.S.R., the concept "value added" is not used and its closest equivalent measure is "gross industrial output" which is defined as "the sum of the gross outputs of all industrial enterprises" (Alec Nove, The Soviet Economy, New York: Frederick A. Praeger, 1961, p. 257).

11. Yakut A.S.S.R. handbook was published in 1964 but was not available at the Library of Congress.

12. See Bibliography for the complete list of handbooks used in this study, including handbooks for major cities (Moscow and Leningrad), R.S.F.S.R., and the U.S.S.R. Periodically, since January, 1959, an updated list of all published handbooks has appeared in Soviet Studies, a quarterly published by the University of Glasgow, indicating the holdings in the major libraries in the United States (Library of Congress) and abroad.

13. U.S.S.R., Tsentral'noye statisticheskoye upravleniye SSSR [Central Statistical Board of the U.S.S.R.], Narodnoye khozyaystvo SSSR v 1964 godu [National Economy of the U.S.S.R. in 1964] (Moscow, 1965).

14. L. N. Telepko, Krupnyye ekonomicheskiye raiony SSSR [Major Economic Regions of the U.S.S.R.] (Moscow: Academy of Sciences of the U.S.S.R., Institute of Economics, 1963), p. 97.

15. U.S.S.R., Tsentral'noye statisticheskoye upravleniye SSSR [Central Statistical Board of the U.S.S.R.], Narodnoye khozyaystvo SSSR v 1960 godu [National Economy of the U.S.S.R. in 1960] (Moscow, 1961).

CHAPTER 2 WORKERS BY MAJOR ECONOMIC REGIONS AND SOVNARKHOZY, 1940

Map 1 shows the location and the boundaries of the major economic regions. The distribution of industrial workers in 1940 is shown in Map 2 and is based on the data for all Soviet-governed territories as of 1940.[1] The visual impression of a massive preponderance of western regions is so strong that it barely needs numerical proof. In 1940 the western U. S. S. R.[2] contained over 80 per cent of industrial workers, while the eastern U. S. S. R.[3] had less than 20 per cent. The Central region and the South (Ukraine) occupy much the same position as the leading industrial centers of the Soviet Union in 1940 as they did in the Russian Empire before the Revolution (see Table 2). The Central region alone accounts for almost one-third of all Soviet industrial workers, while the Central and South regions together represent well over one-half of the U. S. S. R. total. Trailing behind are the next two important regions, Northwest and Ural, the latter slowly catching up with the older industrial complex centered around Leningrad. These four regions constitute the Soviet industrial core as of 1940, together representing 70 per cent of Soviet manufacturing.[4]

The regional figures for Soviet gross industrial output in rubles for 1940 are not available, but the regional breakdown of Soviet gross output for 1937 is given by S. S. Balzak.[5] When the output in rubles is translated into percentages, it is possible to make some comparisons with the distribution of industrial workers in 1940 (see Table 2). It is interesting to note that while Center and Northwest in 1940 constitute together about 42 per cent of workers, in 1937 their share of Soviet industrial output was over one-half of the U. S. S. R. total.[6] Ural and West Siberia had a greater share of the workers in 1940 (about 12 per cent) while their output in 1937

LOCATION MAP: 14 MAJOR ECONOMIC REGIONS

(Boundaries as of September 1, 1958)

MAP 1

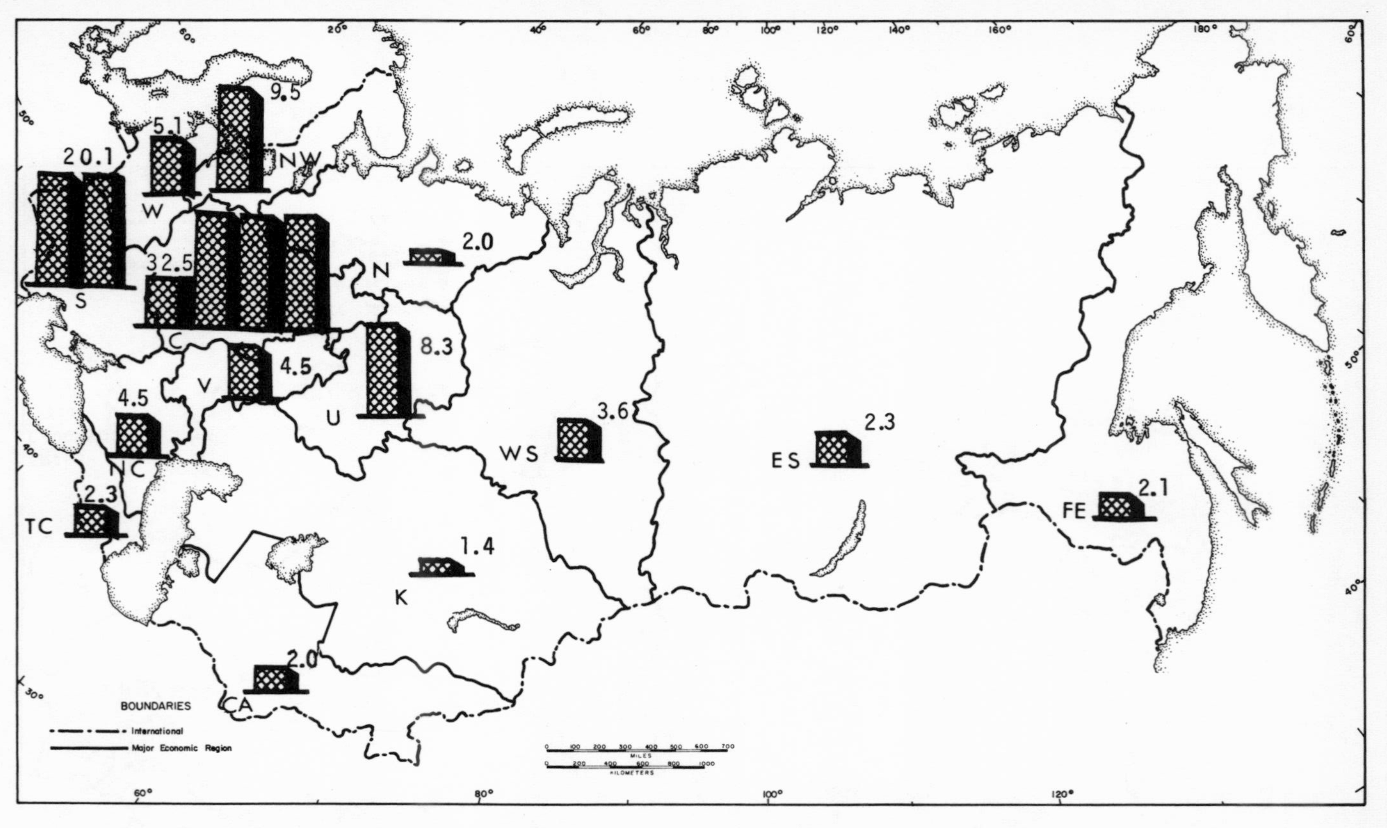

DISTRIBUTION OF INDUSTRIAL WORKERS IN 1940

(Major Economic Regions as Per Cent of U.S.S.R.)

MAP 2

TABLE 2

Major Economic Regions as Per Cent of the U. S. S. R., 1913-40

Regions	Gross Industrial Output 1913	Gross Industrial Output 1937	Industrial Workers 1940
Center and Northwest	50. 6%	50. 2%	42. 0%
Ukraine[a]	20. 2	17. 9	20. 1
Volga	6. 2	5. 3	4. 5
North Caucasus	4. 2	5. 2	4. 2
Trans-Caucasus	4. 2	3. 7	2. 3
North	1. 8	1. 8	2. 0
Belorussian S. S. R. [b]	1. 0	1. 9	2. 8
Western U. S. S. R.	88. 2	86. 0	77. 9 (80. 3)[c]
Ural and West Siberia	6. 1	8. 5	11. 9
Central Asia	2. 9	2. 2	2. 0
East Siberia and Far East	1. 9	3. 2	4. 4
Kazakhstan	0. 5	0. 9	1. 4
Eastern U. S. S. R.	11. 4	14. 8	19. 7

Notes: (a) 1940 data for Ukraine do not include Moldavian S. S. R. (= 0. 1 per cent). (b) The region West is not shown in the table since three of its component union republics (Lithuania, Latvia, and Estonia) were not part of the U. S. S. R. in 1937; thus only the data for its fourth component (Belorussian S. S. R.) are shown. (c) Western U. S. S. R., including Moldavian, Lithuanian, Latvian, and Estonian S. S. R. 's = 80. 3 per cent of the U. S. S. R. Totals may not add to 100 per cent due to rounding.

Sources: Data for 1913 and 1937 computed from Table 17 in S. S. Balzak, V. F. Vasyutin, and Ya. G. Feigin, Economic Geography of the U. S. S. R., translated by Robert M. Hanklin and Olga Adler Titelbaum (New York: Macmillan, 1952). Data for 1940 from Map 2, p. 12.

was less than 9 per cent.[7] Most other regions show a marked parallelism between their share of Soviet gross output in 1937 and their per cent of industrial workers in 1940.

If the analysis is switched from a small scale map (Map 2) showing the distribution by major economic regions, to a larger scale map showing a more detailed pattern indicating the distribution of industrial workers by *sovnarkhozy* in 1940 (Map 3), a more accurate picture of Soviet manufacturing on the eve of World War II is possible. It is unfortunate that data are lacking for the *sovnarkhozy* of the three S. S. R. 's--Ukrainian, Kazakh, and Uzbek--and thus only the totals for these republics are given, concealing the pattern of distribution within them.

At this point the decision to use the maps of per cent of industrial workers in the U. S. S. R. for each *sovnarkhoz* could be questioned. It may be argued, for instance, that the reason Map 3 shows a ring of lower percentages surrounding Moscow may be due to the small size of the *sovnarkhozy* and the choice of the method of calculation (*sovnarkhoz* as per cent of Soviet industrial workers). Thus, it may be suggested that the per cent of industrial workers should be adjusted by population size and therefore an index of industrial workers as a ratio of total *sovnarkhoz* population could be used and plotted on the map.

However, before deciding whether such a map was necessary the two following sets of figures were compared for each *sovnarkhoz*: (1) *sovnarkhoz* as per cent of industrial workers in the U. S. S. R., and (2) industrial workers as a ratio of the total *sovnarkhoz* population. The results showed that there was a very close positive correlation between the two sets of figures and that generally the lower percentage of industrial employment corresponded to the lower ratio of industrial workers in the total population of the *sovnarkhoz*. The following data illustrate this point: Out of a total of forty-nine *sovnarkhozy* in the ranges 0. 1-0. 4 as per cent of the U. S. S. R., thirty-nine *sovnarkhozy* had also a low ratio of industrial workers of 3 per cent or less (3 per cent being the median figure). Conversely, out of twenty-nine *sovnarkhozy* in the ranges of 1 per cent and over, all but one *sovnarkhoz* had a high ratio of industrial workers of over 3 per cent. The four leading *sovnarkhozy*, each with over 3 per cent of the U. S. S. R., had the highest ratio of workers of over

10 per cent. Therefore, it was concluded that the maps of per cent of industrial workers in the U. S. S. R. were adequate and valid and that they would show a meaningful pattern of distribution without any undue distortion. However, if a map had been made based on this second set of data (industrial workers as a ratio of total sovnarkhoz population), there still would be a zone of lesser industrial density surrounding Moscow (eight sovnarkhozy, all with ratios of less than 2 per cent) and the same would be true of all of Central Asia and Kazakhstan.

Map 3 shows Moscow and Leningrad sovnarkhozy (both Moscow sovnarkhozy: Moscow City and Moscow oblast) as the focal industrial areas, connected by a lesser industrial belt stretching from Gorkiy through the northern half of the Central region and extending into Belorussia.[8] The southern half of the Central region shows a marked decrease of industrial activity in contrast to its northern half. This predominantly agricultural belt of the Central Black Earth region is partly divided by the wedge of the Tula industrial complex.

The three industrial concentrations--Moscow-Gorkiy, Central and Northern Ural, and southern Volga-northern part of North Caucasus--do correspond to the generally known economic indicators of Soviet industrial complexes. However, Belorussian and Arkhangel'sk sovnarkhozy show an inflated magnitude. Compared to fourteen sovnarkhozy in the same range of magnitude in the three industrial concentrations, Belorussia stands out because it includes a much larger area and a greater share of total population than any other of the fourteen sovnarkhozy. The explanation of inflated magnitude for Arkhangel'sk sovnarkhoz is that it incorporates the largest area within the range 1. 0-3. 0 per cent (almost four times the size of Belorussia, the second largest in area among the eighteen sovnarkhozy of the same range), and also it is very close to the next lower classification. Inflated magnitude due to the extremely large areas that the two respective sovnarkhozy cover, could be observed also in the cases of Krasnoyarsk and Tyumen'. Krasnoyarsk sovnarkhoz is the second largest in the U. S. S. R. , representing almost 15 per cent of U. S. S. R. territory, while Tyumen' sovnarkhoz with 8 per cent of U. S. S. R. territory is the third largest in area.

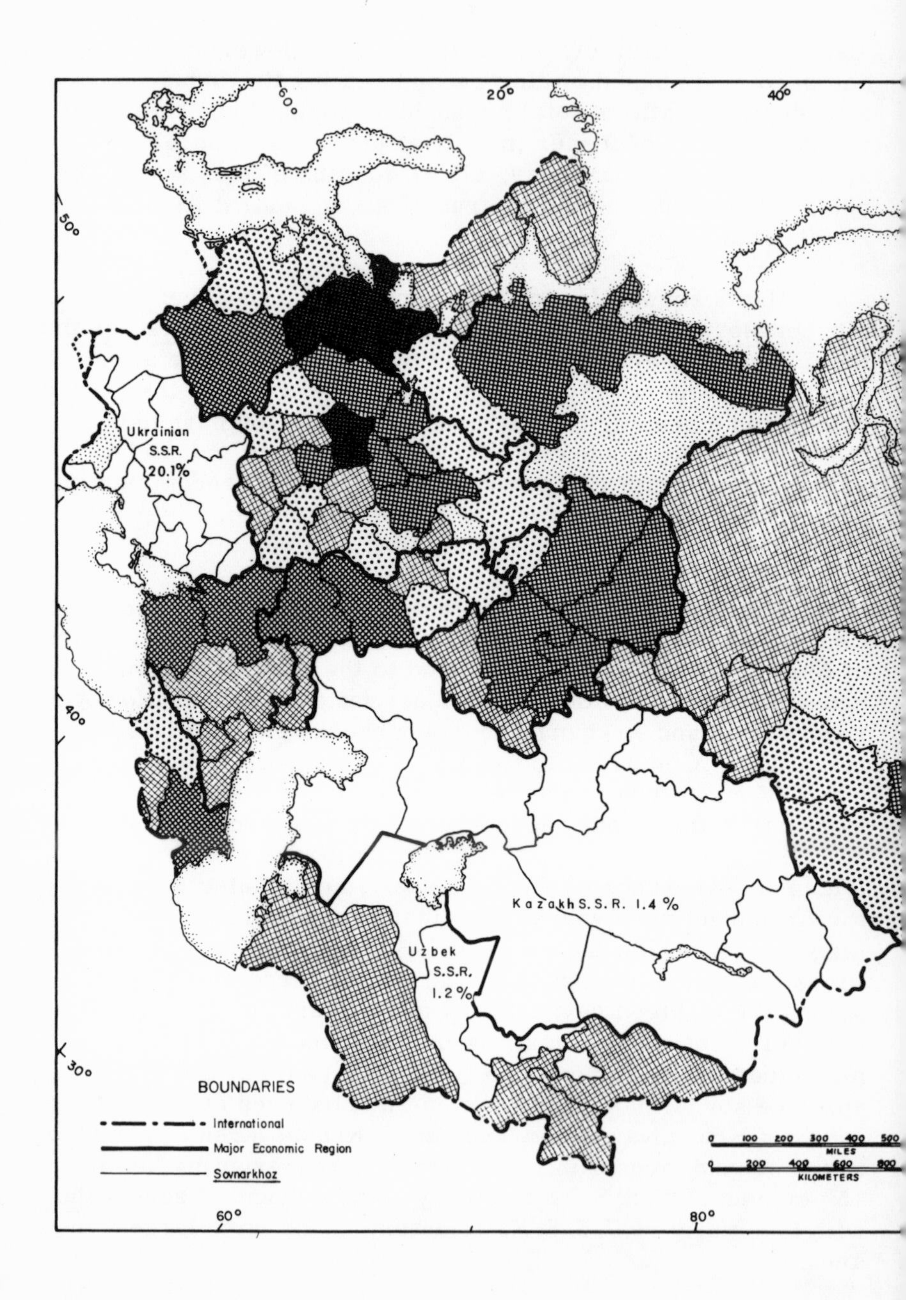
Ukrainian S.S.R. 20.1%
Kazakh S.S.R. 1.4 %
Uzbek S.S.R. 1.2 %
BOUNDARIES
International
Major Economic Region
Sovnarkhoz
MILES
KILOMETERS

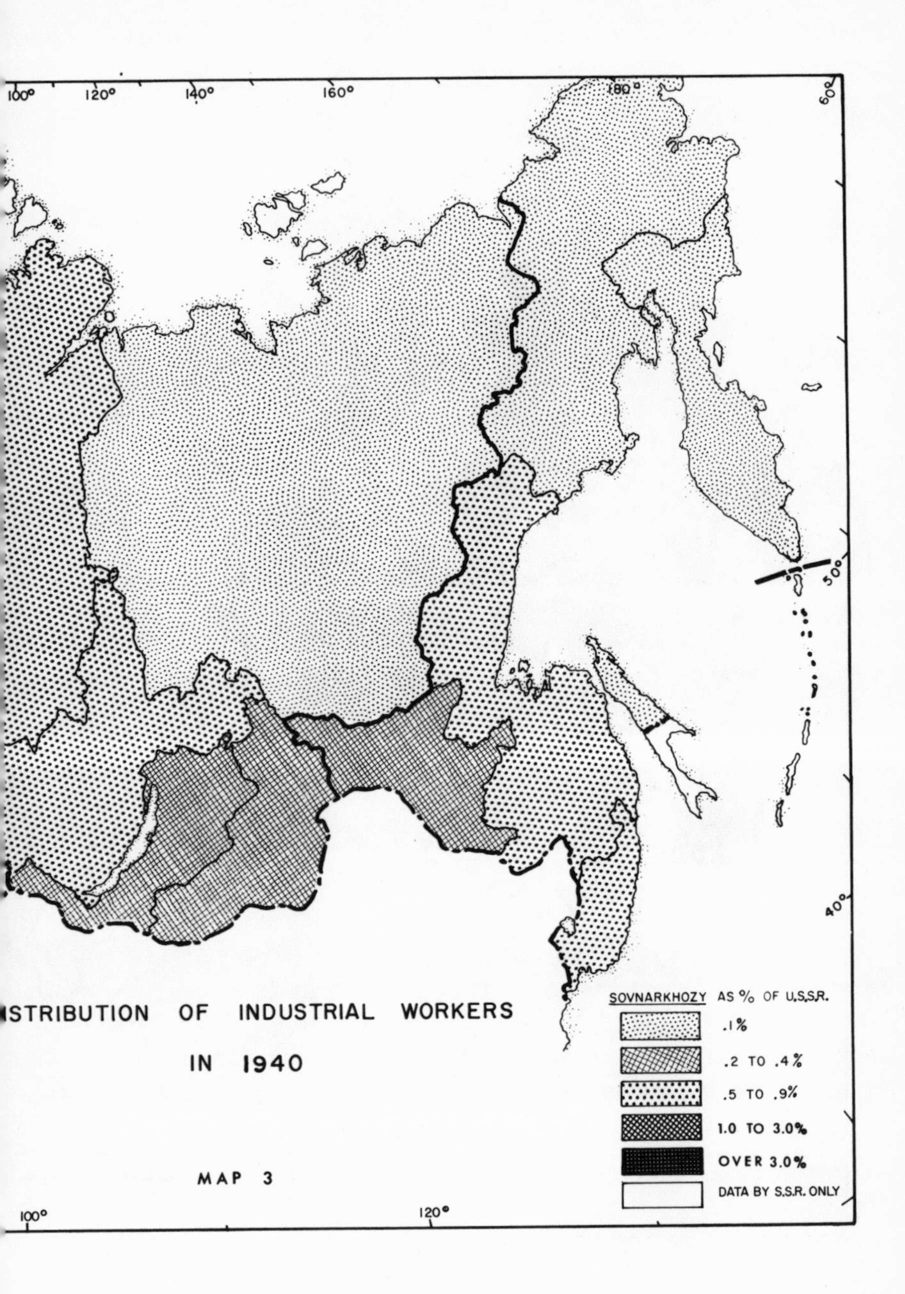
100°
120°
140°
160°
180°
60°
50°
40°
100°
120°
STRIBUTION OF INDUSTRIAL WORKERS
IN 1940
MAP 3
SOVNARKHOZY AS % OF U.S.S.R.
.1%
.2 TO .4%
.5 TO .9%
1.0 TO 3.0%
OVER 3.0%
DATA BY S.S.R. ONLY

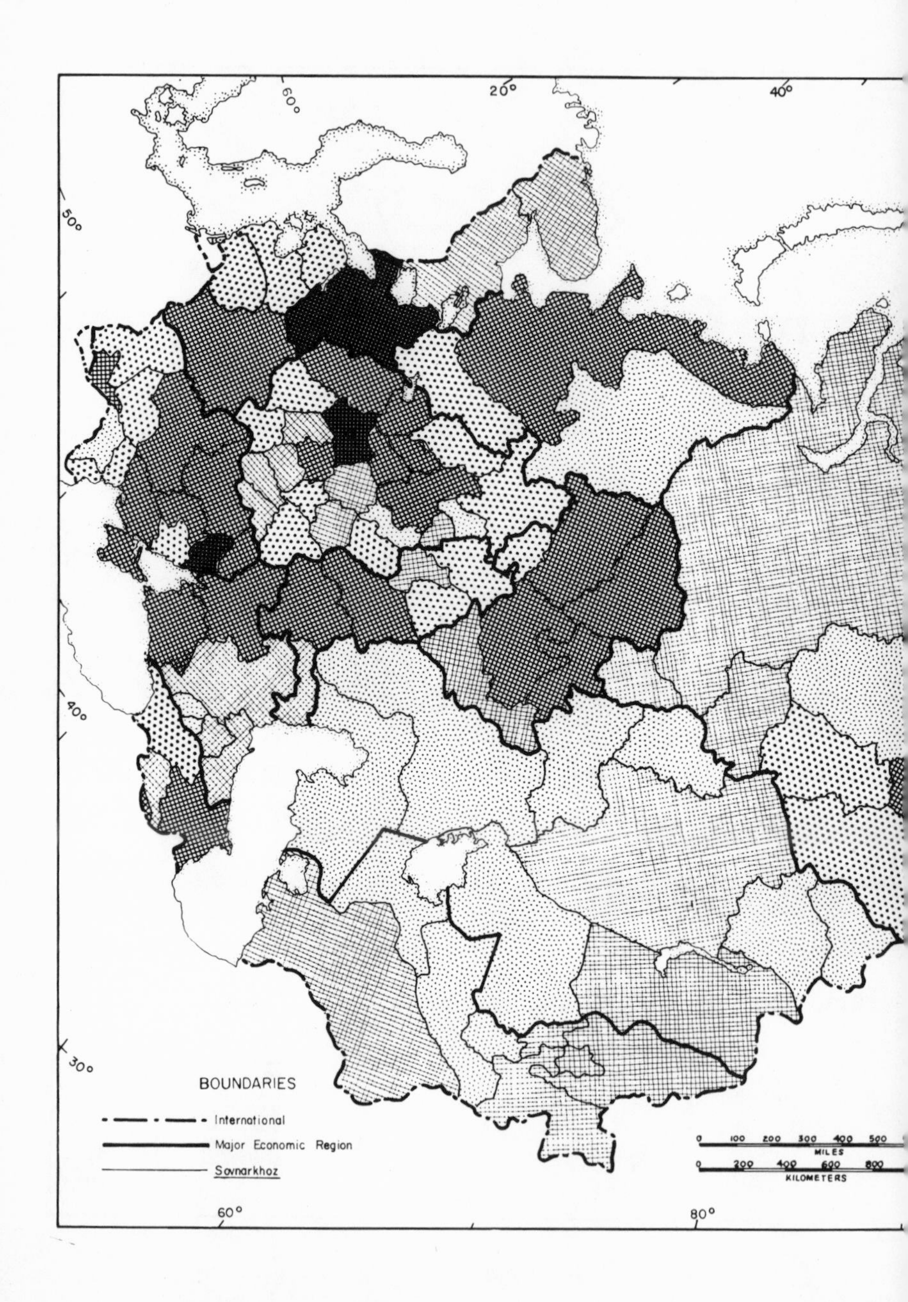
BOUNDARIES
International
Major Economic Region
Sovnarkhoz
MILES
KILOMETERS

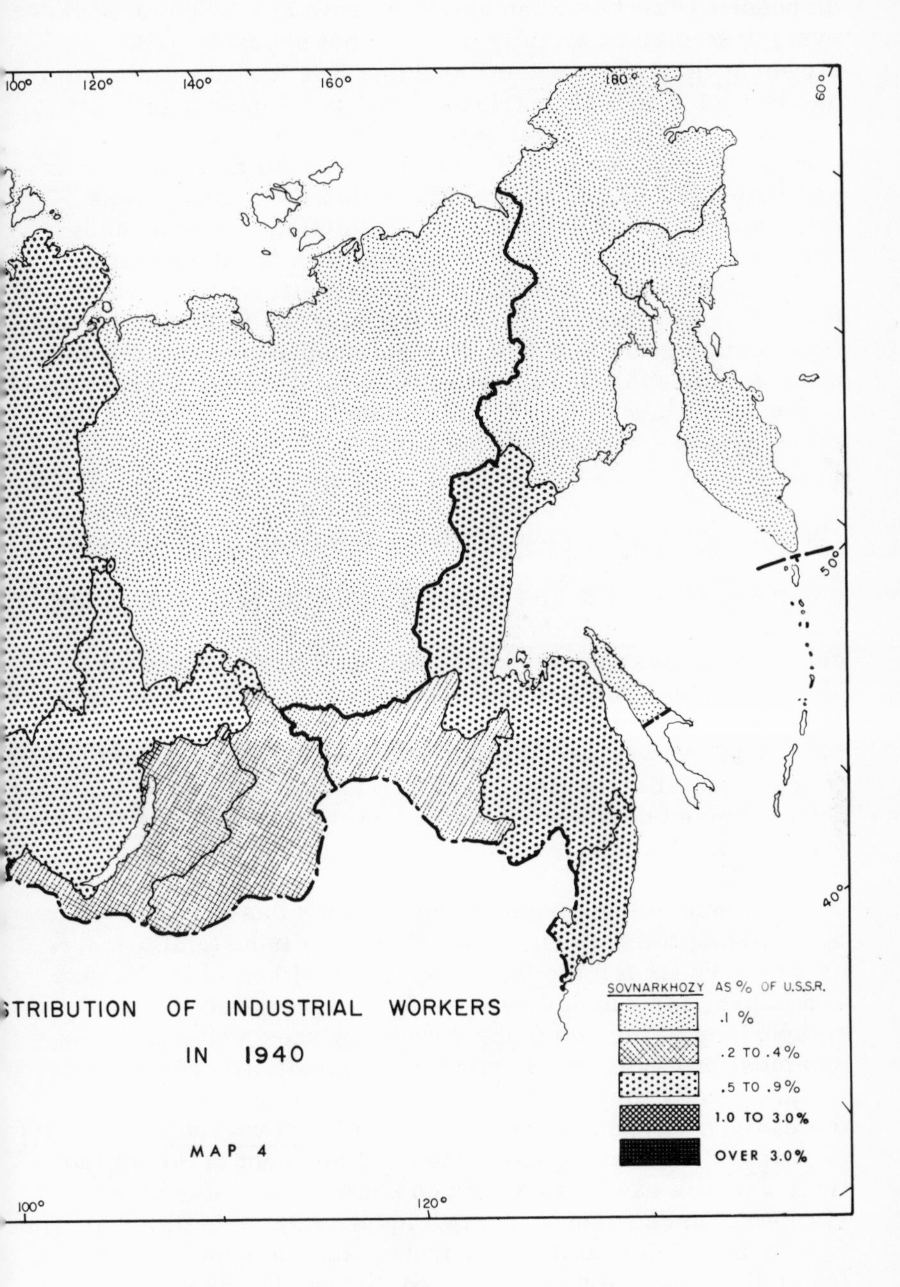

STRIBUTION OF INDUSTRIAL WORKERS IN 1940

MAP 4

The other sovnarkhozy in the range 1.0-3.0 per cent lie outside of the three industrial concentrations already discussed (Azerbaydzhan and Kemerovo sovnarkhoz). However, it is mathematically obvious that probably half of the eleven sovnarkhozy of the Ukrainian S. S. R. (Ukraine = 20.1 per cent of U. S. S. R. workers) must be in the range 1.0-3.0 per cent and therefore an attempt at reconstructing the pattern of distribution in this republic, as well as in the Kazakh and Uzbek S. S. R.'s, where direct data are lacking, was considered to be worthwhile. The solution of this problem (filling-in gaps in the distribution pattern for the Ukrainian, Kazakh, and Uzbek S. S. R.'s) has been attempted by calculating the coefficients of correlation for the following variables (1940 data for the U. S. S. R.): total population, urban population, urban population in the cities over 100,000, rural population, total labor force (employment in all branches of the economy), and number of industrial workers.[9]

The best correlation was the one involving criteria "Industrial workers" and "Urban population," with a coefficient of .97 in 1940.[10] Therefore, if the purpose is to show the distribution of Soviet industry in the three S. S. R.'s for which data by sovnarkhozy are missing, instead of using the criterion "Industrial workers" we could use the data for "Urban population" and probably get very much the same pattern. Urban population by sovnarkhozy as the per cent of the U. S. S. R. was used as the basis for arriving at the pattern of industrial distribution by sovnarkhozy in the three S. S. R.'s. The computed data were accepted as the approximate figures for industrial workers as the per cent of the U. S. S. R.

Based on the computed data, Map 4 has been completed by including the pattern of distribution of industrial workers by sovnarkhozy for the three republics--Ukrainian, Kazakh and Uzbek, for which data by S. S. R. were given in Map 3. A comparison of the two maps shows few unexpected patterns, and most of the distribution seems logically to proceed from the previously mapped areas into the three S. S. R.'s. All of the eastern Ukraine (except Zaporozh'ye sovnarkhoz) consists of sovnarkhozy having more than 1.8 per cent of Soviet industrial workers each. Central and southern Ukraine also has a similar pattern. Thus, the two industrialized belts, that from Gorkiy into Belorussia in the north, and the southern Volga-lower Don belt are now connected through the central and western Ukraine forming a ring around the Central Black Earth region, with two foci centered on Moscow and Donbas (Donetsk _sovnarkhoz_).

The completion of the pattern of distribution within the Kazakh and Uzbek S. S. R. 's shows again the blending of this area with the surrounding regions for which the pattern was shown in Map 3. It would have been logical to expect that most of the nine _sovnarkhozy_ of the Kazakh S. S. R. would have less than 0. 2 per cent each, as the total for the republic is 1. 4 per cent. Thus, we see the five western _sovnarkhozy_ of Kazakhstan blending with a similar zone of underdevelopment in Uzbek S. S. R. Fergana _sovnarkhoz_, on the other hand, shows slightly greater industrial activity and belongs to a wide and long belt of low industrialization with a range of 0. 2-0. 4 per cent of the U. S. S. R. total. This belt extends from West Siberia through Kazakhstan and Central Asia and continues westward to include the Turkmen S. S. R. It ends in the eastern North Caucasus region and the southern Volga region.

Siberia shows a higher stage of industrial development than Kazakhstan and Central Asia, with the greatest concentration in Kemerovo _sovnarkhoz_ (Kuzbas). The industrial activity slowly decreases from Kemerovo both westward, through Novosibirsk and Altay _sovnarkhozy_, and eastward, through Krasnoyarsk and Irkutsk _sovnarkhozy_. The importance of manufacturing again increases in the southern part of the Far East region. The northeastern part of Siberia shows a definite industrial underdevelopment with Yakut, Magadan and Kamchatka _sovnarkhozy_ each contributing only 0. 1 per cent of the U. S. S. R. industry.

Notes to Chapter 2

1. In Maps 2, 5-12, and 14, 18, 20, 22, 24, 26, 28, 30, and 32, simple bar graphs are used representing each region as a per cent of the U. S. S. R. For an easier visual comparison, the maximum length of one bar is equal to 10 per cent, and if there is more than 10 per cent of workers in one region additional bars are used. All regions are identified by initials which are also shown on the location map (Map 1) in parentheses.

2. Western U. S. S. R. includes the following major economic regions: Center, Northwest, North, West, South, Volga, Northern Caucasus, and Trans-Caucasus.

3. Eastern U. S. S. R. includes the following major economic regions: Ural, West Siberia, East Siberia, Far East, Kazakhstan, and Central Asia.

4. The terms manufacturing, industry, industrial-production personnel, and industrial workers are used interchangeably in this study to avoid unnecessary repetitions of the same term "industrial workers" or "industrial-production personnel."

5. S. S. Balzak, V. F. Vasyutin, and Ya. G. Feigin, Economic Geography of the U. S. S. R., translated by Robert M. Hanklin and Olga Adler Titelbaum (New York: Macmillan, 1952), p. 206.

6. Greater labor productivity of these two regions is probably the main reason for the larger share of their industrial output before World War II. See Paul K. Cook, "The Administration and Distribution of Soviet Industry," in Dimensions of Soviet Economic Power (Studies Prepared for the Joint Economic Committee, 87th Congress, 2nd Session, Washington, D. C.: U.S. Government Printing Office, 1962), pp. 197-99.

7. The lower labor productivity of these two regions in the period preceding World War II is probably one of the reasons for their smaller share of industrial output. See Cook, Ibid.

8. See the map and the lists in Appendixes II-IV for the location and the names of 104 sovnarkhozy.

9. For the definition of coefficient of correlation see Note 9 to Chapter 1.

10. For the definition of coefficient of correlation see Note 9 to Chapter 1.

CHAPTER 3 WORKERS BY PRINCIPAL BRANCHES OF INDUSTRY, 1940

The previous chapter was concerned with the distribution of workers in the U. S. S. R. by major economic regions, rather than by types of industry. The present chapter deals with the distribution of industrial workers in each of the eight major branches of industry in the U. S. S. R. : (1) energy and fuel industries, (2) heavy industry, (3) machine manufacturing, (4) chemical industry, (5) building materials industry, (6) forest industries, (7) light industry, and (8) food industry. This arrangement of the eight branches of industry is not in order of their importance but reflects the customary order of listing of these branches in most Soviet publications, including statistical handbooks and economic maps in Soviet atlases. The total employment figures (industrial workers in all industries) were obtained for all the sovnarkhozy and thus warranted an analysis by sovnarkhozy. On the other hand, the data were lacking for some sovnarkhozy for the breakdown by eight branches of industry. Therefore, the discussion of the distribution of workers by industries will be limited to the major economic regions, because our data show much greater accuracy and reliability if analyzed at that level. One map for each industry (Maps 5-12) will show the pattern of distribution by major economic regions.

ENERGY AND FUEL INDUSTRIES (MAP 5)

This group of industries includes electric power stations, coal mining, petroleum refining, gas, and other fuels. In 1940, the industrial workers in these industries represented 7. 4 per cent of the total Soviet manufacturing employment.[1] Out of this figure, the fuel industries (principally coal mining) accounted for 6. 4 per cent while the electric power stations represented only about 1 per cent.

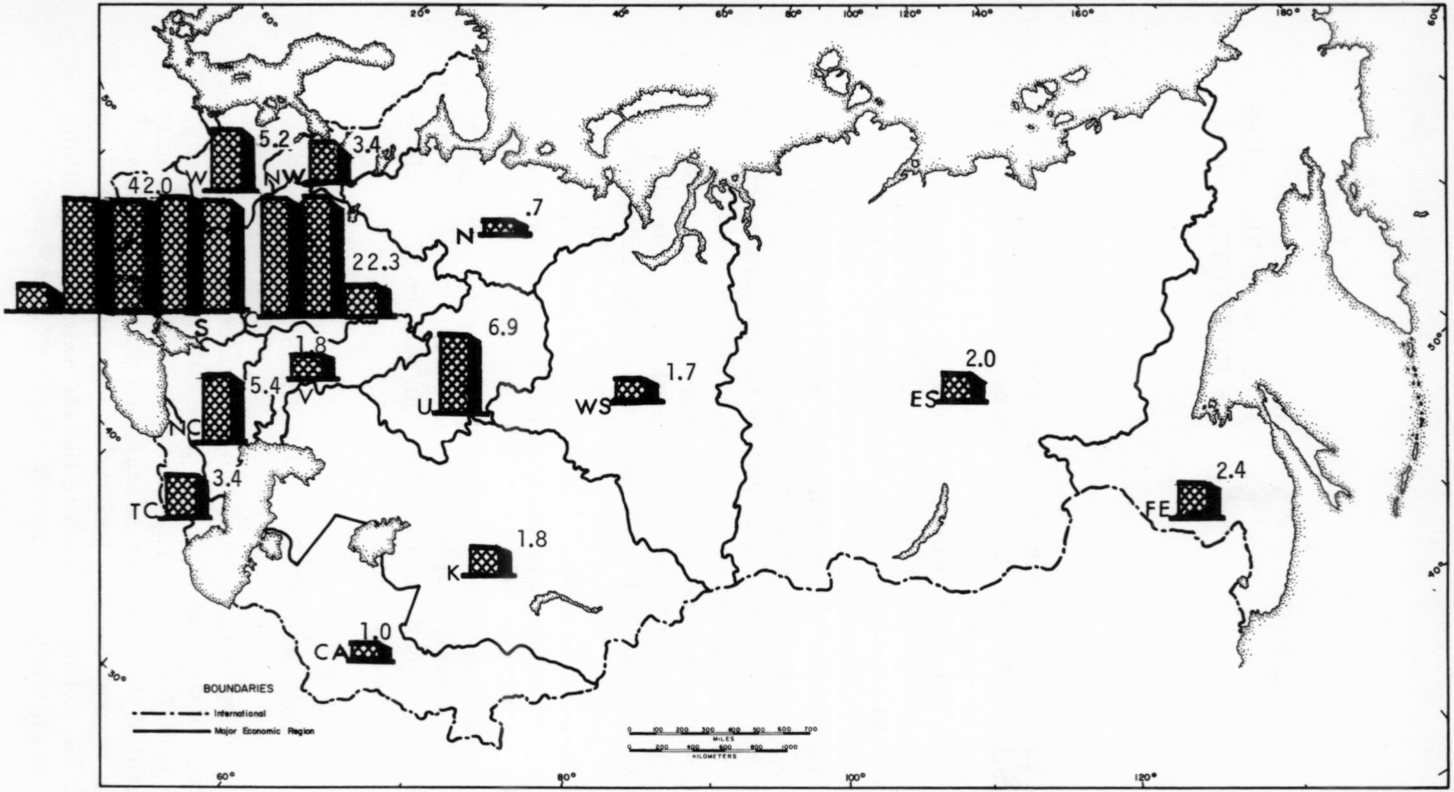

DISTRIBUTION OF INDUSTRIAL WORKERS IN 1940: ENERGY AND FUEL INDUSTRIES

(Major Economic Regions as Per Cent of U.S.S.R.)

MAP 5

Almost 84 per cent of the workers were in the western U. S. S. R. (regions west of the Urals) and about 16 per cent were in the eastern regions. The South was leading with 42 per cent, followed by the Center with over 22 per cent; these two regions were the leaders in the production of hard and soft coal, respectively. The impact of the Kuzbas and Karaganda coal fields had not yet been felt, and thus the share of Kazakhstan and West Siberia was under 2 per cent each. The regions having between 3 and 5 per cent included the Trans-Caucasus and North Caucasus (their share was due to the Caucasus oil and gas fields, as well as coal in the lower Don region), and also the West whose share has been increased by the contribution of the Estonian oil shale industry. The Ural, the third largest, had its share based mainly on coal mining, while in the Northwest the basis was the peat industry. The Pechora coal and oil fields were only beginning to produce, thus the North contributed less than 1 per cent in 1940. The share of the Far East region was based on the oil production in northern Sakhalin.

HEAVY INDUSTRY (MAP 6)

This industrial branch is composed of ferrous metallurgy (iron and steel), nonferrous metallurgy, and the mining of minerals such as iron, copper, and others. In 1940, this branch accounted for 5. 4 per cent of the Soviet manufacturing employment, ranking sixth among the eight principal branches of industry.[2] The western U. S. S. R. had about 71 per cent while the eastern regions had about 29 per cent of all workers. The leading region was the South with 29 per cent, followed by the Center, Ural, and the Northwest. The importance of the first three regions is based on their metallurgical complexes, mainly the iron and steel industry, while nonferrous minerals (nickel, copper) partly reflect the share of the Northwest region. Nonferrous minerals and their mining accounted for the moderate shares of Kazakhstan and East Siberia. The Kuzbas metallurgical complex was then in the early stages of development, and thus the share of West Siberia was still relatively small.

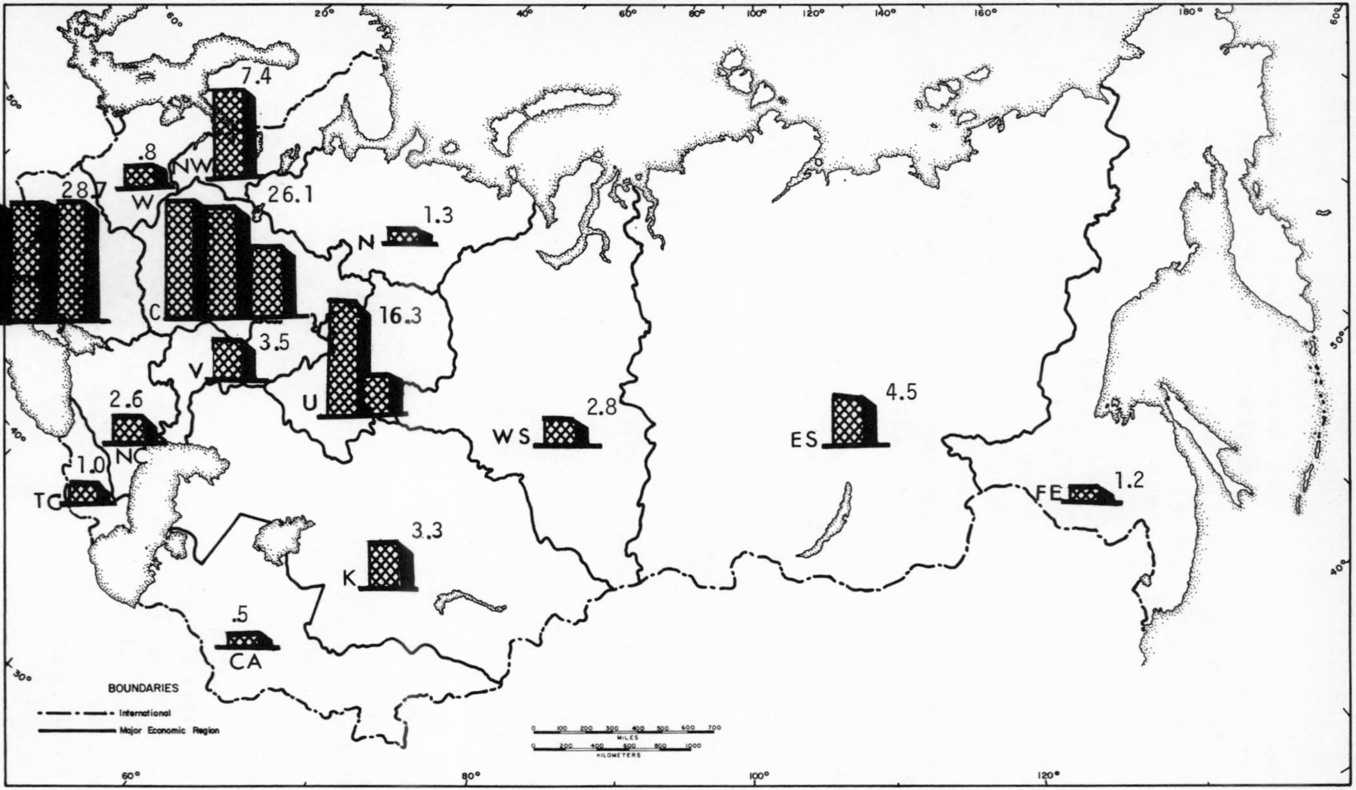

DISTRIBUTION OF INDUSTRIAL WORKERS IN 1940: HEAVY INDUSTRY

(Major Economic Regions as Per Cent of U.S.S.R.)

MAP 6

MACHINE MANUFACTURING (MAP 7)

Machine manufacturing in the U. S. S. R. includes machine tools, and other metal-working industries, agricultural machinery and tractors, shipbuilding, automobile industry (trucks, passenger cars, buses), railroad rolling stock, and airplane manufacturing. It is the most important industrial branch in the U. S. S. R. and it represented in 1940 28. 9 per cent of the total Soviet industrial working force.[3] The western regions accounted for 83 per cent of the workers and the eastern regions contained 17 per cent.

The Central region and the South contained together over one-half of the workers in Soviet machine manufacturing. If the two other leading regions, Ural and Northwest, are added, then these four regions contained almost 77 per cent of the industrial workers in the machine building industries. There seems to be a high correlation between the share of the regions in the total Soviet industrial work force and the per cent figures for machine manufacturing. Also it should be noted that no region had a share smaller than 1. 1 per cent of Soviet machine manufacturing.

CHEMICAL INDUSTRY (MAP 8)

The chemical industry ranked next to the last among the eight principal branches in the U. S. S. R. in 1940 and represented only 3. 3 per cent of Soviet industrial workers.[4] The shares of the western and eastern U. S. S. R. were comparable to those of the energy and fuels industries: The western regions had about 83 per cent and the eastern regions contained about 17 per cent.

The Center contained over 40 per cent of the chemical industry. Together with the three other leading regions (South, Ural, and Northwest), these four areas contained almost 80 per cent of the Soviet chemical workers. On the other hand, the five smallest regions had a combined total of only 5 per cent. The uneven distribution of the industry reflected to some extent the uneven distribution of raw materials.

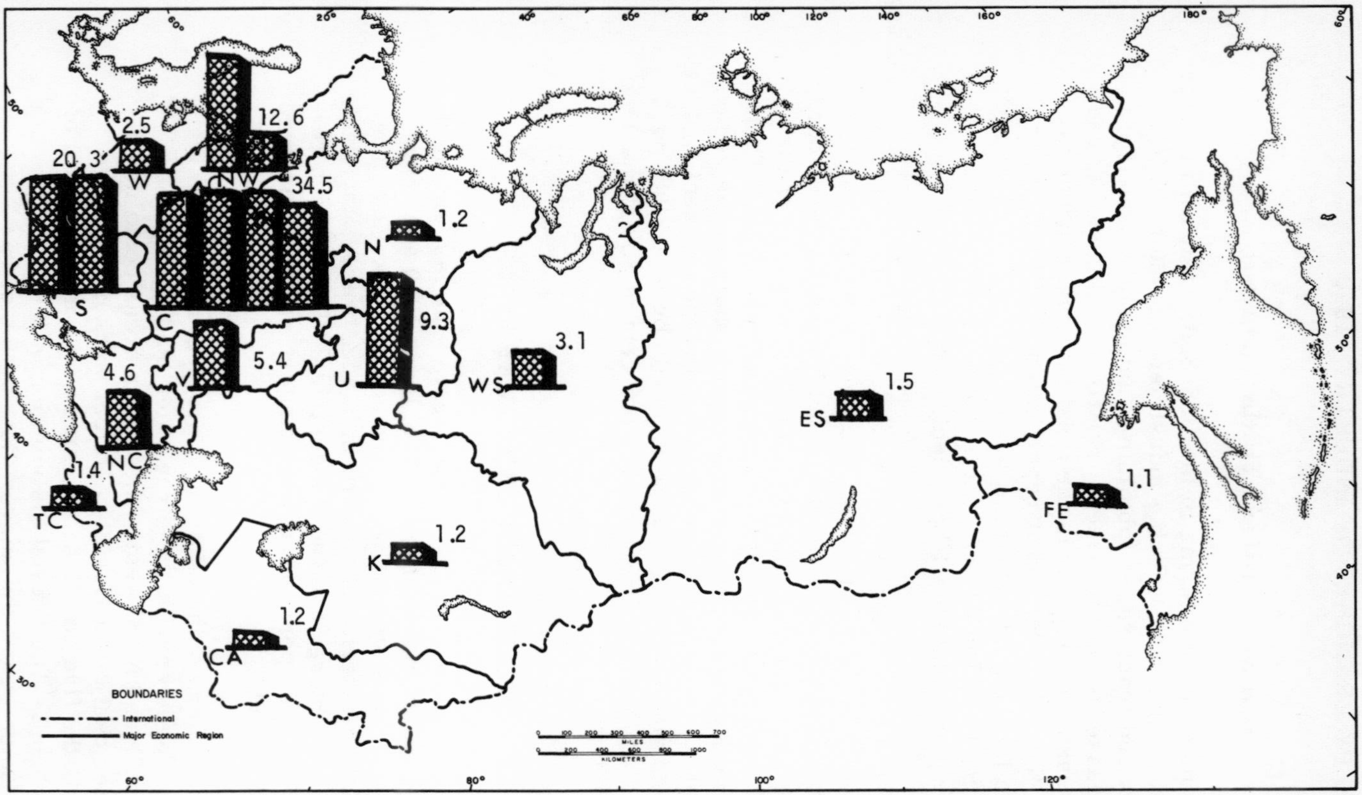

DISTRIBUTION OF INDUSTRIAL WORKERS IN 1940: MACHINE MANUFACTURING

(Major Economic Regions as Per Cent of U.S.S.R.)

MAP 7

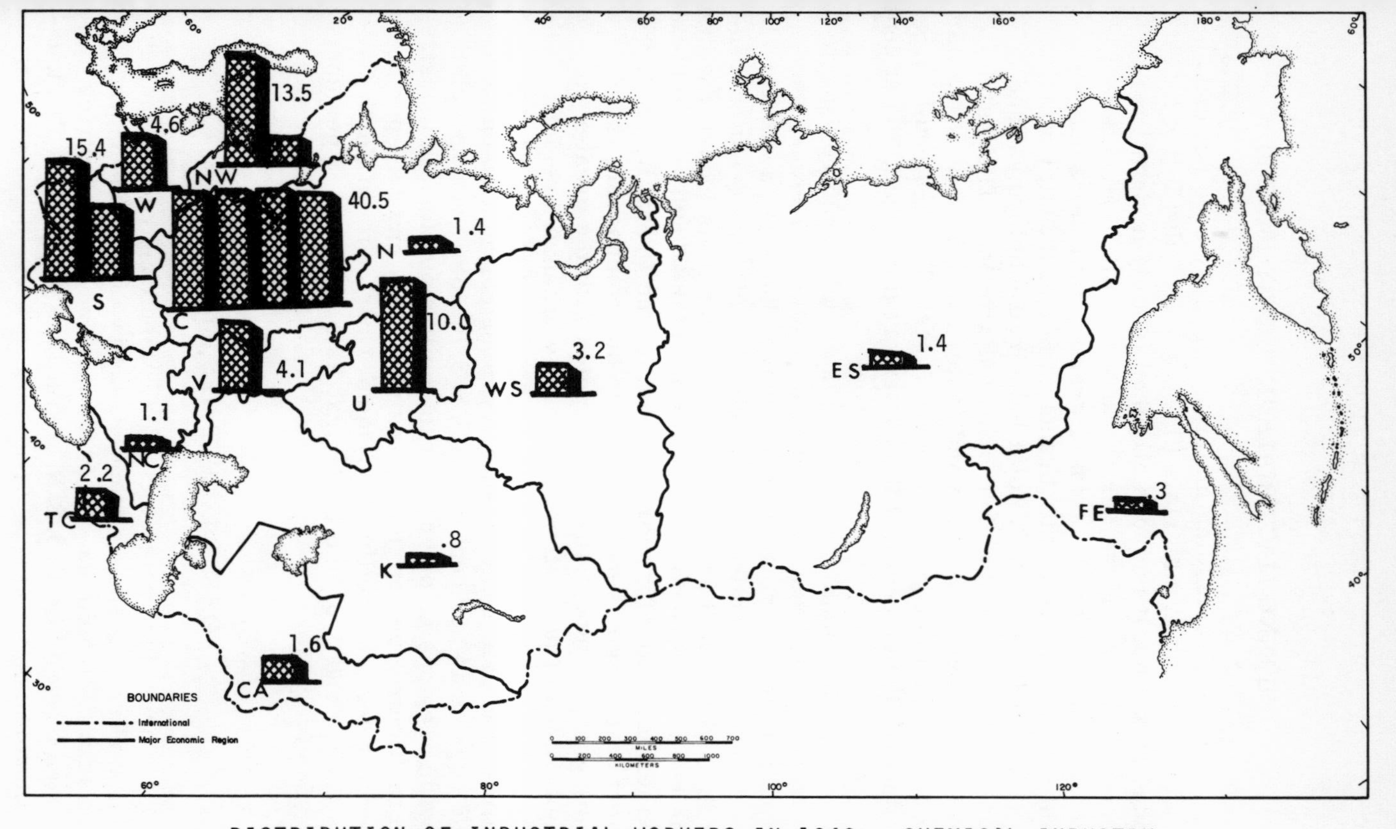

DISTRIBUTION OF INDUSTRIAL WORKERS IN 1940: CHEMICAL INDUSTRY

(Major Economic Regions as Per Cent of U.S.S.R.)

MAP 8

BUILDING MATERIALS INDUSTRY (MAP 9)

The Soviet building materials industry does not include wood construction materials (these are included in the forest industries), but it includes all other (mainly mineral) materials: cement, glass, brick, as well as the extraction of building raw materials--stone, granite, marble, sand, and others. The share of this branch of Soviet industry was 3.0 per cent of the U. S. S. R. total industrial employment and it ranked last among the eight principal groups.[5] The distribution between the western and eastern U. S. S. R. was similar to that of the total industrial work force: The western U. S. S. R had about 80 per cent and the eastern regions about 20 per cent

The distribution of building materials could be expected to be relatively even, since the raw materials, stone, sand, even granite, are found in more places than the raw materials for heavy and chemical industries. Despite the great concentration of the workers in the building materials industry within the two leading regions, the Center and the South, which together accounted for more than half of the U. S. S. R. total, most other regions had a moderate but comparable share. This group of industries is associated with the greater concentrations of population in the highly urbanized regions. The needs for construction materials are greater in the large cities, and indeed there is a very close correlation between the regions as per cent of the U. S. S. R. total urban population and the regions as per cent of the building materials industry. In the Central region the figures were 23.7 and 23.4 per cent respectively, in the Ural 7.7 and 7.1 per cent, in North Caucasus 5.1 and 5.0, and in Central Asia 4.0 and 4.2 per cent respectively.

FOREST INDUSTRIES (MAP 10)

Forest industries include all wood construction materials, timber processing, paper industry, furniture-making, and related industries. In 1940, this group of industries ranked third in the U. S. S. R., with 15.9 per cent of all industrial workers.[6]

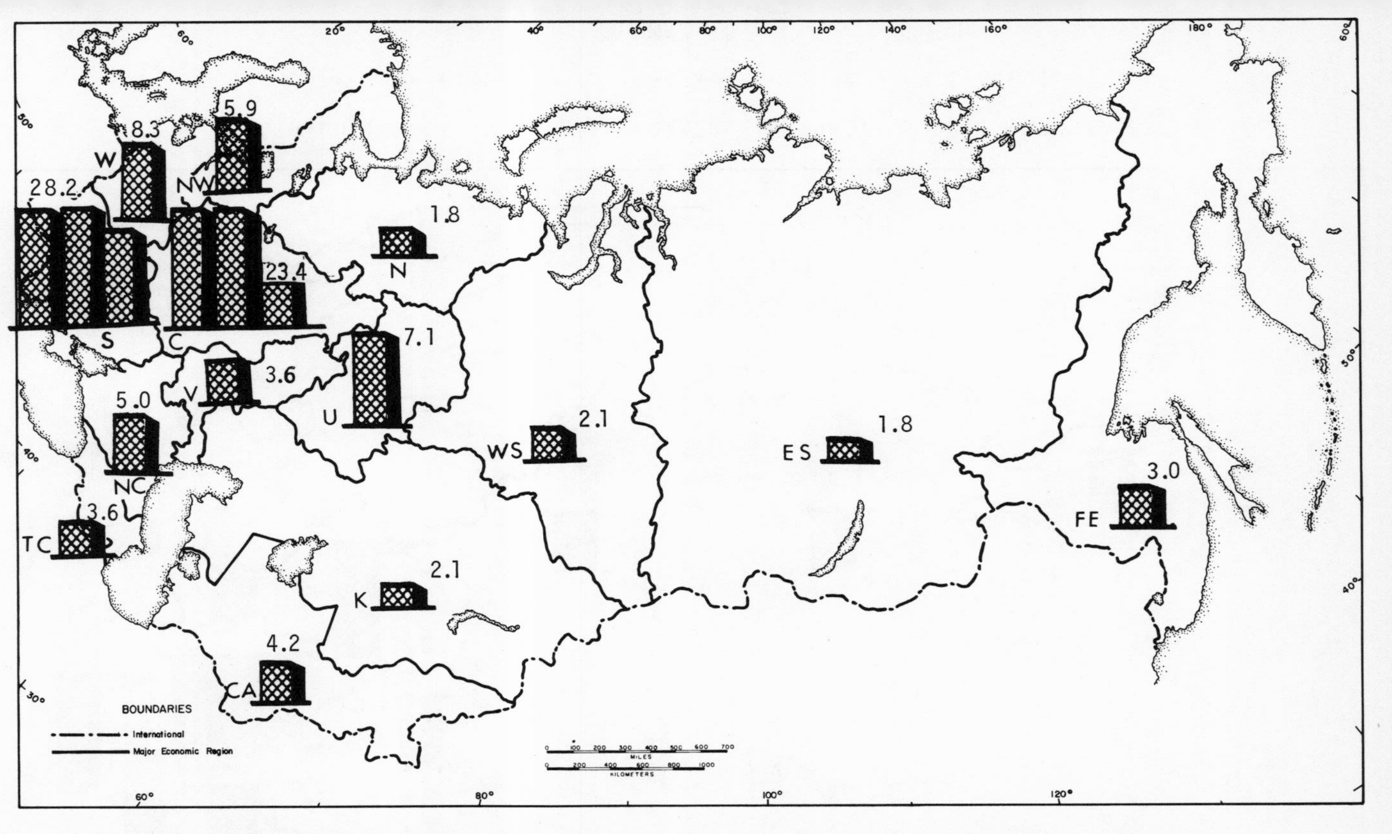

DISTRIBUTION OF INDUSTRIAL WORKERS IN 1940: BUILDING MATERIALS INDUSTRY

(Major Economic Regions as Per Cent of U.S.S.R.)

MAP 9

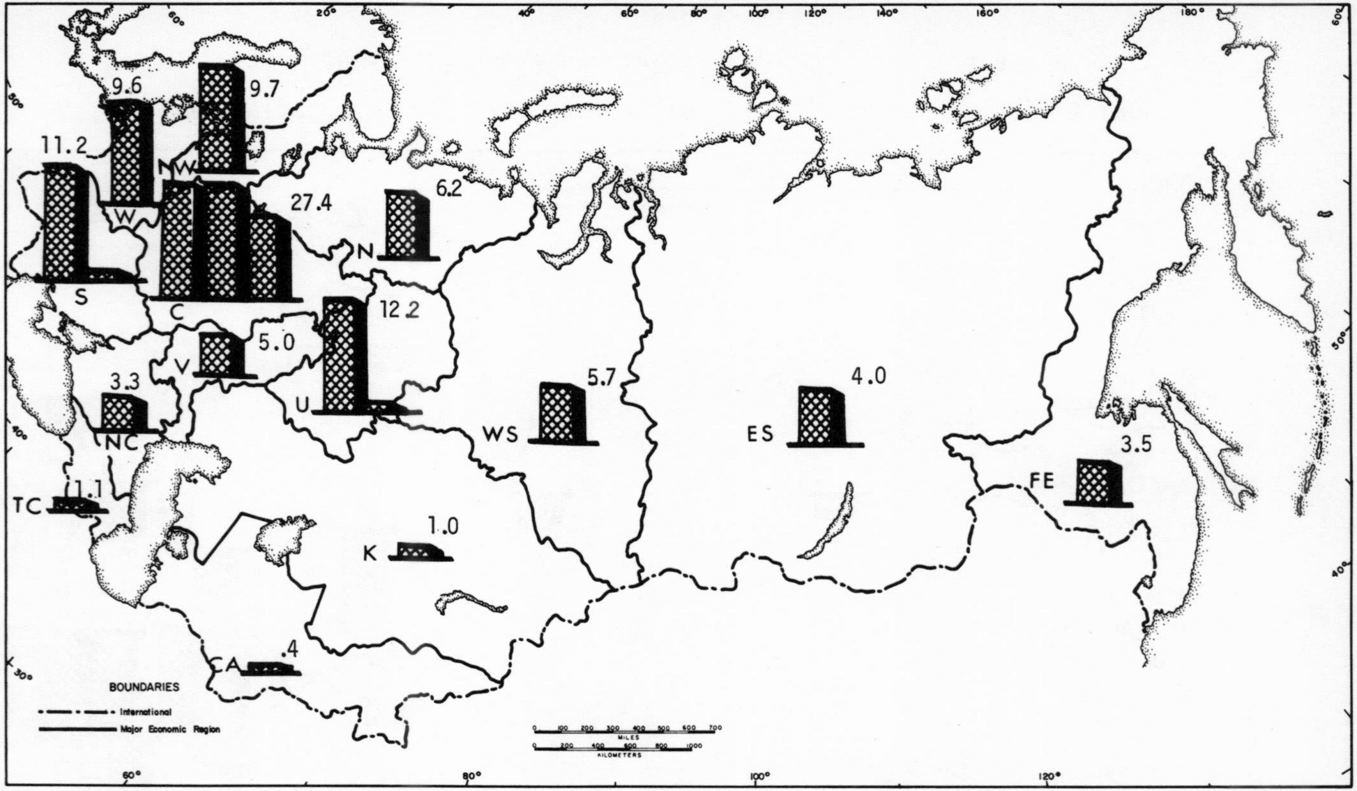

DISTRIBUTION OF INDUSTRIAL WORKERS IN 1940: FOREST INDUSTRIES

(Major Economic Regions as Per Cent of U.S.S.R.)

MAP 10

As the map shows, there is a clear correlation between climate and vegetation on one hand, and the distribution of forest industries on the other. The steppe and the semi-desert climate of the south of the U. S. S. R. explain the low shares of the regions Central Asia and Kazakhstan, as well as the Volga-Caucasus area. The low figures for the Siberian area (East Siberia and the Far East) do not have the same meaning as those for Central Asia and Kazakhstan. Here it is not the lack of raw materials, as Siberia contains the great timber resources of the taiga. It is rather the case of underdevelopment due largely to the inaccessibility of the raw materials and the difficulties in transportation caused by permafrost and the severe climate of the interior.

The Center led in the share of forest industries with over one-fourth of the U. S. S. R. total, while the Northwest and North together accounted for almost 16 per cent. The steppe in the Ukraine partly explains the relatively low figure of 11. 2 per cent for the region South (the lowest share of any of the eight industries in this region). The western U. S. S. R. contained about 73 per cent and the eastern regions had about 27 per cent of the U. S. S. R. total.

LIGHT INDUSTRY (MAP 11)

Light industry includes the textile industry (cotton, linen, wool, silk, and synthetic fibers) and several branches of consumer-oriented industries (shoe manufacturing, clothing and apparel industry, and others). In 1940, the workers in the light industries represented almost one-fifth of the total Soviet industrial work force, and this branch ranked second among the eight principal branches following machine manufacturing.[7] About 86 per cent of the workers were in the western U. S. S. R., while the eastern regions contained about 14 per cent of the Soviet employment in this industry.

The greatest concentration was in the Central region which alone contained over 40 per cent of the workers in light industry. The Central region, with the South and the region Northwest, accounted together for two-thirds of Soviet light industry. The importance of the Central region reflects the fact that the greatest part of light industry is in the textile industry, which has been traditionally overconcentrated in the

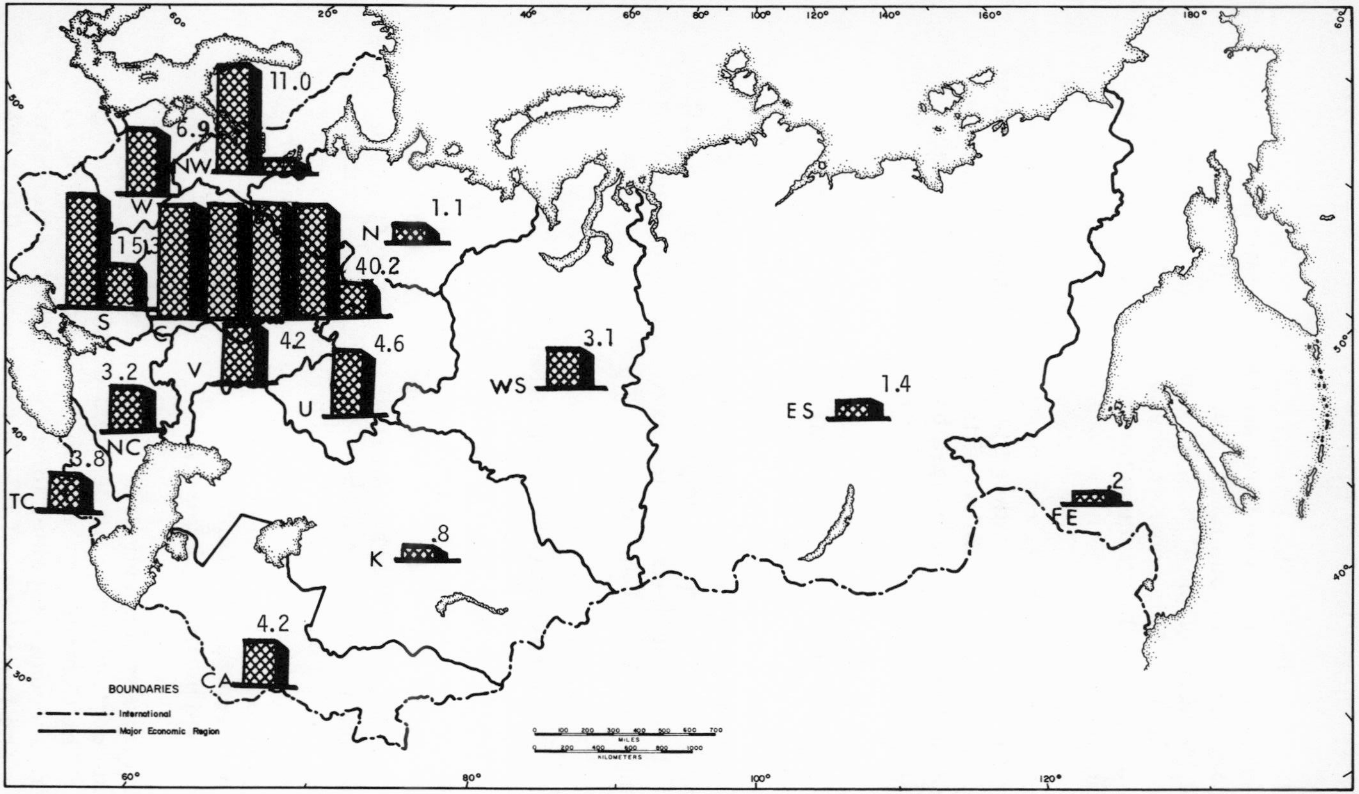

DISTRIBUTION OF INDUSTRIAL WORKERS IN 1940: LIGHT INDUSTRY

(Major Economic Regions as Per Cent of U.S.S.R.)

MAP 11

Moscow-Ivanovo area even before the Revolution of 1917 and continued to be concentrated there in 1940.

FOOD INDUSTRY (MAP 12)

The following food-processing industries are included under the heading "Food industry": flour milling, bread making, meat packing, fish canning, milk and dairy products, butter and margarine, sugar refining, vegetable canning, and the wine industry. As the fourth ranking industry in the U. S. S. R. in 1940, the food industry employed about 13 per cent of Soviet industrial workers.[8] The western U. S. S. R. had about 77 per cent, while the eastern regions had about 23 per cent of the workers in the food industry. These figures follow closely the distribution of Soviet population in 1939-40: 76 per cent in the western, 24 per cent in the eastern regions.

The two leading regions, Center and South, contained about one-half of the workers in the food industry. This figure corresponds to the concentrations of farming and of population: The bread-baskets of the Ukraine and the Central Black Earth region were in 1940 the main producers of grains, meat, milk, sugar, and fats in the U. S. S. R., while the Center and South contained nearly one-half of the Soviet population. On the whole, the distribution of workers in the food industry very closely follows the distribution of population. For example, the figures for the regions' share of the Soviet food industry and per cent of U. S. S. R. population respectively were 22. 5 and 22. 5 per cent in the South, 1. 7 and 1. 6 for the region North, 5. 2 and 5. 5 in the Volga region, and 5. 0 and 5. 2 per cent in West Siberia.

CONCLUDING REMARKS

From Figure 1 it is evident that all the industries, except the forest industries, were overwhelmingly concentrated in three regions: Center, South, and Northwest. While their combined share of all the workers was 62 per cent of the U. S. S. R., the combined share in seven industries ranged from 56 per cent in food industry to 69 per cent in chemical industry, with five industries having a combined share of over 62 per cent. Only the forest industries had a combined

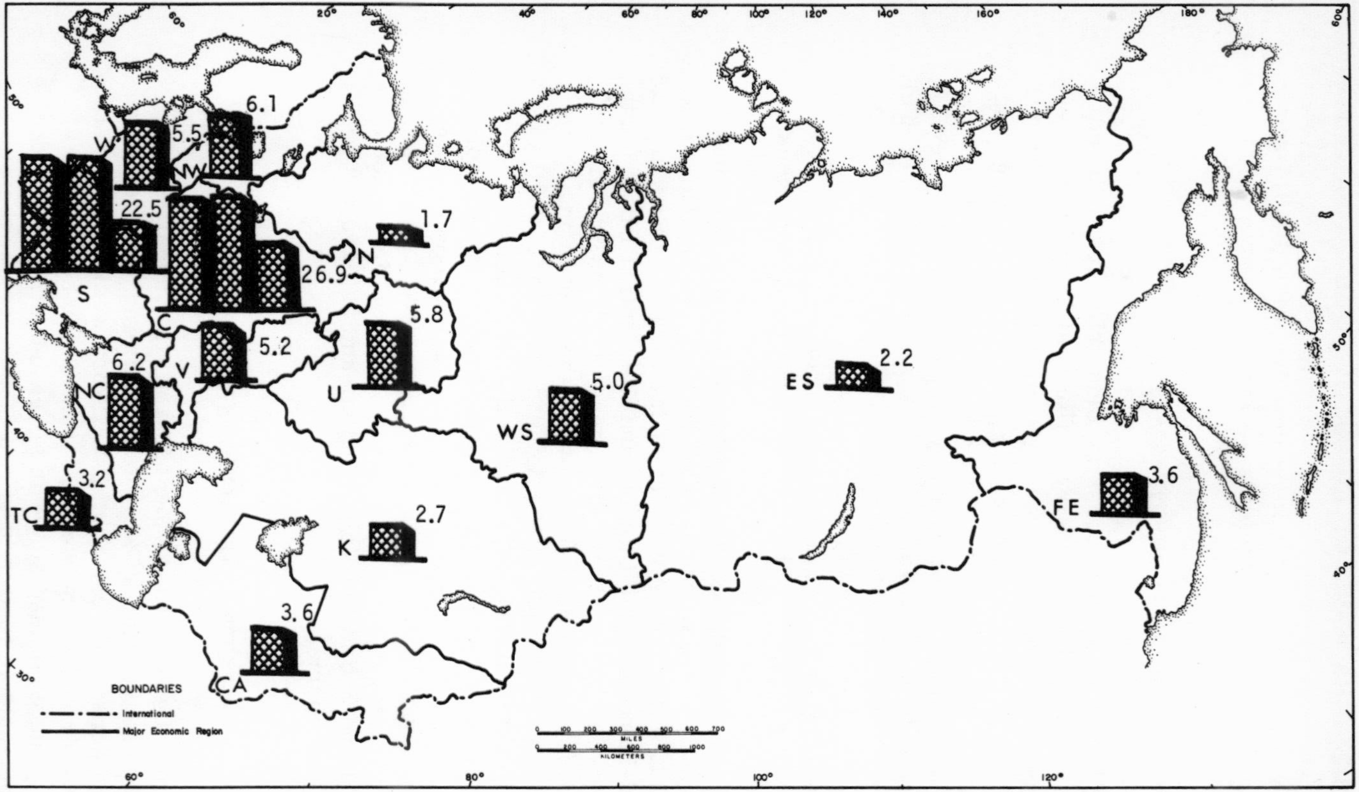

DISTRIBUTION OF INDUSTRIAL WORKERS IN 1940: FOOD INDUSTRY

(Major Economic Regions as Per Cent of U.S.S.R.)

MAP 12

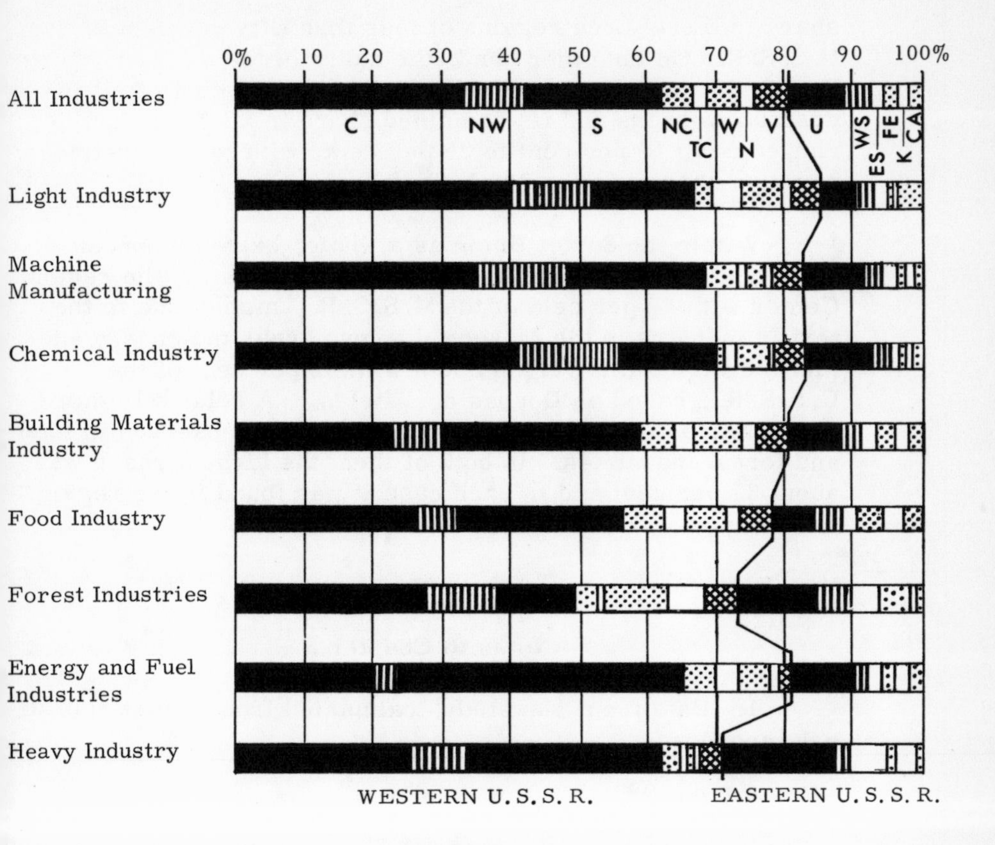

FIGURE 1

WORKERS IN PRINCIPAL BRANCHES OF INDUSTRY AS A PER CENT OF THE U. S. S. R., BY MAJOR ECONOMIC REGIONS, 1940

Key:

C	=	Center	V	=	Volga
NW	=	Northwest	U	=	Ural
S	=	South	WS	=	West Siberia
NC	=	North Caucasus	ES	=	East Siberia
TC	=	Trans-Caucasus	FE	=	Far East
W	=	West	K	=	Kazakhstan
N	=	North	CA	=	Central Asia

share in these three regions of less than fifty per cent of the U. S. S. R. On the other hand, the share of the eastern U. S. S. R. (including the Ural) was twenty per cent of all industrial workers and its combined share in all the industries ranged from 14 per cent to 29 per cent, with four industries having a share of over 20 per cent.

Within the Soviet Union as a whole, extreme concentration occurred in two industries: light industry (the region Center with 40 per cent of the U. S. S. R., mainly due to the textile industry in the Moscow-Ivanovo area) and energy and fuel industries (the region South with 42 per cent of the U. S. S. R., based on Donbas coal fields). A relatively more even distribution among the regions could be observed in food and forest industries. In both of them the highest share was about 27 per cent and in each case it was found in the region Center.

Notes to Chapter 3

1. Data from our study, calculated from Soviet statistical handbooks.

2. *Ibid.*

3. *Ibid.*

4. *Ibid.*

5. *Ibid.*

6. *Ibid.*

7. *Ibid.*

8. *Ibid.*

CHAPTER 4 STRUCTURE OF MAJOR ECONOMIC REGIONS, 1940

While in the previous chapter the discussion was centered on the eight principal branches of industry and the distribution of industrial workers within each of the branches by major economic regions, the focus in this chapter is on the fourteen major economic regions and their internal industrial structure. The data are graphically presented in a bar chart and there are also fourteen tables, one for each major economic region.

In Figure 2 the regions are arranged according to the decreasing share of machine manufacturing (industry #1), ranging from 39 per cent in the region Northwest to 14 per cent in the region West. A visual comparison of the regional industrial structure with that of the U. S. S. R. (top bar in the chart) shows that several industrial branches had approximately the same share of most of the regions as well as of the U. S. S. R. in 1940. For example, industrial workers in the chemical industry represented about 3 per cent of all industrial workers in the U. S. S. R. and eight major regions had about the same share. On the other hand, in machine manufacturing the regional share was similar to the national share in only four regions, comparing their shares, ranging from 29 to 32 per cent, to the national share of 29 per cent. Two regions had a share of between 34 and 39 per cent, while eight regions had a smaller share from 25 down to 14 per cent.

In analyzing briefly the internal industrial structure of the major economic regions, a few comments summarizing Tables 3 through 16 might be of some interest (see also Figure 2). If we compare workers as per cent of the region (Row C in each table) we could conclude that there is a positive correlation between higher percentage of workers in machine

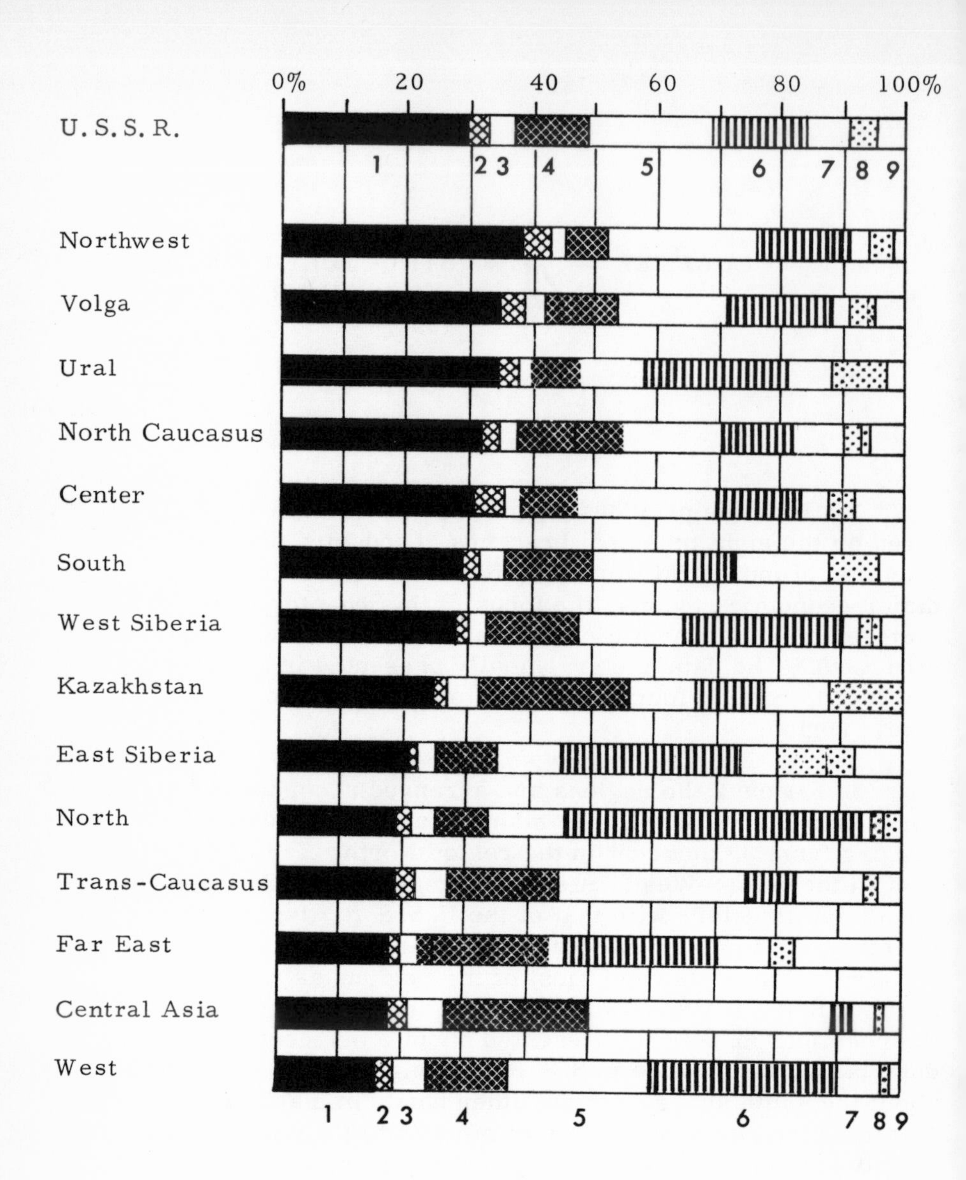

FIGURE 2

INDUSTRIAL WORKERS BY BRANCHES OF INDUSTRY AS A PER CEN[T]
OF THE MAJOR ECONOMIC REGIONS, 1940

Key: 1 = Machine Manufacturing
2 = Chemical Industry
3 = Building Materials Industry
4 = Food Industry
5 = Light Industry
6 = Forest Industries
7 = Energy and Fuel Industrie[s]
8 = Heavy Industry
9 = Other Industries

TABLE 3

Breakdown of Industrial Workers in the

Central Region in 1940

	All Industries	Number of Industry							
		1	2	3	4	5	6	7	8
(A) Workers as Per Cent of the U.S.S.R.	33%	22%	26%	35%	41%	23%	27%	40%	27%
(B) Rank among the Major Regions	1	2	2	1	1	2	1	1	1
(C) Workers as Per Cent of the Region	100%	5%	4%	31%	4%	2%	13%	22%	11%
(D) Rank among the Major Regions[a]	----	9	5	5	2	12	9	4	12
(E) Location Quotient (LQ)[b]	----	.7	.8	1.1	1.3	.7	.8	1.2	.8

Key to Industries:

1 - Energy and Fuel Industries
2 - Heavy Industry
3 - Machine Manufacturing
4 - Chemical Industry
5 - Building Materials Industry
6 - Forest Industries
7 - Light Industry
8 - Food Industry

Note: All per cent figures are rounded values (decimal points have been omitted).

[a]Row D: Rank (among the 14 major regions) of the share of a given industry as per cent of the region (Row C above). See also Fig. 2: e.g., Central Region ranks fifth in machine manufacturing.

[b]"The location quotient measures the degree to which a specific region has more or less than its share of any particular industry...." [John W. Alexander, Economic Geography (Englewood Cliffs, New Jersey: Prentice-Hall, 1963), p. 406]. See Appendix V for a more complete definition of this term.

TABLE 4

Breakdown of Industrial Workers in the

Region South in 1940

	All Industries	Number of Industry							
		1	2	3	4	5	6	7	8
(A) Workers as Per Cent of the U.S.S.R.	20%	42%	29%	20%	15%	28%	11%	15%	23%
(B) Rank among the Major Regions	2	1	1	2	2	1	3	2	2
(C) Workers as Per Cent of the Region	100%	15%	8%	29%	3%	4%	9%	14%	14%
(D) Rank among the Major Regions[a]	----	1	4	6	9	6	12	9	8
(E) Location Quotient (LQ)[b]	----	2.1	1.4	1.1	.8	1.4	.6	.8	1.1

Key to Industries:

1 - Energy and Fuel Industries
2 - Heavy Industry
3 - Machine Manufacturing
4 - Chemical Industry
5 - Building Materials Industry
6 - Forest Industries
7 - Light Industry
8 - Food Industry

Note: All per cent figures are rounded values (decimal points have been omitted).

[a]Row D: Rank (among the 14 major regions) of the share of a given industry as per cent of the region (Row C above). See also Fig. 2: e.g., Central Region ranks fifth in machine manufacturing.

[b]"The location quotient measures the degree to which a specific region has more or less than its share of any particular industry. . ."(Alexander, loc. cit.). See Appendix V for a more complete definition of this term.

TABLE 5

Breakdown of Industrial Workers in the

Northwest Region in 1940

	All Industries	Number of Industry							
		1	2	3	4	5	6	7	8
(A) Workers as Per Cent of the U.S.S.R.	10%	3%	7%	13%	14%	6%	10%	11%	6%
(B) Rank among the Major Regions	3	6	4	3	3	5	4	3	4
(C) Workers as Per Cent of the Region	100%	3%	4%	39%	5%	2%	16%	21%	8%
(D) Rank among the Major Regions[a]	----	14	6	1	1	13	8	5	14
(E) Location Quotient (LQ)[b]	----	.4	.8	1.3	1.4	.6	1.0	1.2	.6

Key to Industries:

1 - Energy and Fuel Industries
2 - Heavy Industry
3 - Machine Manufacturing
4 - Chemical Industry
5 - Building Materials Industry
6 - Forest Industries
7 - Light Industry
8 - Food Industry

Note: All per cent figures are rounded values (decimal points have been omitted).

[a]Row D: Rank (among the 14 major regions) of the share of a given industry as per cent of the region (Row C above). See also Fig. 2: e.g., Central Region ranks fifth in machine manufacturing.

[b]"The location quotient measures the degree to which a specific region has more or less than its share of any particular industry. . ."(Alexander, loc. cit.). See Appendix V for a more complete definition of this term.

TABLE 6

Breakdown of Industrial Workers in the

Ural Region in 1940

	All Industries	Number of Industry							
		1	2	3	4	5	6	7	8
(A) Workers as Per Cent of the U.S.S.R.	8%	7%	16%	9%	10%	7%	12%	5%	6%
(B) Rank among the Major Regions	4	3	3	4	4	4	2	5	5
(C) Workers as Per Cent of the Region	100%	6%	11%	32%	4%	3%	23%	10%	9%
(D) Rank among the Major Regions[a]	----	8	2	3	3	9	6	12	13
(E) Location Quotient (LQ)[b]	----	.8	2.0	1.1	1.2	.9	1.5	.6	.7

Key to Industries:

1 - Energy and Fuel Industries
2 - Heavy Industry
3 - Machine Manufacturing
4 - Chemical Industry
5 - Building Materials Industry
6 - Forest Industries
7 - Light Industry
8 - Food Industry

Note: All per cent figures are rounded values (decimal points have been omitted).

[a]Row D: Rank (among the 14 major regions) of the share of a given industry as per cent of the region (Row C above). See also Fig. 2: e.g., Central Region ranks fifth in machine manufacturing.

[b]"The location quotient measures the degree to which a specific region has more or less than its share of any particular industry. . ."(Alexander, loc. cit.). See Appendix V for a more complete definition of this term.

TABLE 7

Breakdown of Industrial Workers in the

Region West in 1940

	All Industries	Number of Industry							
		1	2	3	4	5	6	7	8
(A) Workers as Per Cent of the U.S.S.R.	5%	5%	1%	3%	5%	8%	10%	7%	6%
(B) Rank among the Major Regions	5	5	13	8	5	3	5	4	6
(C) Workers as Per Cent of the Region	100%	8%	1%	14%	3%	5%	30%	24%	14%
(D) Rank among the Major Regions[a]	----	6	14	14	5	2	2	3	9
(E) Location Quotient (LQ)[b]	----	1.0	.2	.5	.9	1.6	1.9	1.4	1.1

Key to Industries:

1 - Energy and Fuel Industries
2 - Heavy Industry
3 - Machine Manufacturing
4 - Chemical Industry
5 - Building Materials Industry
6 - Forest Industries
7 - Light Industry
8 - Food Industry

Note: All per cent figures are rounded values (decimal points have been omitted).

[a]Row D: Rank (among the 14 major regions) of the share of a given industry as per cent of the region (Row C above). See also Fig. 2: e.g., Central Region ranks fifth in machine manufacturing.

[b]"The location quotient measures the degree to which a specific region has more or less than its share of any particular industry. . ."(Alexander, loc. cit.). See Appendix V for a more complete definition of this term.

TABLE 8

Breakdown of Industrial Workers in the

Volga Region in 1940

	All Industries	Number of Industry							
		1	2	3	4	5	6	7	8
(A) Workers as Per Cent of the U.S.S.R.	5%	2%	4%	5%	4%	4%	5%	4%	5%
(B) Rank among the Major Regions	6	11	6	5	6	8	8	6	7
(C) Workers as Per Cent of the Region	100%	3%	4%	34%	3%	2%	18%	17%	15%
(D) Rank among the Major Regions[a]	----	12	8	2	7	10	7	6	7
(E) Location Quotient (LQ)[b]	----	.4	.8	1.2	.9	.8	1.1	.9	1.2

Key to Industries:

1 - Energy and Fuel Industries
2 - Heavy Industry
3 - Machine Manufacturing
4 - Chemical Industry
5 - Building Materials Industry
6 - Forest Industries
7 - Light Industry
8 - Food Industry

Note: All per cent figures are rounded values (decimal points have been omitted).

[a]Row D: Rank (among the 14 major regions) of the share of a given industry as per cent of the region (Row C above). See also Fig. 2: e.g., Central Region ranks fifth in machine manufacturing.

[b]"The location quotient measures the degree to which a specific region has more or less than its share of any particular industry. . ."(Alexander, loc. cit.). See Appendix V for a more complete definition of this term.

TABLE 9

Breakdown of Industrial Workers in the

North Caucasus Region in 1940

	All Industries	Number of Industry							
		1	2	3	4	5	6	7	8
(A) Workers as Per Cent of the U.S.S.R.	4%	5%	3%	5%	1%	5%	3%	3%	6%
(B) Rank among the Major Regions	7	4	9	6	12	6	11	9	3
(C) Workers as Per Cent of the Region	100%	10%	3%	32%	1%	4%	12%	14%	19%
(D) Rank among the Major Regions[a]	----	3	10	4	13	7	10	8	4
(E) Location Quotient (LQ)[b]	----	1.3	.6	1.1	.3	1.2	.8	.8	1.5

Key to Industries:

1 - Energy and Fuel Industries
2 - Heavy Industry
3 - Machine Manufacturing
4 - Chemical Industry
5 - Building Materials Industry
6 - Forest Industries
7 - Light Industry
8 - Food Industry

Note: All per cent figures are rounded values (decimal points have been omitted).

[a]Row D: Rank (among the 14 major regions) of the share of a given industry as per cent of the region (Row C above). See also Fig. 2: e.g., Central Region ranks fifth in machine manufacturing.

[b]"The location quotient measures the degree to which a specific region has more or less than its share of any particular industry. . ."(Alexander, _loc. cit._). See Appendix V for a more complete definition of this term.

TABLE 10

Breakdown of Industrial Workers in the

Region West Siberia in 1940

	All Industries	Number of Industry							
		1	2	3	4	5	6	7	8
(A) Workers as Per Cent of the U.S.S.R.	4%	2%	3%	3%	3%	2%	6%	3%	5%
(B) Rank among the Major Regions	8	12	8	7	7	11	7	10	8
(C) Workers as Per Cent of the Region	100%	4%	4%	25%	3%	2%	25%	15%	18%
(D) Rank among the Major Regions[a]	----	11	7	7	6	14	5	7	6
(E) Location Quotient (LQ)[b]	----	.5	.8	.9	.9	.6	1.6	.9	1.4

Key to Industries:

1 - Energy and Fuel Industries
2 - Heavy Industry
3 - Machine Manufacturing
4 - Chemical Industry
5 - Building Materials Industry
6 - Forest Industries
7 - Light Industry
8 - Food Industry

Note: All per cent figures are rounded values (decimal points have been omitted).

[a]Row D: Rank (among the 14 major regions) of the share of a given industry as per cent of the region (Row C above). See also Fig. 2: e.g., Central Region ranks fifth in machine manufacturing.

[b]"The location quotient measures the degree to which a specific region has more or less than its share of any particular industry. . ."(Alexander, loc. cit.). See Appendix V for a more complete definition of this term.

TABLE 11

Breakdown of Industrial Workers in the

Region East Siberia in 1940

	All Industries	Number of Industry							
		1	2	3	4	5	6	7	8
(A) Workers as Per Cent of the U.S.S.R.	2%	2%	5%	2%	1%	2%	4%	1%	2%
(B) Rank among the Major Regions	9	9	5	9	10	13	9	11	13
(C) Workers as Per Cent of the Region	100%	7%	11%	19%	2%	2%	28%	11%	12%
(D) Rank among the Major Regions[a]	----	7	3	9	11	11	3	10	10
(E) Location Quotient (LQ)[b]	----	.9	2.0	.7	.6	.8	1.7	.6	1.0

Key to Industries:

1 - Energy and Fuel Industries
2 - Heavy Industry
3 - Machine Manufacturing
4 - Chemical Industry
5 - Building Materials Industry
6 - Forest Industries
7 - Light Industry
8 - Food Industry

Note: All per cent figures are rounded values (decimal points have been omitted).

[a]Row D: Rank (among the 14 major regions) of the share of a given industry as per cent of the region (Row C above). See also Fig. 2: e.g., Central Region ranks fifth in machine manufacturing.

[b]"The location quotient measures the degree to which a specific region has more or less than its share of any particular industry. . ."(Alexander, <u>loc. cit.</u>). See Appendix V for a more complete definition of this term.

TABLE 12

Breakdown of Industrial Workers in the

Trans-Caucasus Region in 1940

	All Industries	Number of Industry							
		1	2	3	4	5	6	7	8
(A) Workers as Per Cent of the U.S.S.R.	2%	3%	1%	1%	2%	4%	1%	4%	3%
(B) Rank among the Major Regions	10	7	12	10	8	9	12	8	11
(C) Workers as Per Cent of the Region	100%	11%	2%	19%	3%	5%	8%	30%	18%
(D) Rank among the Major Regions[a]	----	2	12	10	4	3	13	2	5
(E) Location Quotient (LQ)[b]	----	1.5	.4	.6	1.0	1.6	.5	1.7	1.4

Key to Industries:

1 - Energy and Fuel Industries
2 - Heavy Industry
3 - Machine Manufacturing
4 - Chemical Industry
5 - Building Materials Industry
6 - Forest Industries
7 - Light Industry
8 - Food Industry

Note: All per cent figures are rounded values (decimal points have been omitted).

[a]Row D: Rank (among the 14 major regions) of the share of a given industry as per cent of the region (Row C above). See also Fig. 2: e.g., Central Region ranks fifth in machine manufacturing.

[b]"The location quotient measures the degree to which a specific region has more or less than its share of any particular industry. . ."(Alexander, loc. cit.). See Appendix V for a more complete definition of this term.

TABLE 13

Breakdown of Industrial Workers in the

Region Far East in 1940

	All Industries	Number of Industry							
		1	2	3	4	5	6	7	8
(A) Workers as Per Cent of the U.S.S.R.	2%	2%	1%	1%	1%	3%	4%	1%	4%
(B) Rank among the Major Regions	11	8	11	14	14	10	10	14	9
(C) Workers as Per Cent of the Region	100%	9%	3%	15%	1%	4%	26%	2%	22%
(D) Rank among the Major Regions[a]	----	5	11	13	14	5	4	14	3
(E) Location Quotient (LQ)[b]	----	1.1	.6	.5	.1	1.4	1.7	.2	1.7

Key to Industries:

1 - Energy and Fuel Industries
2 - Heavy Industry
3 - Machine Manufacturing
4 - Chemical Industry
5 - Building Materials Industry
6 - Forest Industries
7 - Light Industry
8 - Food Industry

Note: All per cent figures are rounded values (decimal points have been omitted).

[a]Row D: Rank (among the 14 major regions) of the share of a given industry as per cent of the region (Row C above). See also Fig. 2: e.g., Central Region ranks fifth in machine manufacturing.

[b]"The location quotient measures the degree to which a specific region has more or less than its share of any particular industry. . ."(Alexander, _loc. cit._). See Appendix V for a more complete definition of this term.

TABLE 14

Breakdown of Industrial Workers in the

Region Central Asia in 1940

	All Industries	Number of Industry							
		1	2	3	4	5	6	7	8
(A) Workers as Per Cent of the U.S.S.R.	2%	1%	1%	1%	2%	4%	1%	4%	4%
(B) Rank among the Major Regions	12	13	14	11	9	7	14	7	10
(C) Workers as Per Cent of the Region	100%	4%	1%	18%	3%	6%	3%	38%	23%
(D) Rank among the Major Regions[a]	----	10	13	12	8	1	14	1	2
(E) Location Quotient (LQ)[b]	----	.5	.3	.6	.8	2.1	.2	2.1	1.8

Key to Industries:

1 - Energy and Fuel Industries
2 - Heavy Industry
3 - Machine Manufacturing
4 - Chemical Industry
5 - Building Materials Industry
6 - Forest Industries
7 - Light Industry
8 - Food Industry

Note: All per cent figures are rounded values (decimal points have been omitted).

[a]Row D: Rank (among the 14 major regions) of the share of a given industry as per cent of the region (Row C above). See also Fig. 2: e.g., Central Region ranks fifth in machine manufacturing.

[b]"The location quotient measures the degree to which a specific region has more or less than its share of any particular industry. . ."(Alexander, loc. cit.). See Appendix V for a more complete definition of this term.

TABLE 15

Breakdown of Industrial Workers in the

Region North in 1940

	All Industries	Number of Industry							
		1	2	3	4	5	6	7	8
(A) Workers as Per Cent of the U.S.S.R.	2%	1%	1%	1%	1%	2%	6%	1%	2%
(B) Rank among the Major Regions	13	14	10	12	11	14	6	12	14
(C) Workers as Per Cent of the Region	100%	3%	4%	18%	2%	3%	49%	10%	11%
(D) Rank among the Major Regions[a]	----	13	9	11	10	8	1	13	11
(E) Location Quotient (LQ)[b]	----	.4	.7	.6	.7	.9	3.1	.6	.9

Key to Industries:

1 - Energy and Fuel Industries
2 - Heavy Industry
3 - Machine Manufacturing
4 - Chemical Industry
5 - Building Materials Industry
6 - Forest Industries
7 - Light Industry
8 - Food Industry

Note: All per cent figures are rounded values (decimal points have been omitted).

[a]Row D: Rank (among the 14 major regions) of the share of a given industry as per cent of the region (Row C above). See also Fig. 2: e.g., Central Region ranks fifth in machine manufacturing.

[b]"The location quotient measures the degree to which a specific region has more or less than its share of any particular industry. . ."(Alexander, loc. cit.). See Appendix V for a more complete definition of this term.

TABLE 16

Breakdown of Industrial Workers in the

Kazakhstan Region in 1940

	All Industries	Number of Industry							
		1	2	3	4	5	6	7	8
(A) Workers as Per Cent of the U.S.S.R.	1%	2%	3%	1%	1%	2%	1%	1%	3%
(B) Rank among the Major Regions	14	10	7	13	13	12	13	13	12
(C) Workers as Per Cent of the Region	100%	10%	13%	25%	2%	4%	11%	11%	24%
(D) Rank among the Major Regions[a]	----	4	1	8	12	4	11	11	1
(E) Location Quotient (LQ)[b]	----	1.3	2.4	.9	.6	1.5	.7	.6	1.9

Key to Industries:

1 - Energy and Fuel Industries
2 - Heavy Industry
3 - Machine Manufacturing
4 - Chemical Industry
5 - Building Materials Industry
6 - Forest Industries
7 - Light Industry
8 - Food Industry

Note: All per cent figures are rounded values (decimal points have been omitted).

[a]Row D: Rank (among the 14 major regions) of the share of a given industry as per cent of the region (Row C above). See also Fig. 2: e.g., Central Region ranks fifth in machine manufacturing.

[b]"The location quotient measures the degree to which a specific region has more or less than its share of any particular industry. . ."(Alexander, loc. cit.). See Appendix V for a more complete definition of this term.

manufacturing and more industrialized regions. Of the seven regions having the highest share of workers in this industry (25-39 per cent), four were the leading industrial regions (Center, South, Northwest, and Ural) while the other three were also more industrialized (Volga, North Caucasus and West Siberia). These seven more industrialized regions had significant shares of the total Soviet industrial production in 1940 and their combined share amounted to 100 per cent of the pig iron production, 98 per cent of crude steel, 99 per cent of iron ore, about 99 per cent of coke, 83 per cent of coal, 86 per cent of the electric power, and 87 per cent of the gross industrial output.[1]

On the other hand, the other seven regions (East Siberia, Far East, Central Asia, Kazakhstan, North, Trans-Caucasus, and West) with a much smaller share of workers in machine manufacturing (14-25 per cent) could be considered as less industrialized in 1940 since each one of them had an insignificant share (less than 1 per cent of the total Soviet production, or none at all) of the key industrial raw materials or products (pig iron, crude steel, iron ore, coke). These regions were slightly better off in the coal production, and at least four of them had small shares with a combined total of 14 per cent of the Soviet production. The electric power was distributed about evenly with six of the regions having each about 1 per cent of the U. S. S. R. total output, while Trans-Caucasus region accounted for about 6 per cent. In six regions the share of the Soviet gross industrial output was between 1 and 2 per cent, while Trans-Caucasus again had a slightly higher share of about 4 per cent.[2]

The seven more industrialized regions had not only the seven highest shares of workers in machine manufacturing (over 25 per cent), but in each of the regions this same industry had the largest share among the eight industrial branches (see Figure 2). In the other seven regions an industry other than machine manufacturing had the largest percentage of the workers in the region. The exception was Kazakhstan where the food industry had 24. 1 per cent of the region's workers while machine manufacturing had almost the same share-- 24. 7 per cent.

A negative correlation between the level of industrialization in a region and the share of workers in forest industries, light industry, and food industry can also be noted. The last two industries, consumer-oriented and largely neglected by the Soviet economic planners, could almost serve as an index of industrialization. The regions with the highest percentage of workers in the food industry (22-24 per cent), light industry (38 per cent), and forest industries (26-49 per cent), were among the least industrialized regions of the Soviet Union in 1940. Kazakhstan had the highest share of the workers in the food industry alone, Central Asia the highest share in light industry and high share in the food industry, the Far East had high shares in both food industry and forest industries, and the region North the highest share in forest industries alone.

In almost all cases, those industries which could be considered most characteristic of a region may be easily identified with the three industries having the highest shares of the workers in the region (see Row C in Tables 3-16). Among the most characteristic industries in the fourteen major economic regions (on the average three different characteristic industires per region) more than one-half were those industries that had over 20 per cent of the workers in the region. Since the Soviet Union regards machine manufacturing as the most important industrial branch and a key to the full industrialization and development of all the regions in the country, it is not surprising to find in the Tables 3-16 that this was the only branch which was characteristic of all the major economic regions in 1940. Machine manufacturing had the highest share of the workers in eight regions, and second or third highest share in the other six regions.

There were also a few cases of industries that were unquestionably very important and characteristic in several of the regions despite the fact that their share of workers was very low. Both chemical industry (4 per cent of the region Center, 5 per cent of the Northwest) and heavy industry (8 per cent of the region South, 11 per cent of the Ural) have lower manpower requirements than machine manufacturing and this could partly explain these low percentage figures.

Notes to Chapter 4

1. Data for gross industrial output (for 1937) from S. S. Balzak, V. F. Vasyutin, and Ya. G. Feigin, Economic Geography of the U. S. S. R., translated by Robert M. Hanklin and Olga Adler Titelbaum (New York: Macmillan, 1952), p. 206. Data for coke and electric power from John Stanley Hoyt, Jr., "An Investigation of the Economics of Soviet Locational Doctrine, Policy, and Practice--With Special Emphasis on Heavy Industry" (unpublished Ph. D. dissertation, Department of Economics, The American University, 1959), pp. 101-2 and 134. Other data from Paul E. Lydolph, Geography of the U. S. S. R. (New York: John Wiley and Sons, 1964), p. 355.

2. Data from the same sources as given in Note 1 to Chapter 4.

CHAPTER 5 MANPOWER REDISTRIBUTION DURING WORLD WAR II

On August 15, 1941, eight weeks after the German attack on the Soviet Union, the Soviet Government adopted the "war economic plan":

> For the purpose of the most rapid expansion and material supplying of war production in the regions of the Volga, Urals, Western Siberia, Kazakhstan, and Central Asia, the war economic plan provided for the relocation in the eastern regions of hundreds of industrial enterprises in machine-building, for the production of ammunition, armaments, tanks, and aircraft, and for the transfer to them of construction projects and enterprises from other branches of the economy.[1]

The magnitude of the proposed plan of relocation of industry can be seen if the Soviet territorial losses are compared at the time of the plan's adoption and four months later when the German Blitzkrieg came to a temporary halt in December of 1941. By the middle of August, 1941, the German front had reached a line from Leningrad through Smolensk to Kiev, Dnepropetrovsk and Odessa.[2] Four months later the front extended from Leningrad to Moscow, Kharkov and Rostov.[3] Thus before the end of 1941, all of the regions South and West and parts of the Northwest and Center regions were under German occupation. This area accounted for approximately 35 per cent of Soviet industrial workers in 1940, and its loss was a very serious blow to the Soviet industrial war effort. With minor changes, the area west of the line Leningrad-Smolensk-Kharkov-Rostov remained under German occupation for almost two years until the summer of 1943.[4] An additional area, including most of the region North Caucasus, was under German control from August, 1942, until February, 1943, but was recovered by the Soviets after the German debacle at Stalingrad.[5] These regions of the U. S. S. R. which were under German occupation from six months to two years accounted for 45 per cent of the Soviet population and 33 per cent of the gross output of industry in 1940.[6] This same area also contained about 43 per cent of Soviet industrial workers in 1940 (see Table 17).

Except for Voznesensky's account, little has been written about the changes in the regional distribution of Soviet industry during World War II.[7] Even Voznesensky gives limited data and then only for the changes during 1940-43. Table 17 shows the computed data for the per cent increase or decrease of industrial workers for selected sovnarkhozy for the period 1940-45. The first part of the table (Sovnarkhozy West of the Line of Maximum German Advance) shows the data for sixteen sovnarkhozy and one region (South) but the data are lacking for three sovnarkhozy (Numbers 4, 21, and 50) wholly under German occupation and for three others (Numbers 2, 3, and 17) partially occupied (see the map in Appendix IV). The area west of the line of maximum German advance shows an overall decline of 48 per cent in the number of workers from 1940 to 1945. Including only the sovnarkhozy (and region South) for which the data are available, this area represented 38. 7 per cent of Soviet workers in 1940. However, by adding the rest of the sovnarkhozy for which 1940 data are available but 1945 data are lacking, then the area west of the line contained 43 per cent of Soviet workers. This figure was reduced to 25 per cent by 1945. Thus the actual decline in the number of workers in the areas under German occupation was closer to 50 per cent. The decline in individual regions ranged from 32 per cent in the Center (the part of the region under German occupation) to 62 per cent in the Northwest. The greatest decline among the individual sovnarkhozy was in Leningrad and Belorussia (62 per cent in each) and their share of the Soviet industrial manpower declined from 8. 4 and 2. 8 per cent in 1940 to 3. 5 and 1. 2 per cent in 1945, respectively.

Apart from the decline in the areas under German occupation, according to Alexander Werth,

> Soviet industry also suffered from a serious shortage of manpower. The annual average of workers and employees in the national economy had dropped from 31. 2 million

TABLE 17

Per Cent Increase or Decrease of Industrial Workers for Selected *Sovnarkhozy*, 1940-45

Sovnarkhozy West of the Line of Maximum German Advance (1941-42) and Wholly or Partially under German Occupation (1941-43)				
Number of the *Sovnarkhoz* on Map 33 (Appendix IV)	Name of the *Sovnarkhoz* (See Appendix II)	*Sovnarkhoz* as Per Cent of Soviet Industrial Workers[a] 1940	1945	Change 1940-45: Per Cent Decrease (-) in the Number of Industrial Workers
	NORTHWEST			
25	Leningrad	8.4	3.5	-62
26	Karelian	.4	.2	-63
		8.8	3.7	-62
	WEST			
104	Estonian	.6	.5	-29
102	Lithuanian	.5	.4	-32
103	Latvian	1.0	.7	-35
101	Belorussian	2.8	1.2	-62
		4.9	2.8	-49
	CENTER			
7	Tula	1.5	1.7	- 9
6	Kaluga	.4	.3	-30
20	Kursk	.2	.2	-31
19	Belgorod	.2	.1	-43
5	Bryansk	.7	.3	-58
18	Lipetsk	.5	.2	-60
		3.5	2.8	-32
69-80	SOUTH	19.8	12.6	-45
	NORTH CAUCASUS			
44	Stavropol'	.3	.2	-22
48	Kabardino-Balkar	.1	.1	-36
47	North-Ossetian	.1	.1	-37
45	Krasnodar	1.2	.7	-39
		1.7	1.1	-35
U.S.S.R. West of the Line		38.7	23.0	-48

TABLE 17-Continued

Number of the Sovnarkhoz on Map 33 (Appendix IV)	Name of the Sovnarkhoz (See Appendix II)	Sovnarkhoz as Per Cent of Soviet Industrial Workers[a] 1940	1945	Change 1940-45: Per Cent Increase (+) or Decrease (-) in the Number of Industrial Workers
Sovnarkhozy East of the Line of Maximum German Advance (1941-42) and Not under German Occupation (1941-43)				
	NORTH			
30	Vologda	.7	.7	-14
	CENTER			
14	Gor'kiy	2.4	2.7	- 7
12	Kostroma	.6	.6	-11
15	Tambov	.5	.5	-14
1	Moscow City	8.1	7.6	-23
10	Ivanovo	2.5	1.9	-34
		14.1	13.3	-21
16	Penza	.5	.7	+ 4
9	Vladimir	1.2	1.6	+11
8	Ryazan'	.4	.5	+15
22	Mordva	.1	.2	+18
23	Mari	.2	.2	+24
24	Chuvash	.2	.3	+27
		2.6	3.5	+13
		16.7	16.8	-16
	VOLGA			
43	Astrakhan'	.2	.4	+37
	TRANS-CAUCASUS			
99	Azerbaydzhan	1.0	1.1	- 6
98	Georgian	.9	1.1	+ 9
		1.9	2.2	+ 1
	URAL			
36	Bashkir	1.0	1.5	+17
37	Udmurt	.8	1.1	+23
32	Sverdlovsk	2.5	5.4	+82
		4.3	8.0	+55

TABLE 17-Continued

Number of the Sovnarkhoz on Map 33 (Appendix IV)	Name of the Sovnarkhoz (See Appendix II)	Sovnarkhoz as Per Cent of Soviet Industrial Workers[a] 1940	1945	Change 1940-45: Per Cent Increase (+) or Decrease (-) in the Number of Industrial Workers
	Sovnarkhozy East of the Line of Maximum German Advance (1941-42) and Not under German Occupation (1941-43)			
	WEST SIBERIA			
51	Tyumen'	.3	.5	+ 29
52	Kurgan	.2	.3	+ 32
57	Altay	.6	1.0	+ 33
55	Tomsk	.1	.3	+ 76
54	Novosibirsk	.7	1.5	+ 84
56	Kemerovo	1.1	2.6	+ 88
53	Omsk	.3	.9	+160
		3.3	7.1	+ 74
	KAZAKHSTAN	1.4	2.6	+ 61
	EAST SIBERIA			
61	Buryat	.2	.2	0
59	Irkutsk	.7	.9	+ 5
58	Krasnoyarsk	.7	1.1	+ 30
		1.6	2.2	+ 15
	FAR EAST			
64	Primorskiy	.7	.7	- 19
65	Amur	.2	.3	+ 21
63	Khabarovsk	.5	.7	+ 23
68	Magadan	.1	.3	+ 23
66	Sakhalin (Island)	.1	.2	+178
		1.6	2.2	+ 11
U.S.S.R. East of the Line		31.7	42.2	+ 11
All U.S.S.R. East of the Line		57.0	75.0	+ 14
All U.S.S.R. West of the Line		43.0	25.0	- 50
	TOTAL U.S.S.R.	100.0	100.0	- 13

Note: [a]Data were computed only from those Soviet statistical handbooks (for individual *oblasts*, *krays*, A.S.S.R.'s and S.S.R.'s) which contained the number of industrial workers for both 1940 and 1945.

> in 1940 to 27.3 million in 1941; in November [1941] this figure had dropped to 19.8 million. Some had been left behind in the occupied areas; others were still on their way to the east.[8]

Werth develops "a story of how whole industries and millions of people had been moved to the east," and states that "between July and November 1941 no fewer than 1,523 industrial enterprises . . . had been moved to the east." But he also cautions that "it would . . . be naive to assume that everything of any industrial importance was . . . evacuated in time."[9]

If the figure of 50 per cent decline of Soviet industrial workers in the occupied areas from 1940 to 1945 seems very serious indeed, then the decline in the same area in the period 1940-43 borders on the catastrophic. According to Voznesensky, the decrease in number of workers in the areas of R. S. F. S. R. under German occupation (parts of the regions Northwest, Center, and North Caucasus) was 83 per cent.[10] The Ukrainian S. S. R. decreased also by 83 per cent, while the Belorussian S. S. R. literally lost most of its workers.[11] The decrease in the number of enterprises was also serious in the occupied areas. While many of them could be transferred to the eastern regions, for others the time was too short and when the "war economic plan" was adopted (mid-August, 1941), most of the area of the regions South and West was already under German control. Thus the decrease in the number of enterprises represented a serious loss for the Soviets and not just a transfer from the western U. S. S. R. and a gain for the eastern regions. Between 1940 and 1943, industrial enterprises decreased by 81 per cent in the Ukrainian S. S. R., by 85 per cent in the Belorussian S. S. R., and by 87 per cent in the areas of the R. S. F. S. R. occupied by the German Army.[12]

The second part of Table 17 (pp. 61-62) shows the changes in the number of industrial workers in the *sovnarkhozy* east of the line of maximum German advance. This area was never under German occupation, and it would be an easy and simple assumption to conclude that while the number of workers decreased in the areas under German occupation, the number of workers increased in the unoccupied areas. As the table shows, however, quite a few *sovnarkhozy* in the unoccupied regions showed a marked decrease and not only those immediately bordering on the German front.

For example, it might be possible to explain the decline in Tambov and Vologda _sovnarkhozy_ as a result of their proximity to the front. In Moscow city _sovnarkhoz_ the decline occurred because the political and administrative organs, as well as many ordinary citizens, were evacuated in late 1941. On the other hand, it is more difficult to interpret the decline in the three _sovnarkhozy_ east of Moscow (Gorkiy, Kostroma, and Ivanovo), especially since two _sovnarkhozy_ next to the front (Ryazan and Vladimir) show an increase. It might be suggested that the decision was probably made to concentrate some of the war production, based on metallurgy and machine manufacturing, as near to the front as possible, in the vicinity of Moscow, although the main direction of relocation was toward the eastern regions.

The number of workers in Ivanovo _sovnarkhoz_ declined from 283, 000 in 1940 to 186, 000 in 1945 and this decrease could be interpreted as a switch from light industry, which employed 72 per cent of the workers in the _sovnarkhoz_ in 1940, to more war-oriented industries in the nearby _sovnarkhozy_. The absolute decrease in Moscow city _sovnarkhoz_ amounted to more than 200, 000 workers and this could be explained as either the assignment of workers to front-line military duty both in and near Moscow, or the transfer of workers from non-essential light industries to war production in the eastern regions. In all probability, both factors were involved.

The data for Volga and Ural regions are incomplete for the changes between 1940 and 1945. However, by combining data for the nineteen _sovnarkhozy_ east of the line of maximum German advance (in Volga, Ural, West Siberia, East Siberia, Far East; plus the Kazakhstan region) with the data given by Voznesensky for the five eastern regions (Volga, Ural, West Siberia, Central Asia, and Kazakhstan), some measure could be gained of the pattern of change in eastern regions during the war.

Most of the increase in the eastern regions occurred in the first two years of the war (1941-43).[13] During the same period the share of each of the five eastern regions as a per cent of the U. S. S. R. increased two to four times. In terms of the industrial output, the share of the Volga region increased from 3 to 12 per cent, the Ural increased from 7 to 27 per cent, and West Siberia from 3 to 10 per cent.[14] While the share of the industrial output increased two to four times, the share of Soviet industrial workers increased by slightly more than two times. The Volga region's share increased from 3 to 7.5 per cent, the Ural, 8.5 to 20.5 per cent, West Siberia, 4 to 9 per cent, and Central Asia and Kazakhstan together, from 3.5 to 8 per cent.[15]

For decades the Soviet economists have been writing about an industrial shift to the eastern regions, but this remained a dream that is only slowly becoming a partial reality in the late 1960's. However, during the first two years of the Russo-German conflict, that dream almost became a reality under the abnormal conditions of a war economy.

The five eastern regions (Volga, Ural, West Siberia, Central Asia, and Kazakhstan) successfully fulfilled the "war economic plan" of August 1941. From less than 20 per cent of the total Soviet industrial output in 1940, their combined share in 1943 exceeded 50 per cent of the Soviet industrial production. Even though this share did not remain the same after the war, it did impress Soviet economic planners in the postwar period to such an extent that in the 1950's they presented the desirability of an industrial shift to the eastern regions as a reality already achieved. The complete data for 1945 are available for only one eastern region--West Siberia--and they reveal how its share quickly declined. From 1940 to 1943 it increased from 4 to 9 per cent of all Soviet industrial workers but it decreased to 7 per cent in 1945. By 1960 (see Chapter 6), West Siberia's share declined even further, to 5.6 per cent of Soviet workers.

The greatest increase in individual *sovnarkhozy* for which data for both 1940 and 1945 are available, occurred in the Ural and West Siberia regions. The highest increase was observed in Omsk *sovnarkhoz*--an increase of 160 per cent (see Table 17). The share of Omsk was still less than 1 per cent of U.S.S.R. industrial workers in 1945; but two other *sovnarkhozy* stand out, although their rate of increase was only between 82 and 88 per cent. Kemerovo, in the Kuznetsk basin, increased its share of Soviet industrial manpower from 1.1 in 1940 to 2.6 per cent in 1945, while Sverdlovsk's share increased even more significantly, from 2.5 to 5.4 per cent exceeding Leningrad sovnarkhoz which was the largest Soviet manufacturing area in 1940.[16]

Although the data are incomplete for the three eastern regions (Volga, Ural, and Central Asia), there is indication that the 1940-45 increase did proceed according to the "war economic plan" of 1941. The other two regions (West Siberia and Kazakhstan) for which the data are available, also indicate substantial increase in the period 1940-45. Moving further east of the Kuznetsk basin area, the increase begins to fall off in the regions of East Siberia and the Far East, and one sovnarkhoz even registers a decline. A 19 per cent decline in Primorskiy sovnarkhoz (a loss of about 20,000 workers) could be interpreted as a possible military decision to remove some workers from a vulnerable zone that could be overrun in case of a Japanese attack and transfer them to the interior of the Far East region, to some of the more important industrial centers of war production (for example, Komsomol'sk). The maximum increase shown in Table 17 is in Sakhalin Island sovnarkhoz--178 per cent. However, this increase is misleading since the data for 1940 included only the northern (Soviet) half of the island, while the 1945 data include the whole island after the Japanese lost the southern half to the U. S. S. R. at the end of World War II.

In summarizing the observations of the effects of World War II on the redistribution of Soviet industrial workers, several important changes should be noted. First, while the areas of the U. S. S. R. under German occupation decreased by 50 per cent in the number of industrial workers during the period 1940-45, those areas in the Soviet Union that were never occupied showed an over-all increase of 14 per cent. Second, the share of the occupied areas as a per cent of the U. S. S. R. industrial workers decreased from 43 to 25 per cent, while the share of the unoccupied regions increased from 57 to 75 per cent. Third, the U. S. S. R. as a whole had a 13 per cent decrease in the total number of industrial workers: Their number fell from almost 11 million in 1940 to about 9.5 million in 1945. Finally, it is important to consider the great changes that occurred in the Soviet industry during the war before analyzing the changes that took place in a much longer period from 1940 to 1960.

Notes to Chapter 5

1. Nikolai A. Voznesensky, The Economy of the U.S.S.R. During World War II (Washington, D.C.: Public Affairs Press, 1948), p. 23.

2. Colonel Vincent J. Esposito (ed.), The West Point Atlas of American Wars, Vol. II: 1900-1953 (New York: Frederick A. Praeger, 1959), Map 25b.

3. Ibid., Map 28.

4. Ibid., Map 37.

5. Ibid., Map 32.

6. Voznesensky, op. cit., p. 94.

7. Ibid., pp. 28-31 and 65.

8. Alexander Werth, Russia at War 1941-1945 (New York: E. P. Dutton and Company, 1964), p. 223.

9. Ibid., pp. 216 and 218.

10. Voznesensky, op. cit., p. 32.

11. Ibid., p. 33.

12. Ibid., pp. 32-33.

13. Ibid., p. 65.

14. Ibid., pp. 28-30.

15. Ibid., p. 65.

16. Leningrad sovnarkhoz consists of the city of Leningrad and Leningrad oblast, plus three other oblasts: Pskov, Novgorod, and Velikiye Luki. While Leningrad sovnarkhoz represented 8.4 per cent of Soviet industrial workers in 1940, Moscow city sovnarkhoz alone accounted for 8.1 per cent. If both Moscow city and Moscow oblast sovnarkhozy are added their combined share

of U. S. S. R. industrial workers in 1940 was 14. 6 per cent or almost double the share of Leningrad sovnarkhoz.

CHAPTER 6 WORKERS BY MAJOR ECONOMIC REGIONS AND *SOVNARKHOZY*, 1960

In the previous chapter the evidence has been presented indicating that World War II gave an enormous impetus to the long-desired industrial shift to the eastern regions of the Soviet Union. Of course, it would be difficult to speculate whether or not the intended eastward shift would have taken place without the drastic "war economic plan" of 1941. It is possible, however, to show the actual changes by using the combined industrial manpower of the five eastern regions (Volga, Ural, West Siberia, Kazakhstan, and Central Asia) to which much of the Soviet industry was to be relocated. In 1940 this combined area accounted for less than 20 per cent of Soviet industrial workers; but by 1943, under the pressure of the war, its share more than doubled, to 45 per cent of total industrial work force. However, by 1960, when most of the western regions had recovered from the war, the combined share of the same five eastern regions was down to about 28 per cent. It is reasonable to assume, on the basis of these figures, that since the industrial manpower share of the five eastern regions increased from about one-fifth of the U. S. S. R. in 1940 to slightly more than one-fourth in 1960 (helped in no small measure by the "war economic plan"), then in all probability without the war-induced industrial relocation the same regions would have increased their share on a much more modest scale.

In Chapter 1, the territorial extent of the Soviet Union at the end of 1940 was described. It was stressed that only minor additions, both in terms of territory and industrial manpower, were effected by the U. S. S. R. at the end of the war. Thus for all practical purposes the comparisons between 1940 and 1960 are for virtually the same territory.

Before discussing the changes between 1940 and 1960 by major economic regions, some observations should be made on the changes during the same period in the U. S. S. R. as a whole. Conservatively, it is estimated that the population losses of the Soviet Union due to World War II exceeded 20 million persons.[1] Thus the low Soviet population increase of 13 per cent in the twenty-year period (1940-60) comes as no surprise. However, while the total population increased by only 13 per cent, the urban population increased by 80 per cent, total employment[2] (workers and employees in all branch of the economy) increased by 94 per cent, and the number of industrial workers rose by 99 per cent.[3] During the same period, the rural population decreased by 20 per cent and its share of the total population was reduced from 68 per cent in 1940 to 50 per cent in 1960. From 1940 to 1960 the U. S. S. R. increased the share of urban population in the total population from 32 to 50 per cent, the share of total employment[4] rose from 17 to 29 per cent, and the industrial workers increased their share of the total population from 6 to 10 per cent. At the same time, the industrial workers as a per cent of the total employment increased from 34 to 36 per cent.[5]

A word of caution is necessary at this point. In order to understand the full meaning of the changes in the period 1940-60, the changes in the shorter periods within this time span must be analyzed. For example, although the increase in the number of industrial workers in the U. S. S. R. from 1940 to 1960 seems to be substantial when compared to a small increase in total population, it is in effect misleading since there are two distinct periods during these twenty years. First, there was a 38 per cent decline in the number of industrial workers in the U. S. S. R. from 1940 to 1943, and second, a great increase of close to 135 per cent from 1945 to 1960. Therefore, our conclusion should be not that there was a moderate gain in industrial manpower (1940- 60) but a successful recovery despite the terrible destruction of the Soviet industrial capacity during the war.

While it is true that the western U. S. S. R. increased by 79 per cent (industrial workers 1940-60), and the eastern U. S. S. R. increased in the same period by 182 per cent, these percentages obscure the fact that the western U. S. S. R. actually decreased by about 50 per cent in 1940-45 and then increased by almost 170 per cent in the postwar period. The eastern U. S. S. R., on the other hand, increased by over 50 per cent from 1940 to 1945, but the increase in the postwar period was only about 80 per cent. Thus, although it is true that during the whole period under examination (1940-60) the eastern regions showed a greater increase than the western regions, it should be pointed out that in the postwar period of reconstruction the reverse was true.

INDUSTRIAL WORKERS BY MAJOR ECONOMIC REGIONS

Map 13 shows the key changes among the major regions in the period 1940 to 1960: the greatest increase east of the Ural region and the smallest increase west of it. The two regions showing the highest increase are Kazakhstan (256 per cent) and West Siberia (210 per cent). An additional observation could be made regarding the changes in total population compared to industrial workers: Of the four regions showing the smallest increase of industrial workers, two registered a net decline in total population (Center 5 per cent, West 2 per cent) while Northwest and South had only an increase of 2 and 7 per cent, respectively. At the opposite end, Kazakhstan, which had the highest increase in the number of workers, had the second-highest increase (70 per cent) in total population among the major regions.

A comparison of Maps 2 and 14 makes possible the analysis of the changing share of major economic regions in the period 1940-60. A visual inspection of both maps shows that very few regions have had a significant change--a substantial reduction or increase of their share. The most marked reduction occurred in the Central region which was reduced from 32. 5 to 27. 0 per cent, while two other regions in the western U. S. S. R. were reduced by several percentage points--South from 20. 2 to 18. 6 and Northwest from 9. 5 to 6. 1 per cent. Of the five remaining western regions, four show almost no change in their share, while Volga shows a small increase. On the other hand, all the six eastern regions show an increase in their share.

If the shares of the individual regions changed little from 1940 to 1960, there was a substantial change in the share of the western and eastern parts of the U. S. S. R. (see Table 18). While the share of the western U. S. S. R. decreased from

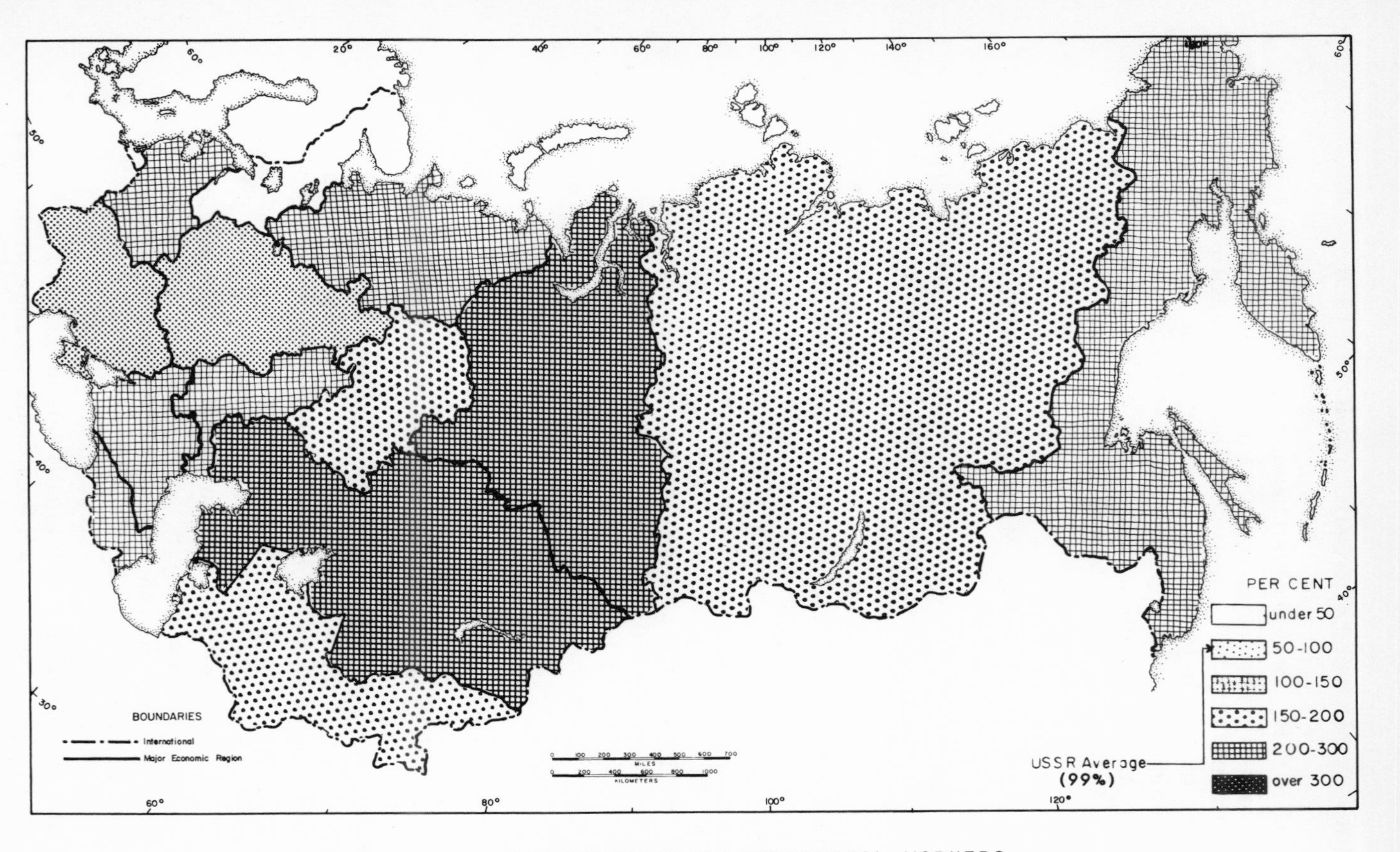

PER CENT INCREASE OF INDUSTRIAL WORKERS

(By Major Economic Regions, 1940 to 1960)

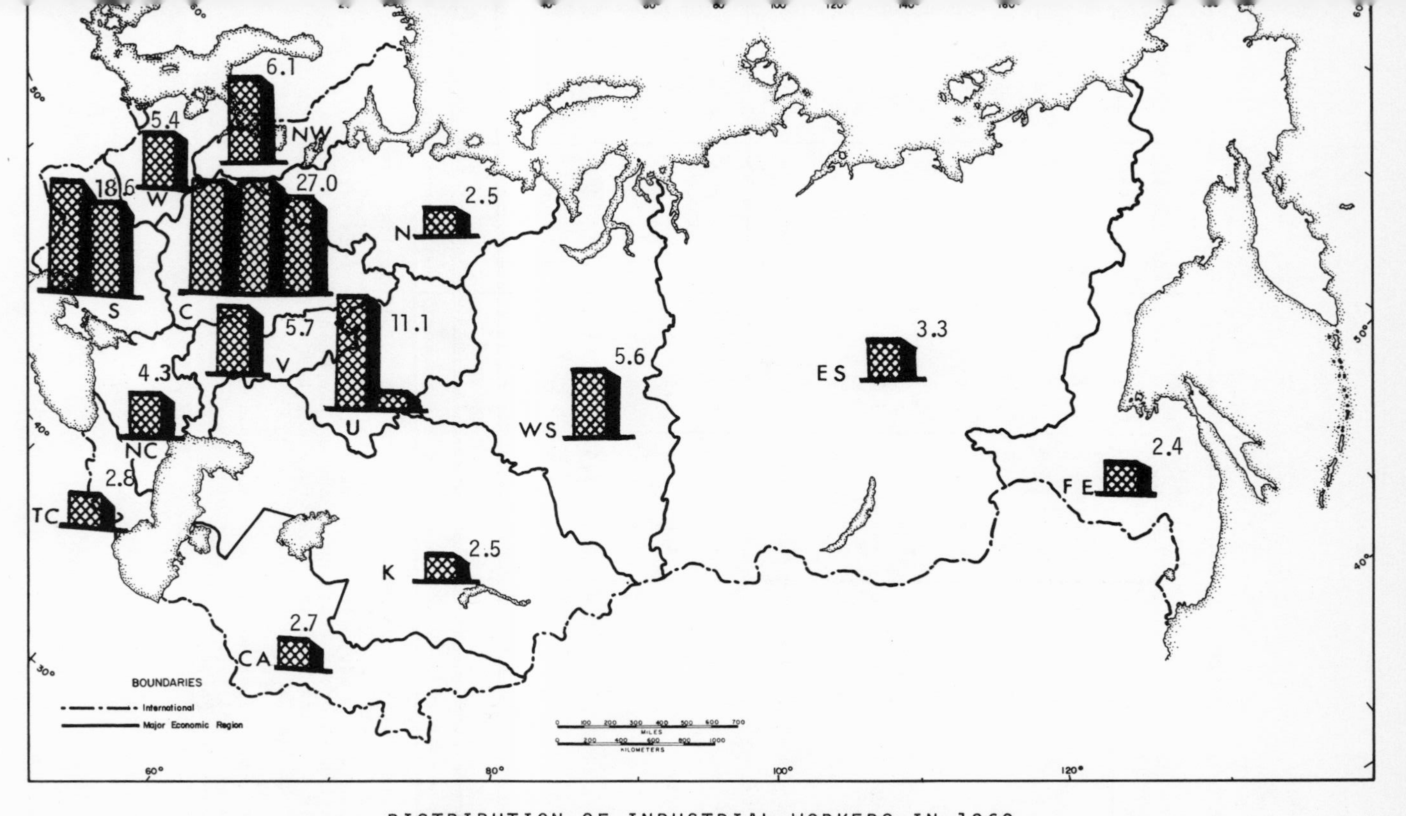

DISTRIBUTION OF INDUSTRIAL WORKERS IN 1960

(Major Economic Regions as Per Cent of U.S.S.R.)

MAP 14

TABLE 18

Major Economic Regions as Per Cent of the U.S.S.R., 1940 and 1960

	Population						Total Employment[a]		Industrial Workers	
	Total		Urban		Rural					
	1940	1960	1940	1960	1940	1960	1940	1960	1940	1960
Center	24.2	20.2	23.7	20.9	24.4	19.5	27.5	23.5	32.5	27.0
South	22.5	21.3	23.0	19.9	22.3	22.8	19.7	17.9	20.2	18.6
Northwest	4.3	3.8	7.6	5.7	2.7	2.0	7.4	5.6	9.5	6.1
West	7.7	6.7	5.8	5.4	8.6	7.9	5.3	6.0	5.1	5.4
Volga	5.5	5.2	5.1	5.6	5.7	4.9	5.3	5.5	4.5	5.7
North Caucasus	5.5	5.8	5.1	5.0	5.7	6.5	5.4	5.3	4.2	4.3
Trans-Caucasus	4.2	4.7	4.3	4.4	4.2	4.9	3.3	3.4	2.3	2.8
North	1.6	1.6	1.2	1.6	1.7	1.6	1.8	2.0	2.0	2.5
Western U.S.S.R.	75.5	69.3	75.8	68.5	75.3	70.1	75.7	69.2	80.3	72.4
Ural	6.5	7.9	7.7	9.7	6.0	6.1	7.6	9.0	8.3	11.1
West Siberia	5.2	5.8	4.4	6.1	5.5	5.6	4.9	6.4	3.6	5.6
East Siberia	2.7	3.4	3.1	3.7	2.6	3.0	3.0	3.8	2.3	3.3
Far East	1.3	2.0	2.1	2.9	1.0	1.1	2.3	2.6	2.1	2.4
Central Asia	5.5	6.8	4.0	4.9	6.2	8.6	3.7	4.2	2.0	2.7
Kazakhstan	3.2	4.8	2.8	4.3	3.4	5.3	2.9	4.8	1.4	2.5
Eastern U.S.S.R.	24.4	30.7	24.1	31.6	24.7	29.7	24.4	30.8	19.7	27.6
U.S.S.R.	100%	100%	100%	100%	100%	100%	100%	100%	100%	100%

Note: [a]The term "Total employment" refers to the total civilian labor force, excluding the military and the agricultural employment in the collective far (kolkhozes) but including the workers in the state farms (sovkhozes) and i the machine-tractor stations. Some of the main branches that are included in this term are industry, construction, transportation, trade, education, public health, and others.

Sources: Data for industrial workers from this study. Other data from U.S.S.R., Results of All-Union Census of 1959--U.S.S.R. (Summary Volume), (Moscow 1962), pp. 20-29.

80 per cent of Soviet industrial workers in 1940 to 72 per cent in 1960, the share of the eastern U. S. S. R. increased from 20 to 28 per cent.

A comparison of the regions as share of Soviet industrial manpower, total employment and of total, urban, and rural population in 1940 and 1960 is shown in Table 18. There is a close correlation between industrial workers and total employment and another close correlation seems to exist between industrial workers and urban population. An even closer correlation exists between the total employment and urban population: Twelve regions have identical or nearly identical shares in both categories.

Table 19 shows a breakdown by major economic regions under the same headings as those in Table 18 except that the columns A through D are expressed as a per cent of the total population of major economic regions (column E is a per cent of the total employment).

An analysis of Table 19 indicates at least three points that should be mentioned. First, the region Northwest had the highest share in four categories in 1940 and in three categories in 1960. This was mainly due to the fact that the city of Leningrad alone accounts for more than 80 per cent of the population of the region Northwest. Thus, the large shares in the four categories reflect predominantly the second largest industrial city in the Soviet Union. Second, Central Asia had the smallest share in three categories and next to the smallest share in another in both 1940 and 1960. The reason, probably, is the fact that Central Asia was in both years the least urbanized region in the U. S. S. R., with 77 per cent of its population classified as rural in 1940 and 64 per cent in 1960. Finally, one of the highest increases of its shares (in three out of four categories) among all the regions was in the Ural following the trend of its urban population which increased by 25 points from 37 to 62 per cent.

Table 20 indicates that from 1940 to 1960 in most of the regions and in the U. S. S. R. as a whole, the industrial workers showed the highest per cent increase, followed by the smaller increase in the total employment and urban population, the smallest increase being in the total population.

TABLE 19

Urban and Rural Population, Total Employment, and Industrial Workers, as Per Cent of Total Population of Major Economic Regions in 1940 and 1960

	Population				Total Employment[a]		Industrial Workers			
	Urban A		Rural B		C		D		E	
	1940	1960	1940	1960	1940	1960	1940	1960	1940	1960
Center	31	52	69	48	19	33	8	14	42	41
South	32	47	68	53	15	24	5	9	36	37
Northwest	57	74	43	26	29	42	13	16	45	39
West	24	41	76	59	11	26	4	8	34	32
Volga	29	53	71	47	16	30	5	11	30	37
North Caucasus	30	44	70	56	16	27	4	8	27	29
Trans-Caucasus	32	47	68	53	13	21	3	6	24	30
North	25	51	75	49	19	35	7	16	39	45
Western U.S.S.R.	32	49	68	51	17	29	6	11	38	37
Ural	37	62	63	38	19	33	7	15	39	44
West Siberia	27	52	73	48	16	31	4	10	26	32
East Siberia	36	55	64	45	18	32	5	10	27	31
Far East	50	72	50	28	29	37	9	12	32	32
Central Asia	23	36	77	64	11	18	2	4	19	24
Kazakhstan	28	44	72	56	15	29	3	5	17	19
Eastern U.S.S.R.	32	52	68	48	17	29	5	9	28	33
U.S.S.R.	32	50	68	50	17	29	6	10	34	36

Note: All per cent figures are rounded values (decimal points have been omitte

Columns A-D: Each column expressed as per cent of total population of t region; columns A + B = 100%.
Column E: Industrial workers as per cent of total employment of the regi

[a]See Note to Table 18, p. 74.

Source: See Table 18.

TABLE 20

Per Cent Change 1940-60 By Major Economic Regions

	Population			Total Employment[a]	Industrial Workers
	Total	Urban	Rural		
Center	- 5	+ 58	- 34	+ 66	+ 65
South	+ 7	+ 55	- 15	+ 76	+ 83
Northwest	+ 2	+ 33	- 40	+ 48	+ 28
West	- 2	+ 65	- 24	+121	+109
Volga	+ 8	+ 96	- 28	+104	+148
North Caucasus	+ 18	+ 74	- 5	+ 92	+105
Trans-Caucasus	+ 25	+ 83	- 2	+101	+149
North	+ 15	+137	- 26	+113	+146
Western U.S.S.R.	+ 4	+ 61	- 29	+ 79	+ 79
Ural	+ 37	+125	- 16	+131	+165
West Siberia	+ 28	+145	+ 16	+153	+210
East Siberia	+ 40	+116	- 2	+144	+189
Far East	+ 72	+149	+ 5	+119	+124
Central Asia	+ 39	+121	+ 14	+122	+176
Kazakhstan	+ 70	+174	+ 31	+226	+256
Eastern U.S.S.R.	+ 40	+127	+ 0	+144	+182
U.S.S.R.	+ 13	+ 80	- 20	+ 94	+ 99

Note: + Indicates per cent increase, - indicates per cent decrease.

[a]See Note to Table 18, p. 74.

Source: See Table 18.

INDUSTRIAL WORKERS BY *SOVNARKHOZY*, 1955

The comparison of Maps 2 and 14 gives a general view of the changes in the distribution of Soviet workers by fourteen major regions. A more detailed pattern begins to emerg when the analysis is made by comparing Maps 4 and 15 showing the distribution by 104 *sovnarkhozy*. This comparison is facilitated by the fact that both maps use the same line or dot patterns representing identical per cent ranges.

Unfortunately, as was explained in Chapter 1, the latest year for which sufficient data are available by *sovnarkhozy* is 1955. Thus the comparisons in this section of Chapter 6 are limited to the changes in the 1940-55 period.

Before a detailed analysis of the maps, a few general observations could be made. Since the number of *sovnarkhozy* increased from 103 to 104 by 1955, the value of an "average" *sovnarkhoz* would have been theoretically just below 1 per cen in both years.[6] The actual median value increased from 0.5 in 1940 to 0.6 per cent in 1955 indicating a general tendency toward a more even distribution of industrial workers among all the *sovnarkhozy*. The breakdown by percentage ranges throws an even better light on this trend. In the lowest range, the number of *sovnarkhozy* decreased from twenty-one in 1940 to thirteen in 1955; in the next higher range (0.2-0.4 per cent the number increased from twenty-eight to thirty-three; it also increased in the next range from twenty-five to twenty-eight; in the next to the highest range (1.0-3.0) the number remained constant (twenty-five); and in the top range (over 3 per cent) the number rose from four to five but the upper limit of the range was reduced from 8.4 to 6.2 per cent. In brief, the reduction occurred at both ends of the scale indicating that both the very small and the very large *sovnarkhozy* (as a per cent of the Soviet industrial workers) gave way to a medium-sized unit of about 0.6 per cent.

Beginning the comparison of Maps 4 and 15, we note that the leading industrial concentrations have remained the same, but one new area has been added. In addition to both Moscow *sovnarkhozy* (city and *oblast*), Leningrad and Stalino, which were the most important industrial areas in the U.S.S.R. in 1940, a fifth *sovnarkhoz* has joined their ranks in 1955--

Sverdlovsk with 3. 4 per cent of Soviet industrial workers (2. 5 per cent in 1940). While these five *sovnarkhozy* are unmistakably the focal centers of Soviet industrial activity, only Sverdlovsk has increased its share in the fifteen-year period while the original four foci show a decrease of their shares.[7] Moscow city decreased from 8. 1 to 6. 2 per cent, Moscow *oblast* decreased from 6. 5 to 5. 3, Leningrad *sovnarkhoz* is down from 8. 4 to 5. 3, and Stalino (now Donetsk) *sovnarkhoz* declined from 4. 1 to 3. 7 per cent of Soviet industrial workers. Although in absolute numbers of industrial workers the combined total of the five *sovnarkhozy* increased from 2. 5 million in 1940 to 3. 5 million in 1955, their combined share of the national industrial manpower dropped from 30 to 24 per cent. The industrial preeminence of the old pre-revolutionary industrial centers is clearly on the decline and the rise of Sverdlovsk indicates a slow but steady direction of the eastward shift of the Soviet center of industrial gravity.

Moving the focus from the *sovnarkhozy* with very high industrialization (top range over 3. 0 per cent) to the range of high industrialization (1. 0-3. 0 per cent), it should be noted that in 1940 this range partly consisted of a zone surrounding the southern part of the region Center. In 1955, the same range shows a different pattern: Instead of a zone separated from the three outliers (Ural, Arkhangel'sk, Azerbaydzhan) the pattern has changed into a continuous zone radiating from Latvia eastward to the Ural and southeastward to the Trans-Caucasus.[8]

The next lower range (0. 5-0. 9 per cent) is that of moderate industrialization. The main changes occurred in four separate areas: three are in western U. S. S. R. and one in eastern U. S. S. R. The moderate zone now extends westward from the highly industrialized Novosibirsk-Kemerovo-Krasnoyarsk area astride the Trans-Siberian railroad line and into the heart of Kazakhstan. The second area of change is from the southeastern part of the region Center, through the lower Volga region, and into the southernmost part of the Ural. This second area now connects the highly industrialized areas of Donbas and Ural and thus completes an industrialized triangle around the Central region. The third area of change is in the western and southern Ukraine where several *sovnarkhozy* represent the less industrialized and more agricultural part of the region South. The last area of change is the region

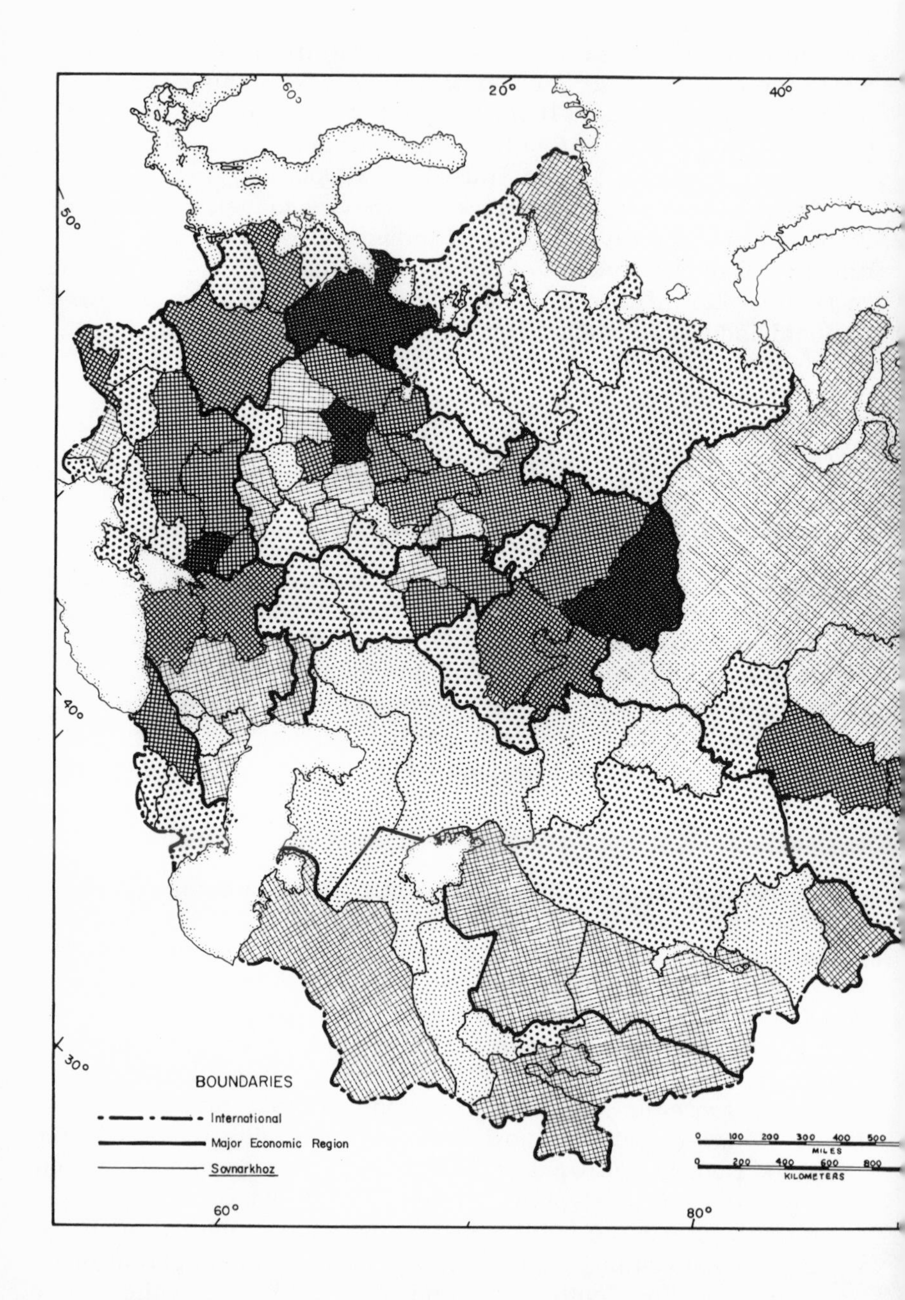
20°
40°
60°
50°
40°
30°
60°
80°
BOUNDARIES
International
Major Economic Region
Sovnarkhoz
0 100 200 300 400 500
MILES
0 200 400 600 800
KILOMETERS

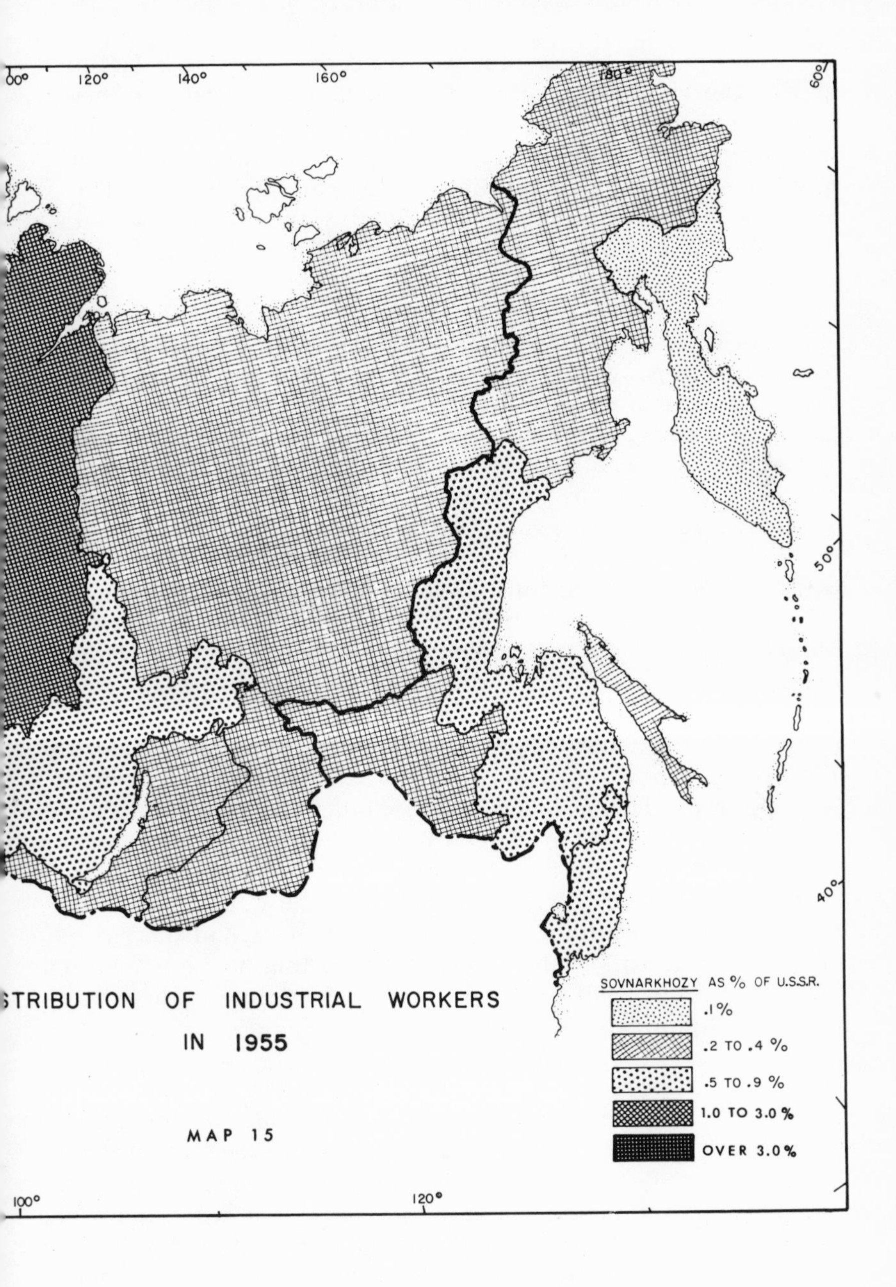
STRIBUTION OF INDUSTRIAL WORKERS
IN 1955
MAP 15
SOVNARKHOZY AS % OF U.S.S.R.
.1%
.2 TO .4 %
.5 TO .9 %
1.0 TO 3.0 %
OVER 3.0 %
100°
120°
140°
160°
180°
60°
50°
40°

North and the central part of the Northwest region. While in 1940 this area showed an uneven industrial manpower distribution, in 1955 the distribution is more uniform.

The areas of low industrialization (range 0.2-0.4 per cent) have replaced many of the *sovnarkhozy* that had the minimum share in 1940. By 1955 there were no *sovnarkhozy* with the very low industrialization (0.1 per cent) in the regions West Siberia, East Siberia, North, and South. The regions Far East, Center, and North Caucasus contained each between one and three *sovnarkhozy* with very low industrialization.

In Chapter 2, the decision to use Map 4 has been explained as opposed to the possible use of maps based on the industrial workers as a ratio of the total *sovnarkhoz* population. The conclusion was that the correlation between the two sets of figures was very close and thus the maps of the percentage of industrial workers in the U. S. S. R. were adequate and valid. An example was given that if a map for 1940 had been made based on the other set of data (industrial workers as a ratio of total *sovnarkhoz* population) there would still be a zone of lower industrial density to the south of Moscow as well as in Kazakhstan and Central Asia. This example is also valid if a similar map had been made for 1955: There are still eight *sovnarkhozy* with lower ratios surrounding Moscow (4 per cent or less, the median ratio in 1955 being 6 per cent), while all of Kazakhstan and Central Asia have the ratios below the median. Out of a total of forty-six *sovnarkhozy* in the ranges 0.1-0.4 per cent of Soviet workers, thirty-four had the ratios below the median. On the other hand, out of thirty *sovnarkhozy* in the ranges of 1 per cent and over of Soviet workers, twenty-five had the ratios above the median. Finally, all five leading *sovnarkhozy* (each with over 3 per cent of Soviet workers) had the highest ratios of over 13 per cent in 1955.

The comparison of Maps 4 and 15 shows the changing shares of the *sovnarkhozy* as a per cent of Soviet industrial work force between 1940 and 1955. Map 16, on the other hand, shows the increase in the absolute numbers of workers by *sovnarkhozy* during the same period. The word increase should be stressed since no *sovnarkhoz* registered a decrease in the number of industrial workers between 1940 and 1955.

Earlier in this chapter the per cent increase by major regions was discussed based on Map 13. The low increase in the western regions and the higher increase in the eastern regions were noted, and the same general pattern can be seen in more detail in Map 16. However, while between 1940 and 1960 no major region registered an increase over 256 per cent, there are five sovnarkhozy with a greater increase in the period 1940-55. About one-half of all sovnarkhozy registered an increase of less than 100 per cent and the other half showed an increase between 100 and 300 per cent, with only three sovnarkhozy having an increase over 300 per cent. The median increase for sovnarkhozy was 99. 6 per cent while the increase for the U. S. S. R. as a whole was 71. 7 per cent.[9]

Map 16 shows that most of the sovnarkhozy with a very small increase (under 50 per cent) in the western regions were under German occupation from 1941 to 1943. Fifteen out of twenty-two were occupied, the other seven were unoccupied but near the front, and they experienced a very serious decrease in the number of workers between 1940 and 1945. Thus their low increase in the period 1940-55 might be misleading since many of these sovnarkhozy show a high increase when the postwar period alone is considered.

Most of the sovnarkhozy with small increase (50-100 per cent) form a wide continuous belt extending from the region North through the regions Center, Volga, and South, into the region North Caucasus. This belt separates most of the regions with very small increase located to the west of it, from the majority of the regions with higher increases (over 100 per cent) that are located to the east.

Many of the sovnarkhozy with moderate increase (100-150 per cent) had most of their increase in the period 1940-45 (see Table 17) and thus their postwar increase is less significant. One of the best examples is Sverdlovsk sovnarkhoz where most of the 131 per cent increase occurred during the war when this area increased its number of industrial workers by 82 per cent.

Only three out of eighteen sovnarkhozy with a high increase (150-200 per cent) are located in the western regions. The fifteen sovnarkhozy in the eastern regions are all grouped together forming a large but compact area extending from the

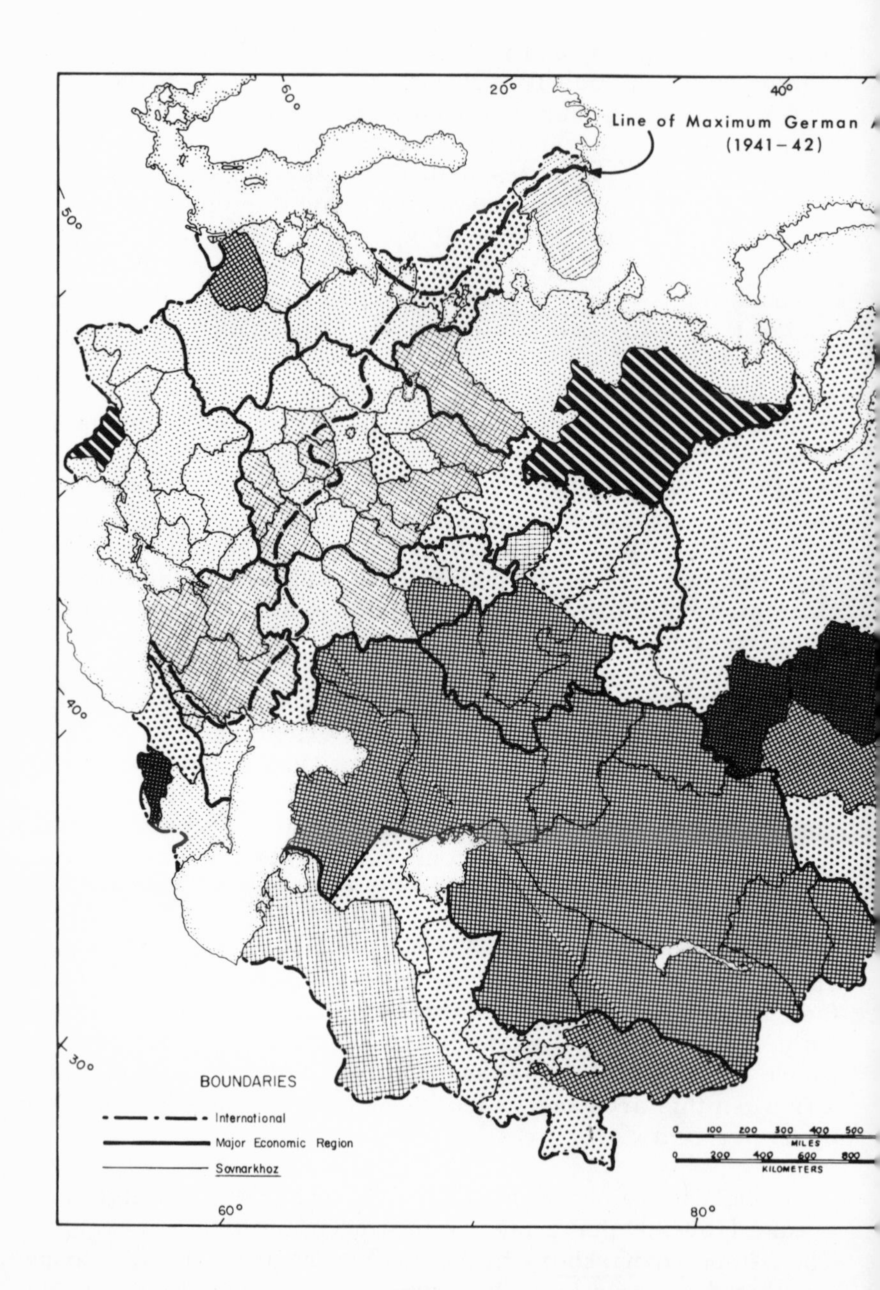

Line of Maximum German A
(1941–42)
BOUNDARIES
International
Major Economic Region
Sovnarkhoz
MILES
KILOMETERS

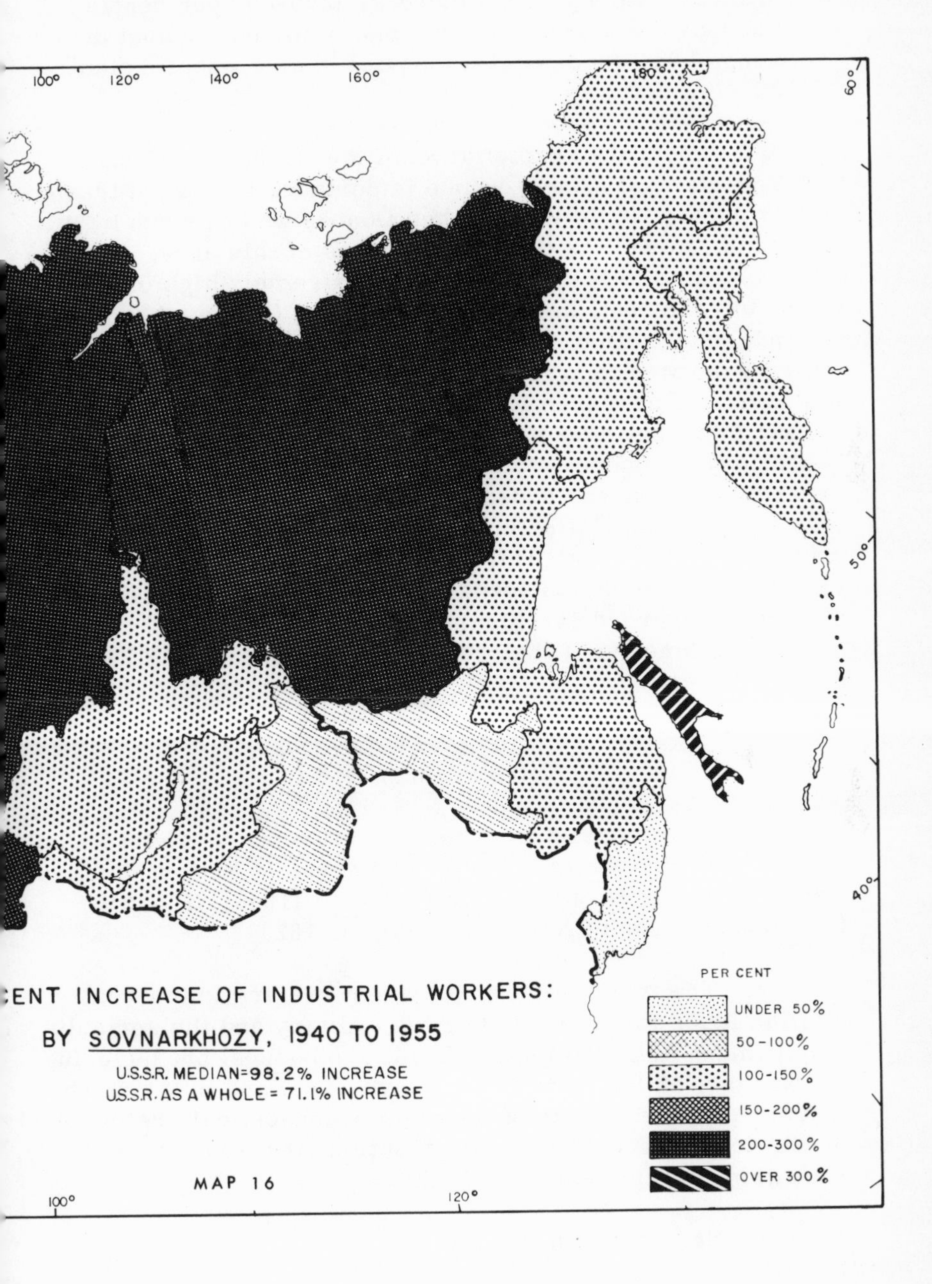

CENT INCREASE OF INDUSTRIAL WORKERS:

BY SOVNARKHOZY, 1940 TO 1955

U.S.S.R. MEDIAN=98.2% INCREASE
U.S.S.R. AS A WHOLE = 71.1% INCREASE

MAP 16

Caspian Sea to the Kuznetsk basin and from the Volga-Ural area to the Kirgiz S. S. R. This area, together with several sovnarkhozy with very high increase (200-300 per cent) in West and East Siberia, presents one of the best visual demonstrations of the success of the Soviet "war economic plan" of 1941.

The increased exploitation of the Pechora coal basin and Vorkuta coal mines, whose importance increased tremendously during World War II when Donbas was overrun by the Germans, as well as timber resources of this area, offer some clues as to the reason for the extremely high increase (over 300 per cent) in Komi sovnarkhoz. On the other hand, the industrialization, however limited, of an area previously entirely devoted to agriculture, could explain the increase in Moldavia. The reason for questioning the validity of the increase in Sakhalin sovnarkhoz is that the southern part of Sakhalin was annexed from Japan in 1945. In this way a large urban population was added which unnaturally increased not only the total population but also the number of industrial workers. Therefore, while accepting as valid the increases in Komi and Moldavian sovnarkhozy, the increase in Sakhalin should be regarded largely as distorted as it would have been much smaller if it were not for the annexation of southern Sakhalin.

Notes to Chapter 6

1. Frank Lorimer, The Population of the Soviet Union: History and Prospects ["Series of League of Nations Publications," Vol. II: Economic and Financial (1946: II. A. 3)] (Geneva: League of Nations, 1946), p. 182.

2. The term "total employment" refers to the total civilian labor force, excluding the military and the agricultural employment in the collective farms (kolkhozes) but including the workers in the state farms (sovkhozes) and in the machine-tractor stations. Some of the main branches that are included in this term are industry, construction, transportation, trade, education, public health, and others.

3. See Table 20, p. 77.

4. See Note 2 to Chapter 6.

5. See Table 19, p. 76.

6. There were only 103 *sovnarkhozy* in 1940 since Kaliningrad was annexed at the end of the war.

7. In almost all the *sovnarkhozy* whose share increased between 1940 and 1955, the increase is attributable to a great extent to a large addition of workers in machine manufacturing. This is a proof of the importance attached to machine manufacturing in the postwar period of rebuilding of the Soviet industry.

8. Compare this zone on Map 15 with the Soviet manufacturing belt (Figure 2) and the Map of Manufacturing in the Soviet Union (Figure 1) in Richard E. Lonsdale and John H. Thompson, "A Map of the U. S. S. R. 's Manufacturing," *Economic Geography,* Vol. 36, No. 1 (January, 1960).

9. Kaliningrad *sovnarkhoz* (northern half of former German East Prussia), which was not annexed by the U. S. S. R. until 1945, is shown blank on the map since the data for it were lacking for 1940 and thus no change between 1940 and 1955 can be indicated.

CHAPTER 7 WORKERS BY PRINCIPAL BRANCHES OF INDUSTRY, 1960

In the previous chapter the changing pattern of distribution of the total Soviet industrial work force was analyzed and now attention is focused on the changing pattern in the eight principal branches of industry. As in Chapter 3, the discussion will be limited to the major economic regions since the data are missing for the breakdown by industries for many sovnarkhozy.

The breakdown of the Soviet industrial work force by eight major industries is shown in Table 21 with the corresponding data for the United States. Although the data for the U. S. are earlier than those for the U. S. S. R., the comparisons are still meaningful.

Machine manufacturing ranks first both in the U. S. S. R. and in the U. S. and it retains the leading position in the twenty-year period (1940-60). Although its share was almost the same in both countries prior to World War II, in the post-war period machine manufacturing increased its share by only 1.5 percentage points in the U. S. S. R. while in the United States its share increased by seven points. The impact of World War II is probably the main cause but the results are quite different. In the United States, coming out of the depression, the share rose during the war when this country became the "arsenal of democracy." In the Soviet Union a relatively high share of machine manufacturing at the end of a decade of stepped-up industrialization was radically reduced during the war as a result of an enormous destruction of industry in the western U. S. S. R. Thus the small increase in the share of machine manufacturing in the U. S. S. R. shows in effect a success in overcoming the setbacks caused by the

TABLE 21

Distribution of Industrial Workers by Principal Branches of Industry
U. S. S. R., 1940-60, and United States, 1937-58

Branch of Industry	Branch of Industry as Percent of All Industrial Workers				Ranking of the Eight Branches			
	U. S. S. R.		U. S.		U. S. S. R.		U. S.	
	1940	1960	1937	1958	1940	1960	1937	1958
Machine Manufacturing	28. 9%	30. 4%	28. 0%	35. 0%	1	1	1	1
Light Industry	18. 0	18. 1	23. 8	18. 0	2	2	2	2
Forest Industries	15. 9	12. 0	8. 4	7. 3	3	3	6	5
Food Industry	12. 7	9. 4	10. 8	11. 0	4	4	4	3
Energy and Fuel Industries	7. 4	8. 0	11. 2	10. 4	5	5	3	4
Heavy Industry	5. 4	5. 8	8. 6	7. 1	6	7	5	6
Chemical Industry	3. 3	3. 1	5. 0	6. 8	7	8	7	7
Building Materials Industry	3. 0	7. 1	4. 2	3. 6	8	6	8	8
Subtotal	94. 6	93. 9	100. 0	99. 2				
Other Industries	5. 4	6. 1	--	0. 8				
TOTAL	100. 0%	100. 0%	100. 0%	100. 0%				

Sources: For the U. S. : data for 1937 from G. Warren Nutter, Growth of Industrial Production in the Soviet Union (Princeton, New Jersey: Princeton University Press, 1962), p. 253. Data for 1958 calculated from U. S., Bureau of the Census, United States Census of Manufactures, 1958, Vol. I: Summary Statistics (Washington, D. C. : U. S. Government Printing Office, 1961), Table 2, pp. 1-4 and 1-5. For the U. S. S. R. : data from this study, calculated from Soviet statistical handbooks.

war and demonstrates a progress rather than a slowdown when compared with the great increase in the share of machine manufacturing in the United States.

The second leading industry is light industry and it has the same rank in both countries at the start and at the end of the twenty-year period. There is a difference here between the two countries in terms of the share of this industry: in 1937 it was higher in the U. S. but by the end of the period it is the same in both countries.

The forest industries rank third in the U. S. S. R. in both years (1940 and 1960) while in the U. S. the rank is much lower during this period. The shares have declined in both countries but the forest industries still have a much more significant place in the Soviet Union.

While it is difficult to interpret all the changes in ranking or in shares in the two countries, a few comments might be warranted. One of the reasons for the increase of the shares of the energy and fuel industries in the U. S. S. R. and the decrease of the same in the U. S. could be suggested by analyzing the structural changes in energy output in both countries between 1940 and 1960. If coal (lignite, bituminous, anthracite) on the one hand, and petroleum and natural gas, on the other, are expressed as a per cent of total fuel balance, it becomes evident that coal actually slightly increased its share in the U. S. S. R. from about 53 per cent in 1940 to about 54 per cent of total energy in 1960, while petroleum and natural gas increased their share in the same period from less than 20 to about 38 per cent.[1] In the U. S. in the same period coal decreased its share from about 50 per cent in 1940 to about 27 per cent in 1960, while petroleum and natural gas increased their share from about 40 to about 70 per cent in 1960.[2] Since coal mining has heavy demands on manpower as opposed to the automated processes that were developed in the oil and gas industry, it is not surprising that the Soviet Union had to more than double the number of workers in energy and fuel industries between 1940 and 1960 (from 830, 000 to 1, 783, 000) and thus increased their share of the total industrial work force. The United States, on the other hand, could afford to cut almost in half the employment in coal mining (from 485, 000 to 268, 000) while the number of workers in oil and gas industries was increased by only

130, 000 (from 225, 000 to 355, 000) in the 1939-54 period.[3] Thus a more modern structure of the energy output in the United States could permit a decrease both in the share and in the absolute numbers of the workers in the energy and fuel industries while at the same time meeting all the demands for an increased energy output.

The continued importance of the forest industries in the U. S. S. R., when compared to the rank they occupy in the United States where their shares are about half of those in the U. S. S. R., can be explained to a large extent by analyzing the main uses of timber in both countries. One of the main uses in the U. S. S. R. is as fuel while this use has almost disappeared in the United States. In the late 1950's one-third of the timber produced was used as fuel in the U. S. S. R.[4] Another measure is the change in the fuel balance in both countries: In the U. S. S. R. fuelwood represented almost 30 per cent of the energy output in 1940 and this share declined to about 8 per cent in 1958.[5] On the other hand, the same share (about 8 per cent) has been achieved in the United States four decades earlier at the time of World War I.[6] The other use is for construction purposes in both countries but a higher technology in the United States has reduced the use of wood considerably while this use was still important in the U. S. S. R. in 1960.

Figures 3 and 4 show in chart form the distribution of industrial workers in eight principal branches of industry by major regions as a per cent of the U. S. S. R. The regions are divided into two groups: western regions (western U. S. S. R.) and eastern regions (eastern U. S. S. R.), separated by a heavy zig-zagging line running from the top to the bottom bar. The reason for a definite grouping of regions and the selection of certain zip patterns used in the bars is this: In the western U. S. S. R., the first three regions (from left to right) are those which have been established well before the revolution of 1917 and the solid black is used for Center and South as the leading regions of the U. S. S. R. both in 1940 and in 1960. The next four regions in the west are those that are of secondary importance in terms of over-all development in this period. Volga is shown in a darker pattern as a promising region with a potential for future development (after 1960). In the eastern U. S. S. R., Ural and West Siberia repeat the solid black pattern because their importance and position

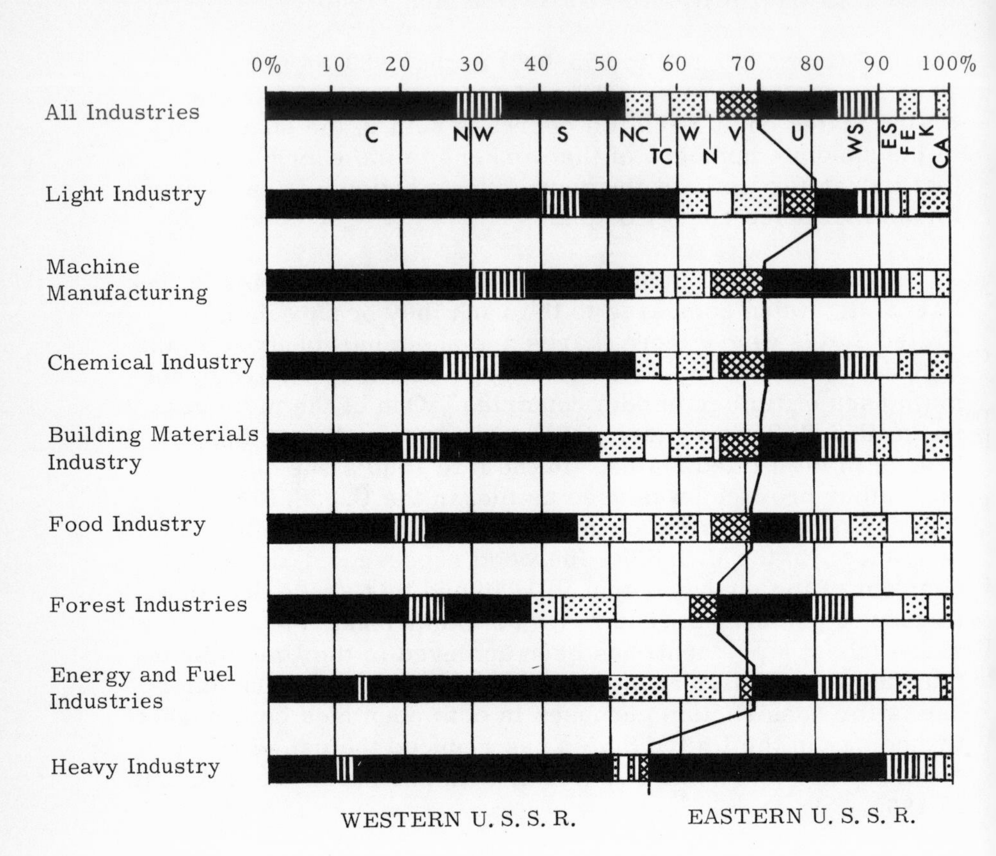

FIGURE 3

WORKERS IN PRINCIPAL BRANCHES OF INDUSTRY AS A PER CENT OF THE U. S. S. R., BY MAJOR ECONOMIC REGIONS, 1960

Key:

C	=	Center
NW	=	Northwest
S	=	South
NC	=	North Caucasus
TC	=	Trans-Caucasus
W	=	West
N	=	North
V	=	Volga
U	=	Ural
WS	=	West Siberia
ES	=	East Siberia
FE	=	Far East
K	=	Kazakhstan
CA	=	Central Asia

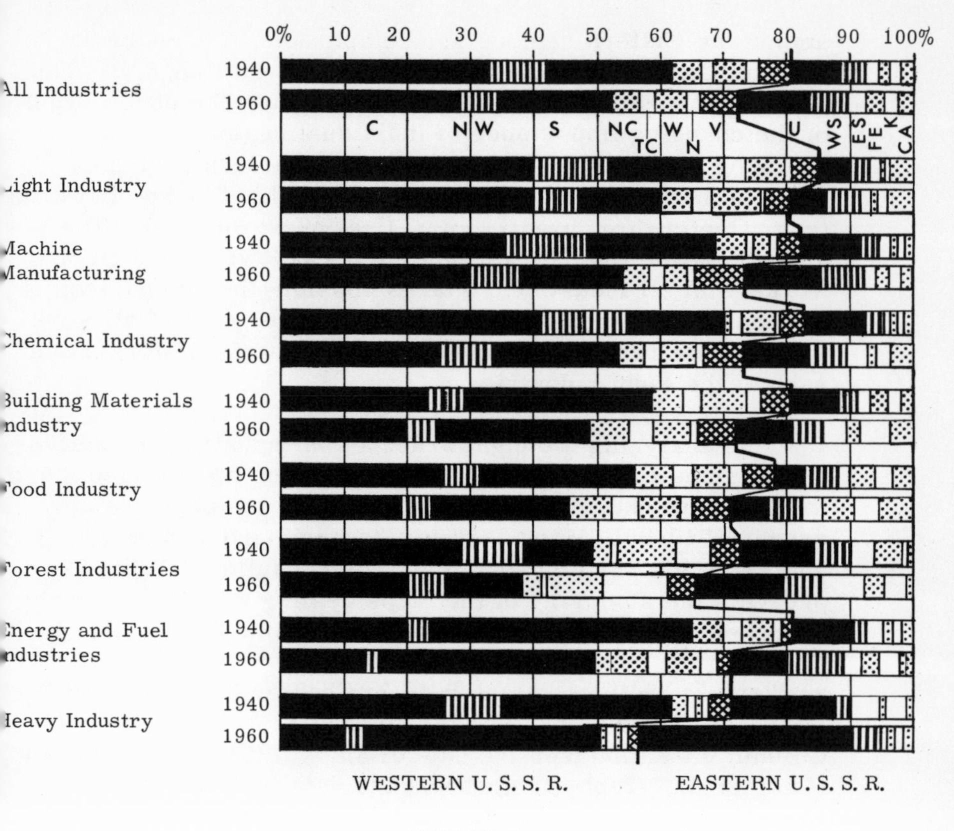

FIGURE 4

WORKERS IN PRINCIPAL BRANCHES OF INDUSTRY AS A PER CENT OF THE U. S. S. R., BY MAJOR ECONOMIC REGIONS: COMPARISON, 1940 AND 1960

Key:

C	= Center	V	= Volga
NW	= Northwest	U	= Ural
S	= South	WS	= West Siberia
NC	= North Caucasus	ES	= East Siberia
TC	= Trans-Caucasus	FE	= Far East
W	= West	K	= Kazakhstan
N	= North	CA	= Central Asia

among the eastern regions are comparable to those of the regions Center and Northwest in the western U. S. S. R. Thus, a visual inspection of Figure 4 can facilitate the observation of the changing importance of individual regions, or of changing aggregates of western versus eastern regions, and can also help in following the changes within blocks of regions (e. g. Center-Northwest-South; Ural-West Siberia). The addition of the top bar showing the breakdown of industrial workers in all industries, makes possible the comparison of the changing shares of each region as a per cent of all workers with the region's shares as a per cent of the workers in each of the eight industries.

In analyzing the eight branches of industry, in addition to two maps for each industry (one showing the distribution of industrial workers in 1960, and the other the per cent increase 1940-60), Maps 5-12 in Chapter 3 and Tables 21, 22, and 23 in this chapter should also be consulted. Table 22 presents the summary of the maps dealing with the separate branches of industry. Columns 1-8 summarize the data included in the maps showing the distribution of industrial workers in 1940 (see Maps 5-12 in Chapter 3) and in 1960 (Maps 18, 20, 22, 24, 26, 28, 30, and 32 in this chapter). Column 0 summarizes the data of Maps 2 (Chapter 2) and 14 (Chapter 6). Table 23 presents the data in Table 22 as the ranking of major economic regions.

Regarding the changes in specific industrial branches, the heavy industry was the one in which probably the greatest regional changes occurred in the Soviet Union between 1940 and 1960 and eleven regions showed a change in rank. The most significant and the most impressive change was evident in the region Ural: it rose from the third place in 1940 to the second place in the U. S. S. R. , more than doubling its share with an increase of 342 per cent. The reasons for the rising significance of some eastern regions in heavy industry can be traced to the effects of the wartime shift to the east but also to the development of new metallurgical centers in the Ural and the Kuzbas (West Siberia).

Some of the highest regional increases occurred in the energy and fuel industries. The spectacular increase in West Siberia (1, 042 per cent) was due to the full exploitation of the Kuzbas coal fields, much of this increase resulting

TABLE 22

Industrial Workers, 1940-60; Major Economic Regions as Per Cent of the U.S.S.R.

	Number of Industry																	
	0		1		2		3		4		5		6		7		8	
	1940	1960	1940	1960	1940	1960	1940	1960	1940	1960	1940	1960	1940	1960	1940	1960	1940	1960
Center	33	27	22	13	26	10	35	31	41	26	23	20	27	21	40	40	27	19
South	20	19	42	34	29	38	20	17	15	19	28	24	11	12	15	14	23	23
Northwest	10	6	3	2	7	3	13	7	14	8	6	5	10	5	11	6	6	5
Ural	8	11	7	8	16	34	9	11	10	12	7	9	12	14	5	5	6	6
West	5	5	5	6	1	(1)	3	4	5	5	8	7	10	8	7	8	6	8
Volga	5	6	2	3	4	2	5	8	4	6	4	6	5	4	4	4	5	6
North Caucasus	4	4	5	7	3	2	5	5	1	4	5	6	3	4	3	4	6	7
West Siberia	4	6	2	9	3	5	3	6	3	5	2	5	6	7	3	4	5	5
East Siberia	2	3	2	3	5	1	2	2	1	3	2	3	4	8	1	2	2	3
Trans-Caucasus	2	3	3	3	1	3	1	2	2	3	4	4	1	1	4	4	3	4
Far East	2	2	2	3	1	(1)	1	2	(1)	2	3	2	4	4	(1)	1	4	5
Central Asia	2	3	1	2	1	(1)	1	2	2	3	4	4	(1)	1	4	5	4	4
North	2	3	1	3	1	(1)	1	1	1	1	2	1	6	11	1	1	2	2
Kazakhstan	1	3	2	5	3	2	1	2	1	3	2	5	1	2	1	2	3	4
U.S.S.R. total (in thousands)	11,218	22,291	830	1,783	606	1,293	3,242	6,776	370	691	337	1,583	1,784	2,675	2,019	4,035	1,425	2,095

Key to Industries:
0-All Industries
1-Energy and Fuel Industries
2-Heavy Industry
3-Machine Manufacturing
4-Chemical Industry
5-Building Materials Industry
6-Forest Industries
7-Light Industry
8-Food Industry

Note: All per cent figures are rounded values (decimal points have been omitted).
(1) = less than 1 per cent.

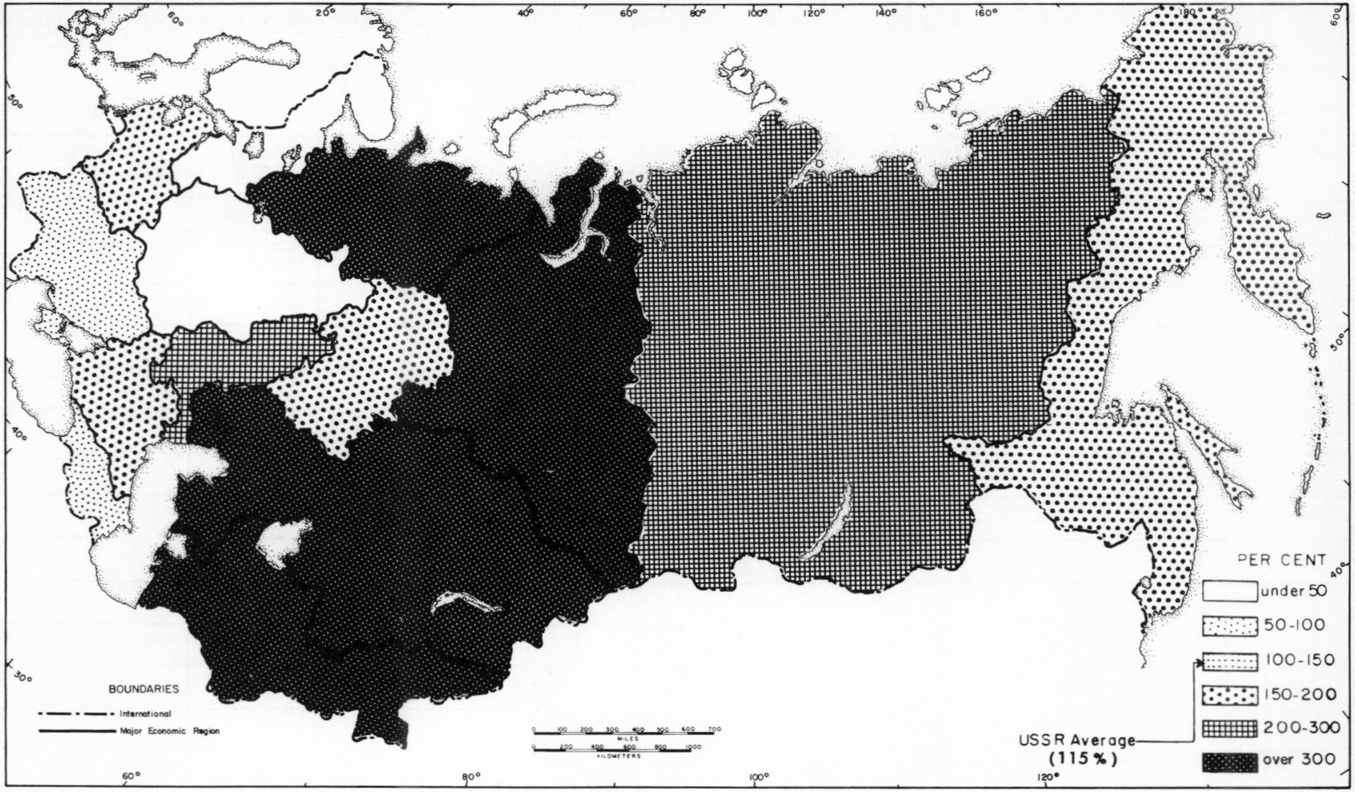

PER CENT INCREASE OF INDUSTRIAL WORKERS: ENERGY AND FUEL INDUSTRIES

(By Major Economic Regions, 1940 to 1960)

MAP 17

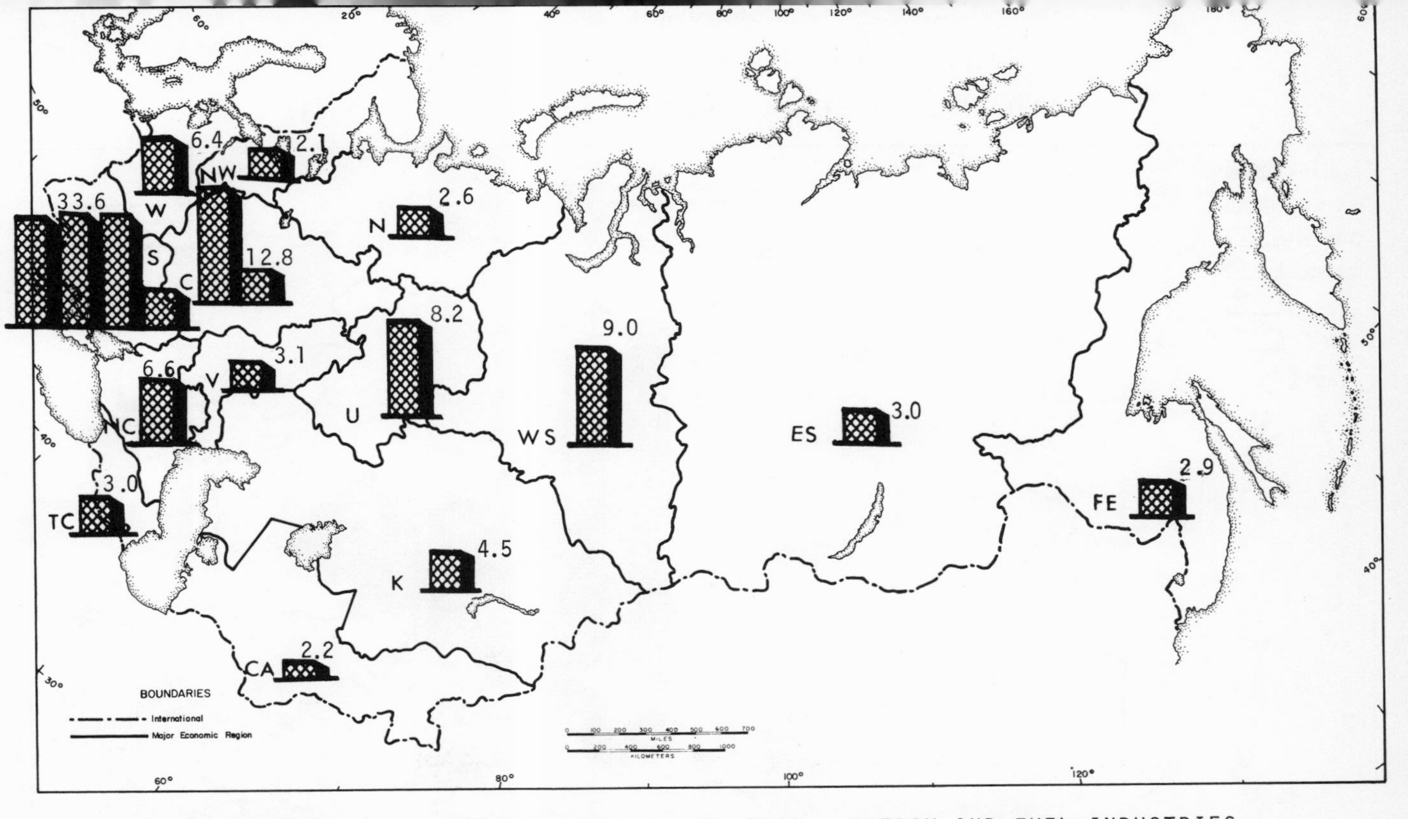

DISTRIBUTION OF INDUSTRIAL WORKERS IN 1960: ENERGY AND FUEL INDUSTRIES

(Major Economic Regions as Per Cent of U.S.S.R.)

MAP 18

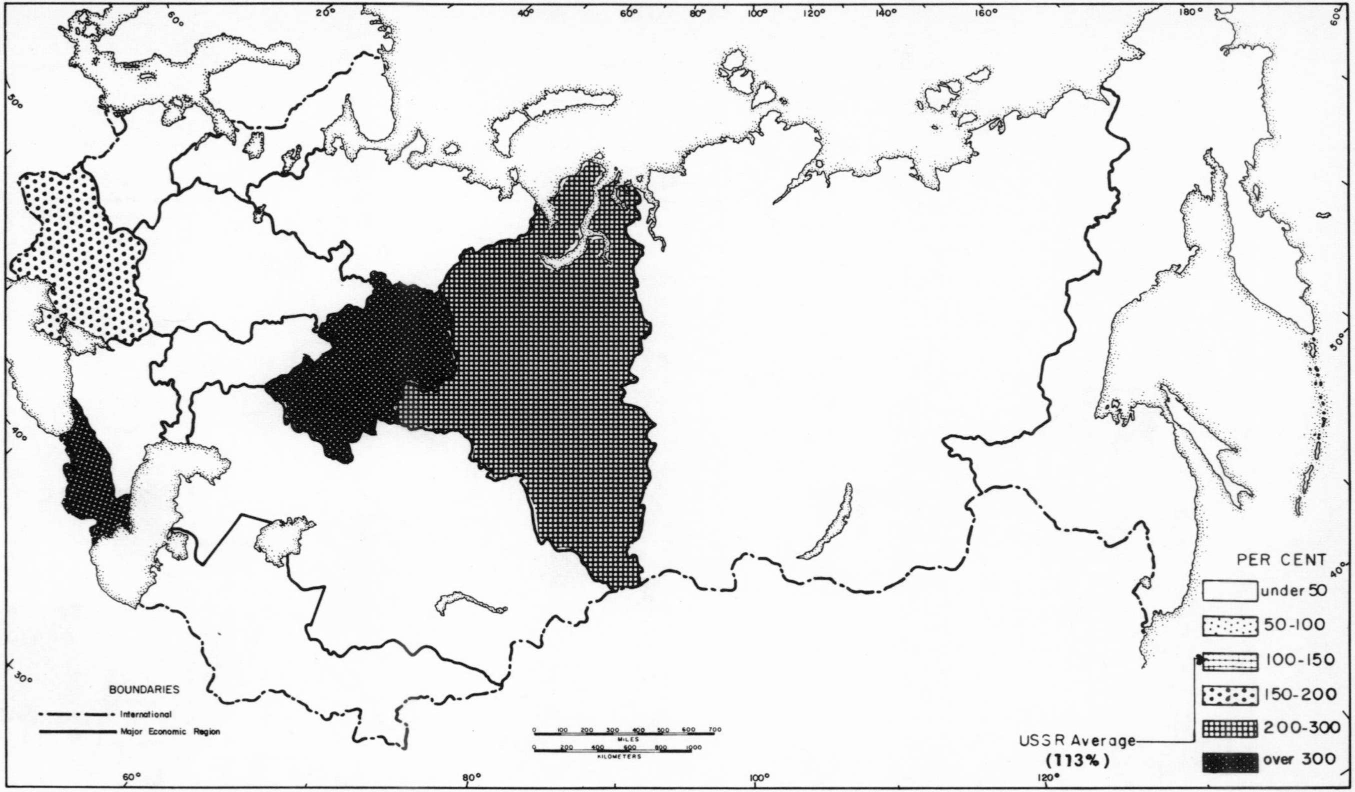

BOUNDARIES
International
Major Economic Region

PER CENT
under 50
50-100
100-150
150-200
200-300
over 300

USSR Average (113%)

MILES 0 100 200 300 400 500 600 700
KILOMETERS 0 200 400 600 800 1000

PER CENT INCREASE OF INDUSTRIAL WORKERS: HEAVY INDUSTRY

(By Major Economic Regions, 1940 to 1960)

MAP 19

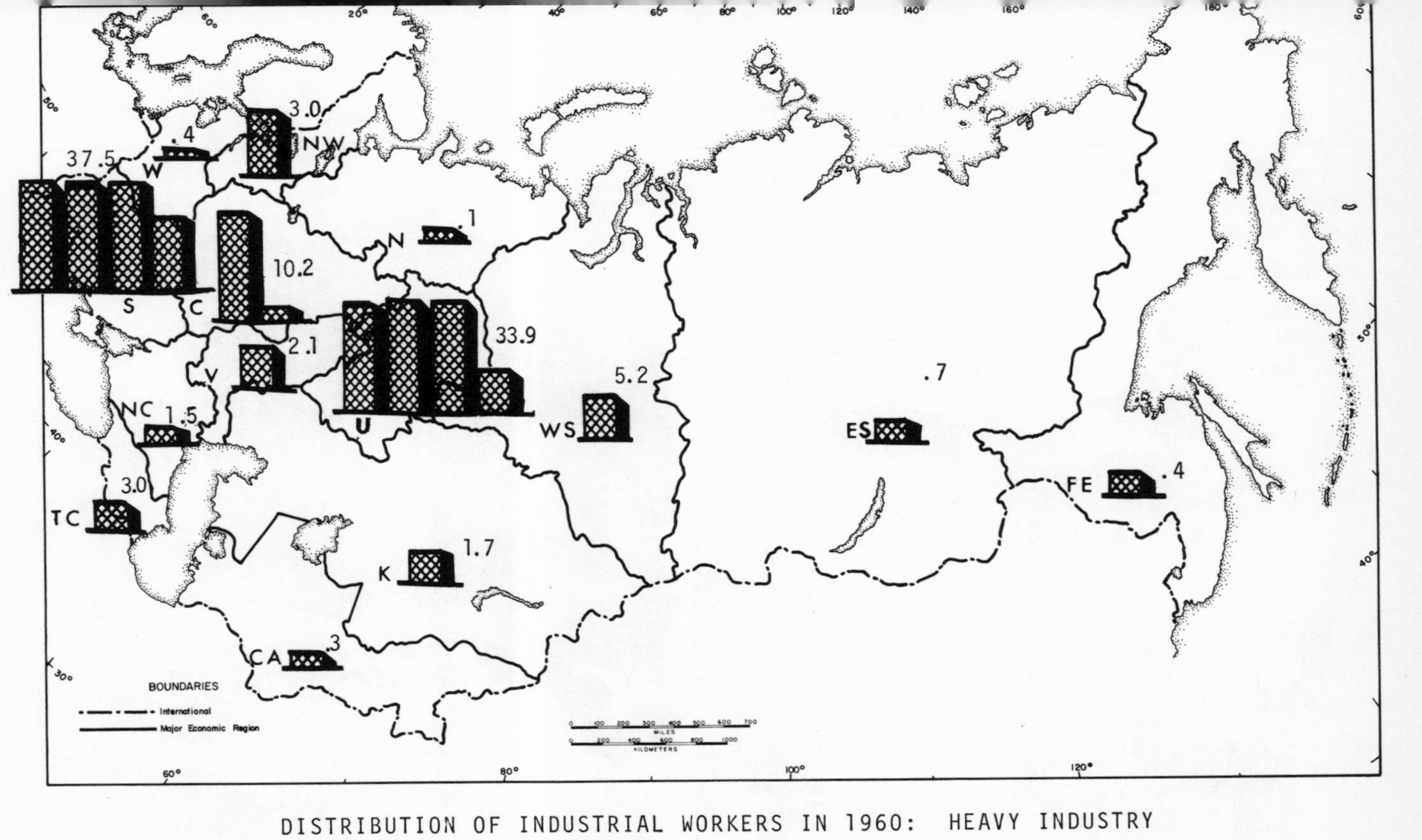

DISTRIBUTION OF INDUSTRIAL WORKERS IN 1960: HEAVY INDUSTRY

(Major Economic Regions as Per Cent of U.S.S.R.)

MAP 20

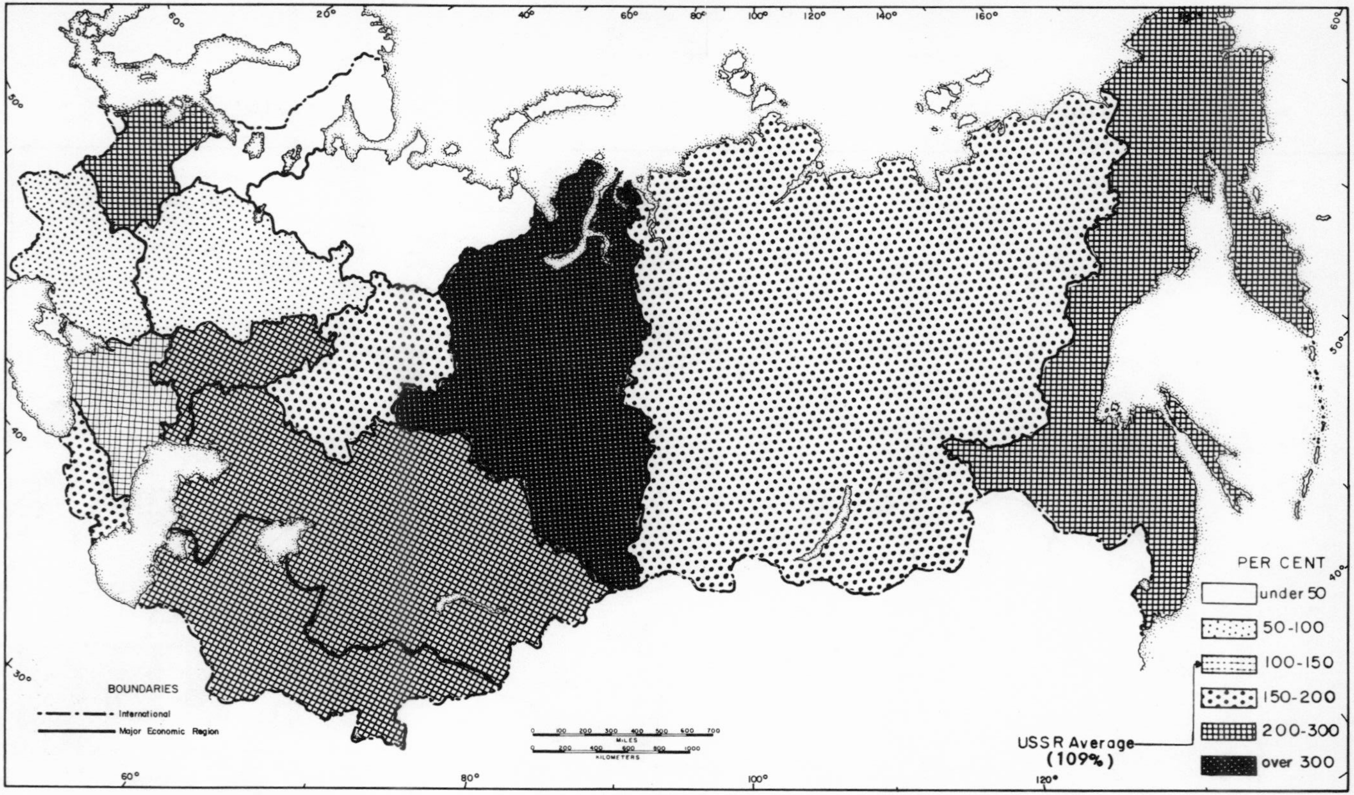
20°
40°
60°
80°
100°
120°
140°
160°
60°
50°
40°
30°
60°
80°
100°
120°
PER CENT
under 50
50-100
100-150
150-200
200-300
over 300
USSR Average
(109%)
BOUNDARIES
International
Major Economic Region
0 100 200 300 400 500 600 700
MILES
0 200 400 600 800 1000
KILOMETERS

PER CENT INCREASE OF INDUSTRIAL WORKERS: MACHINE MANUFACTURING

(By Major Economic Regions, 1940 to 1960)

MAP 21

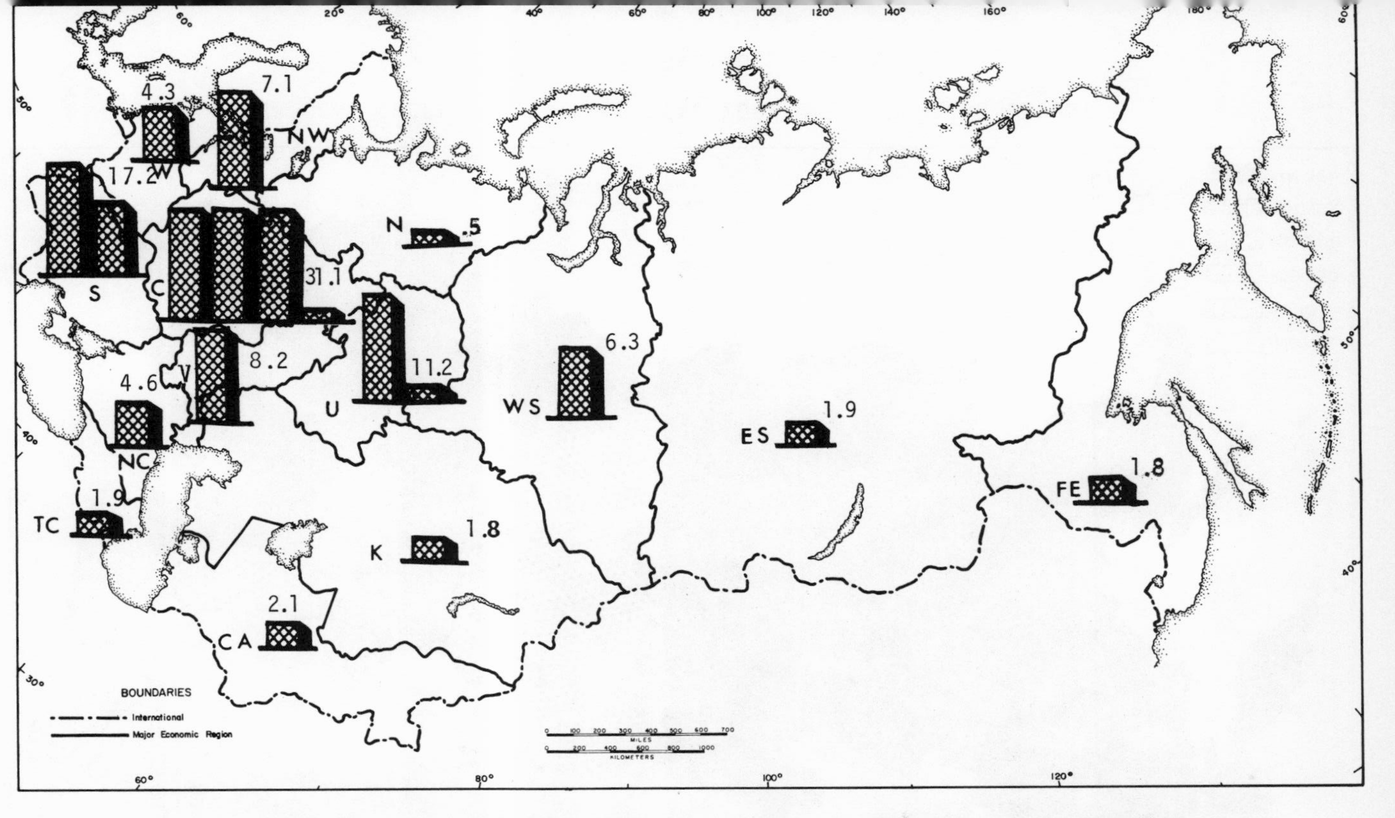

DISTRIBUTION OF INDUSTRIAL WORKERS IN 1960: MACHINE MANUFACTURING

(Major Economic Regions as Per Cent of U.S.S.R.)

MAP 22

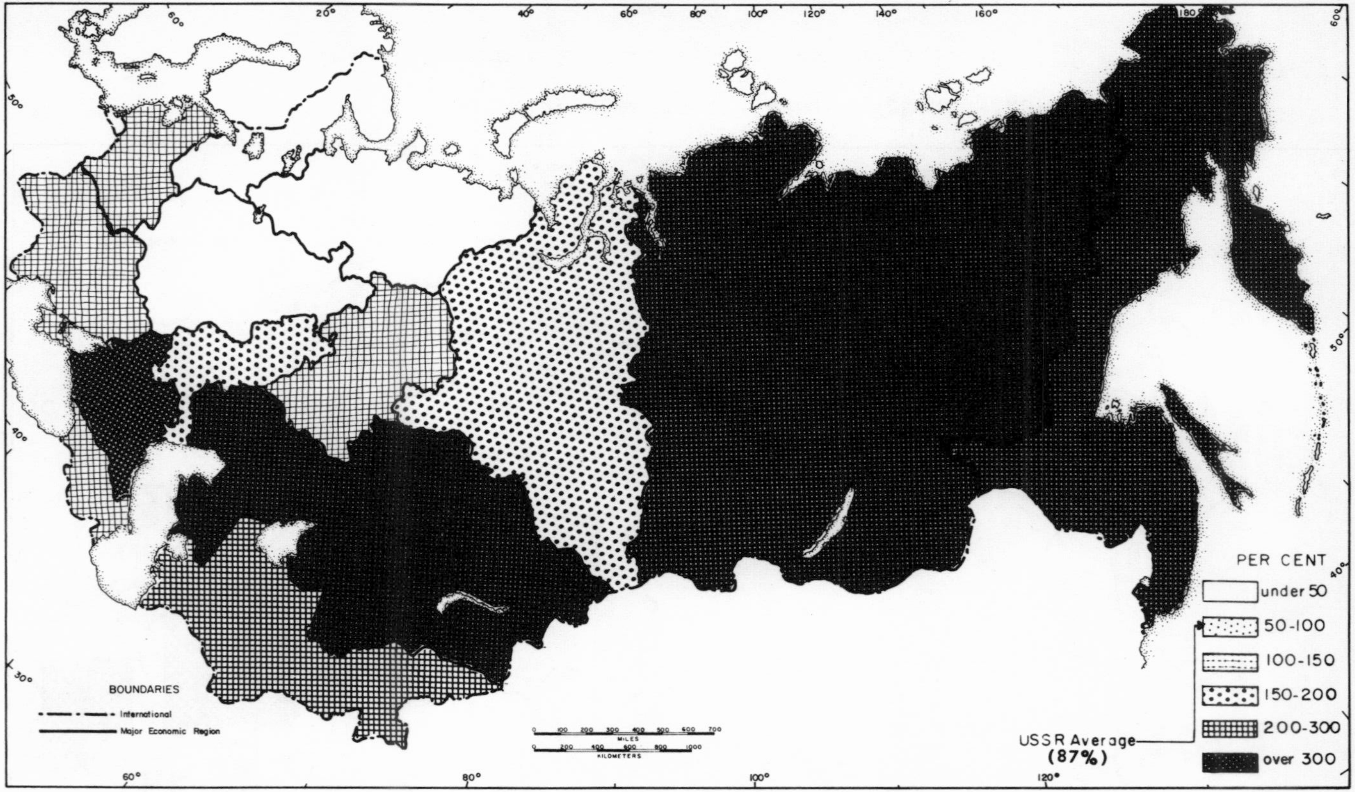

PER CENT INCREASE OF INDUSTRIAL WORKERS: CHEMICAL INDUSTRY

(By Major Economic Regions, 1940 to 1960)

MAP 23

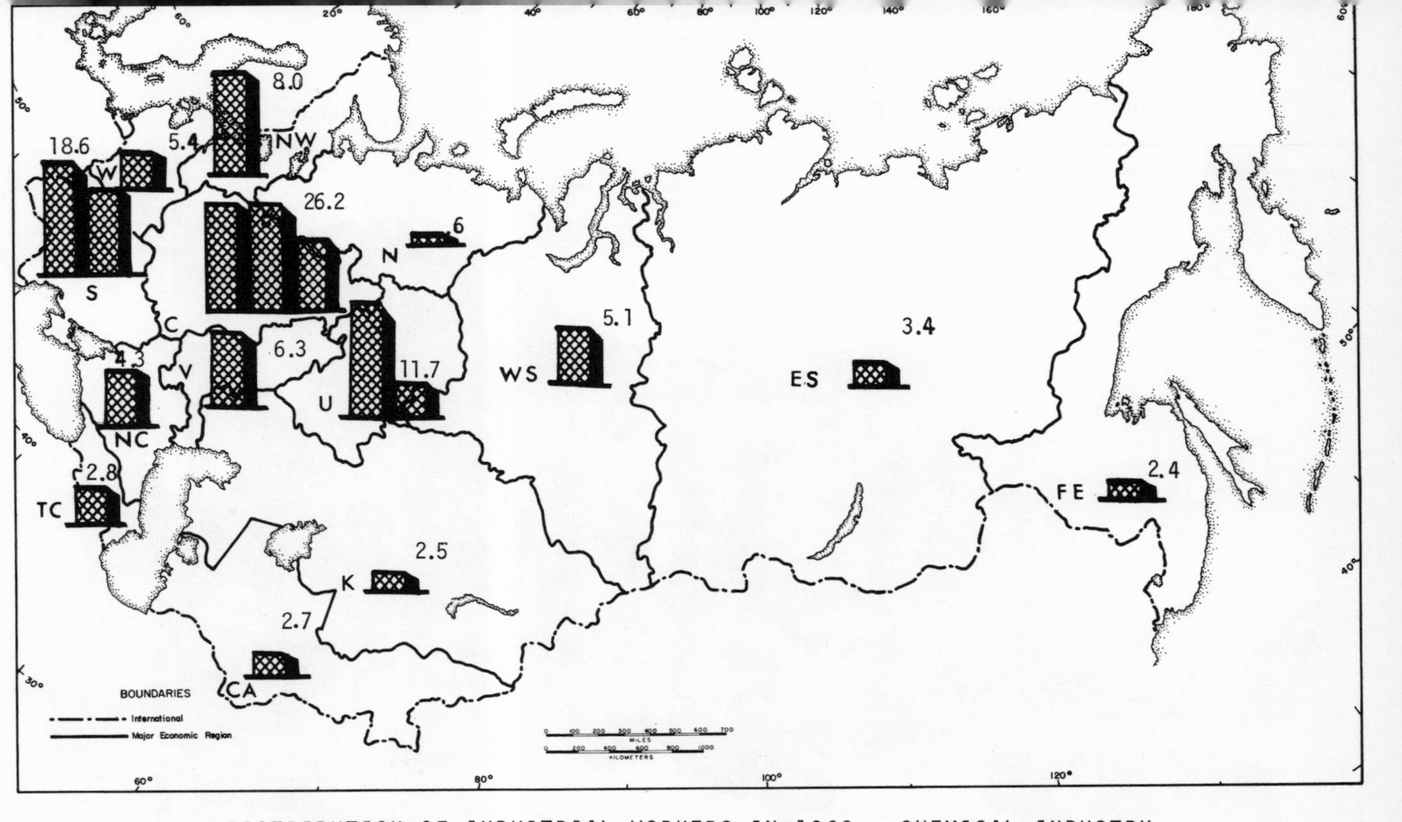

DISTRIBUTION OF INDUSTRIAL WORKERS IN 1960: CHEMICAL INDUSTRY

(Major Economic Regions as Per Cent of U.S.S.R.)

MAP 24

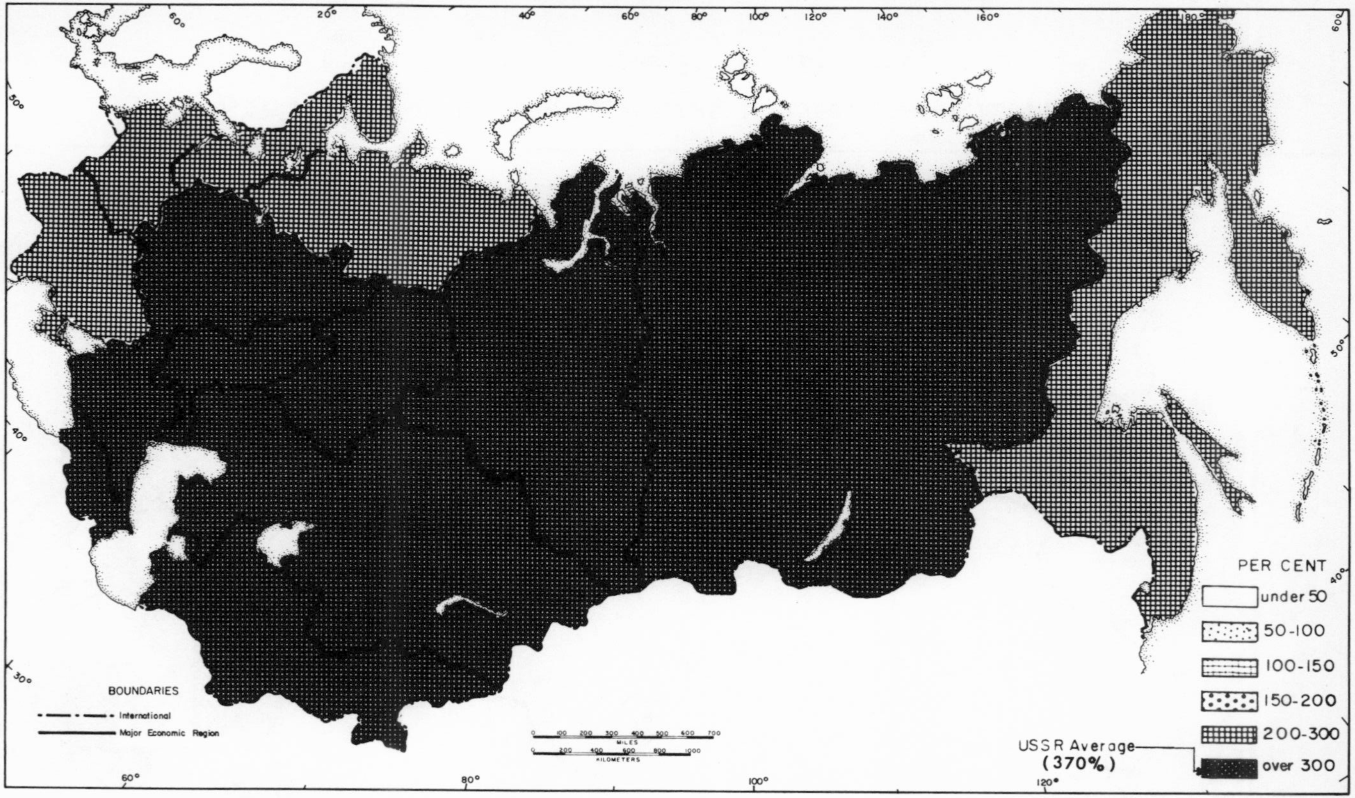

PER CENT INCREASE OF INDUSTRIAL WORKERS: BUILDING MATERIALS INDUSTRY

(By Major Economic Regions, 1940 to 1960)

MAP 25

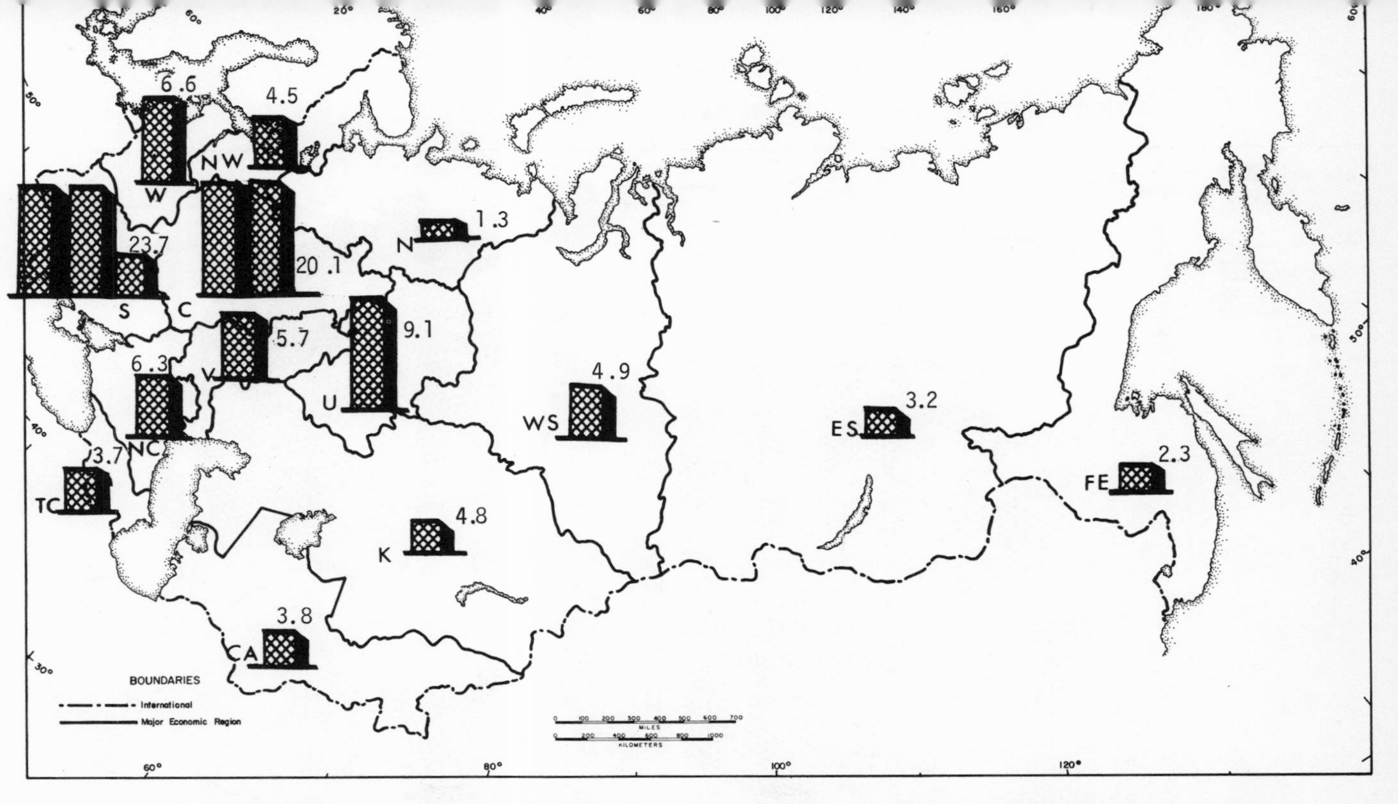

DISTRIBUTION OF INDUSTRIAL WORKERS IN 1960: BUILDING MATERIALS INDUSTRY

(Major Economic Regions as Per Cent of U.S.S.R.)

MAP 26

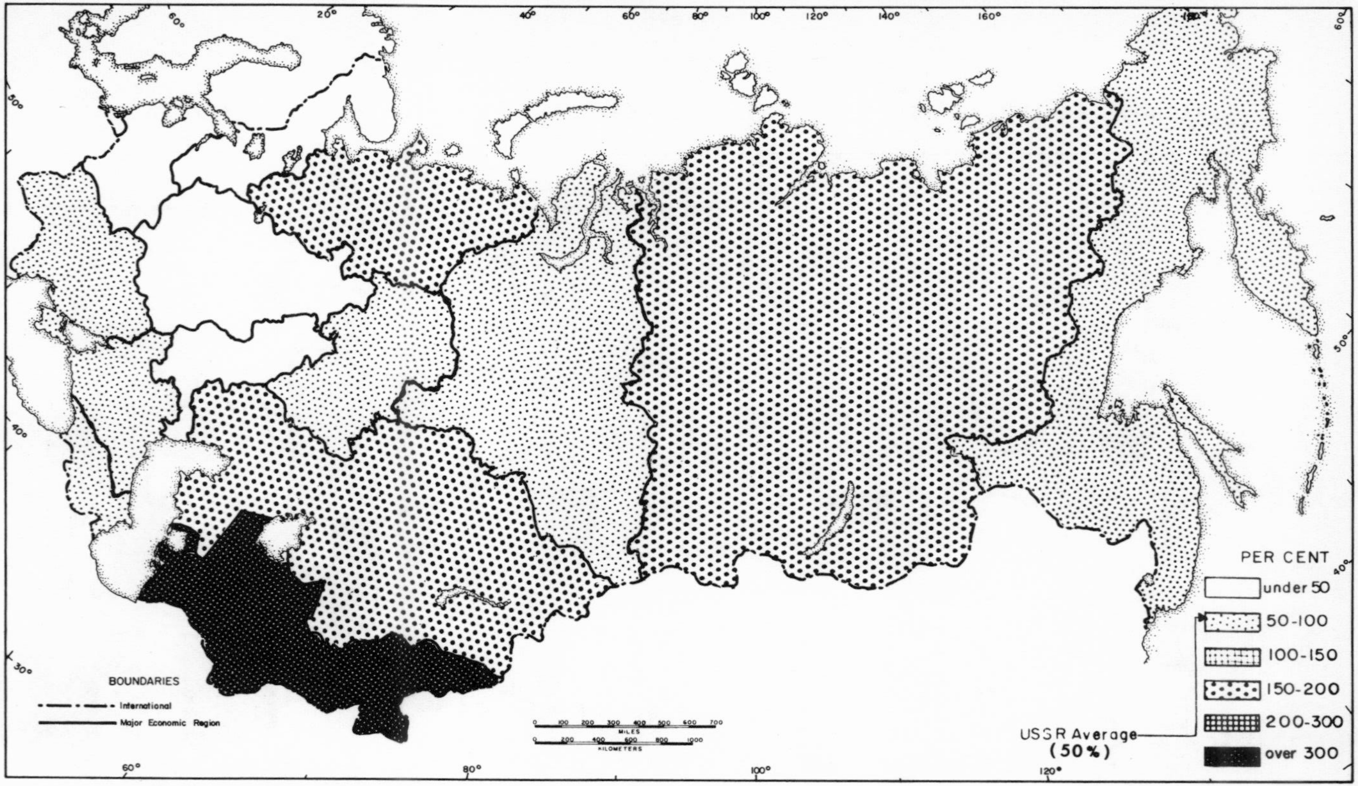

PER CENT INCREASE OF INDUSTRIAL WORKERS: FOREST INDUSTRIES

(By Major Economic Regions, 1940 to 1960)

MAP 27

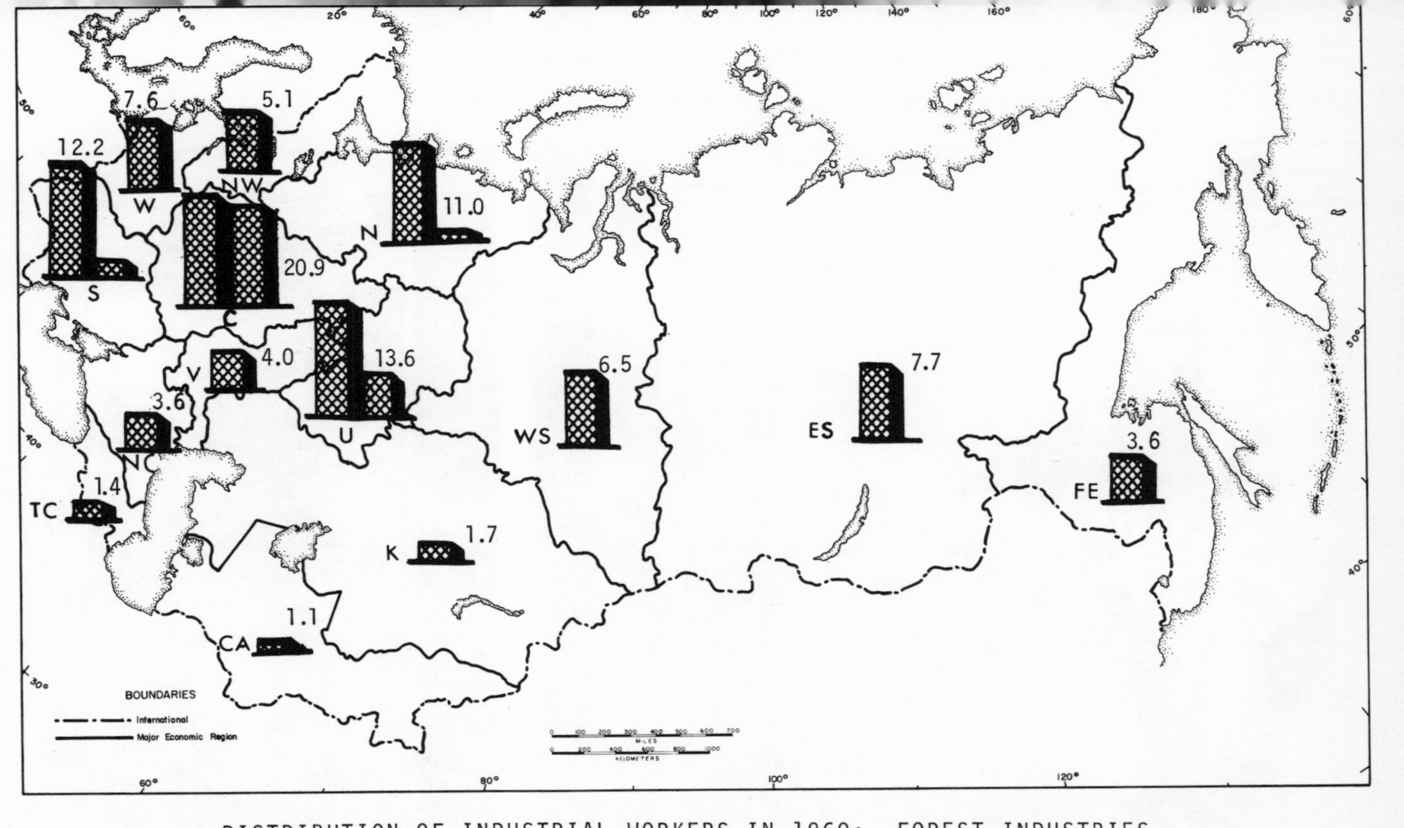

DISTRIBUTION OF INDUSTRIAL WORKERS IN 1960: FOREST INDUSTRIES

(Major Economic Regions as Per Cent of U.S.S.R.)

MAP 28

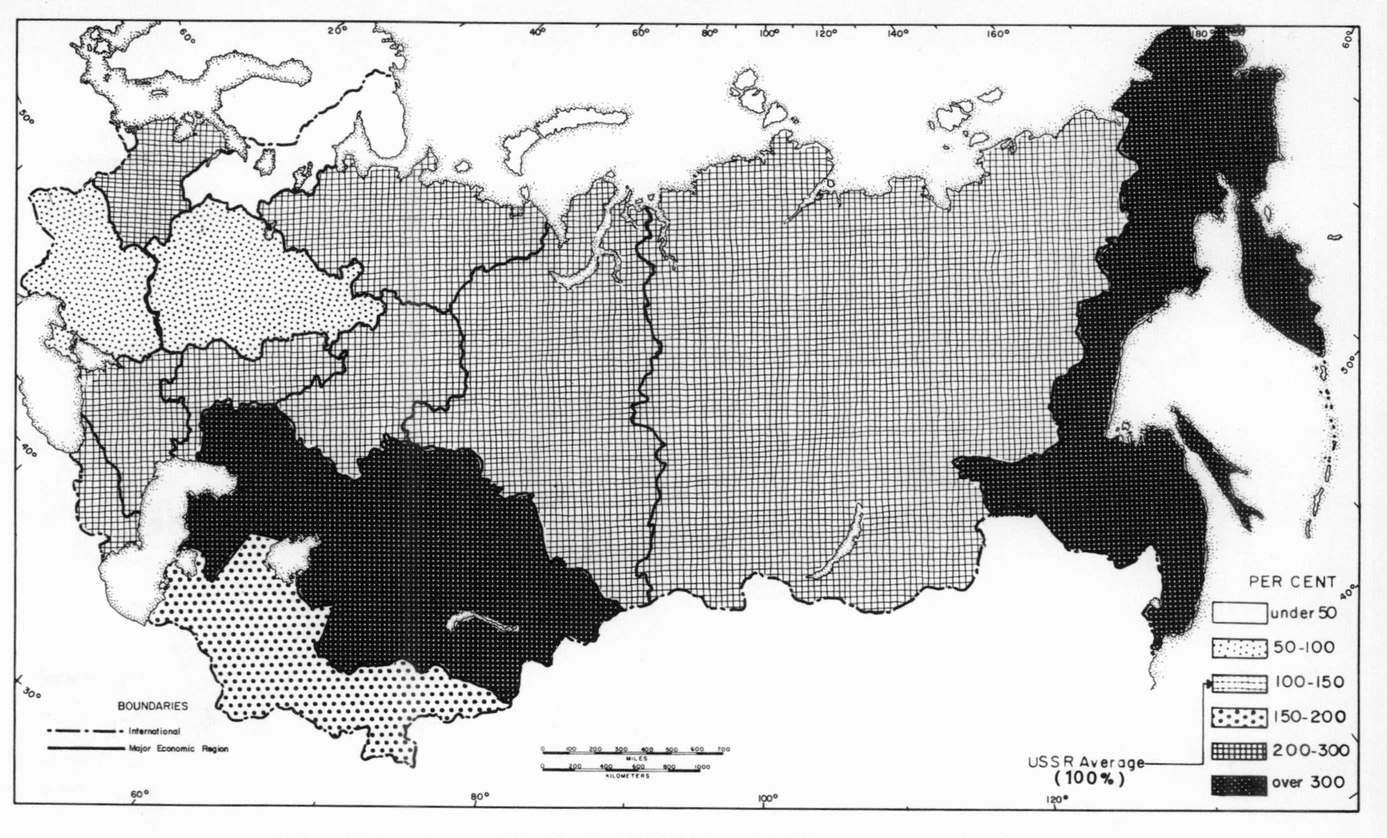

PER CENT INCREASE OF INDUSTRIAL WORKERS: LIGHT INDUSTRY

(By Major Economic Regions, 1940 to 1960)

MAP 29

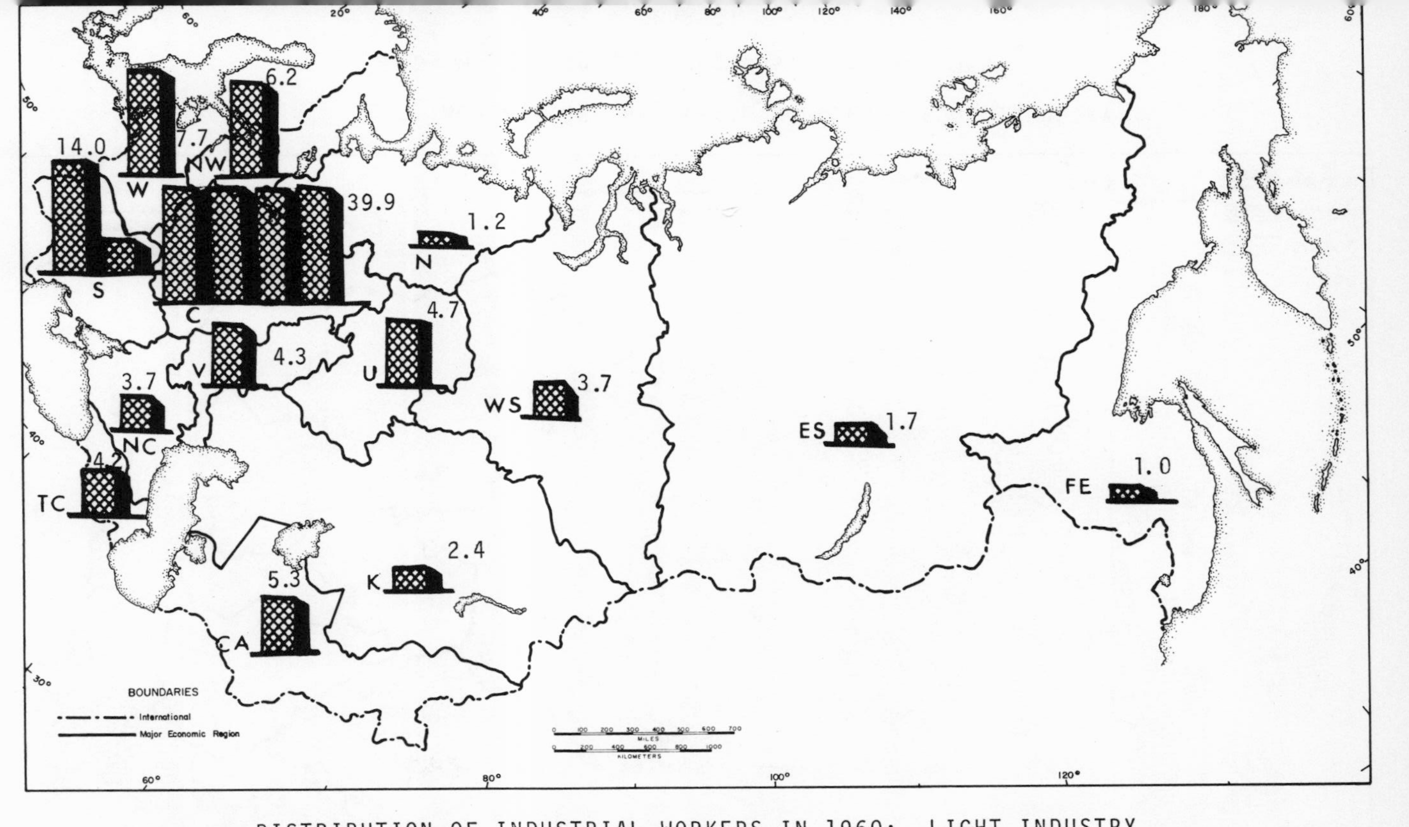

DISTRIBUTION OF INDUSTRIAL WORKERS IN 1960: LIGHT INDUSTRY

(Major Economic Regions as Per Cent of U.S.S.R.)

MAP 30

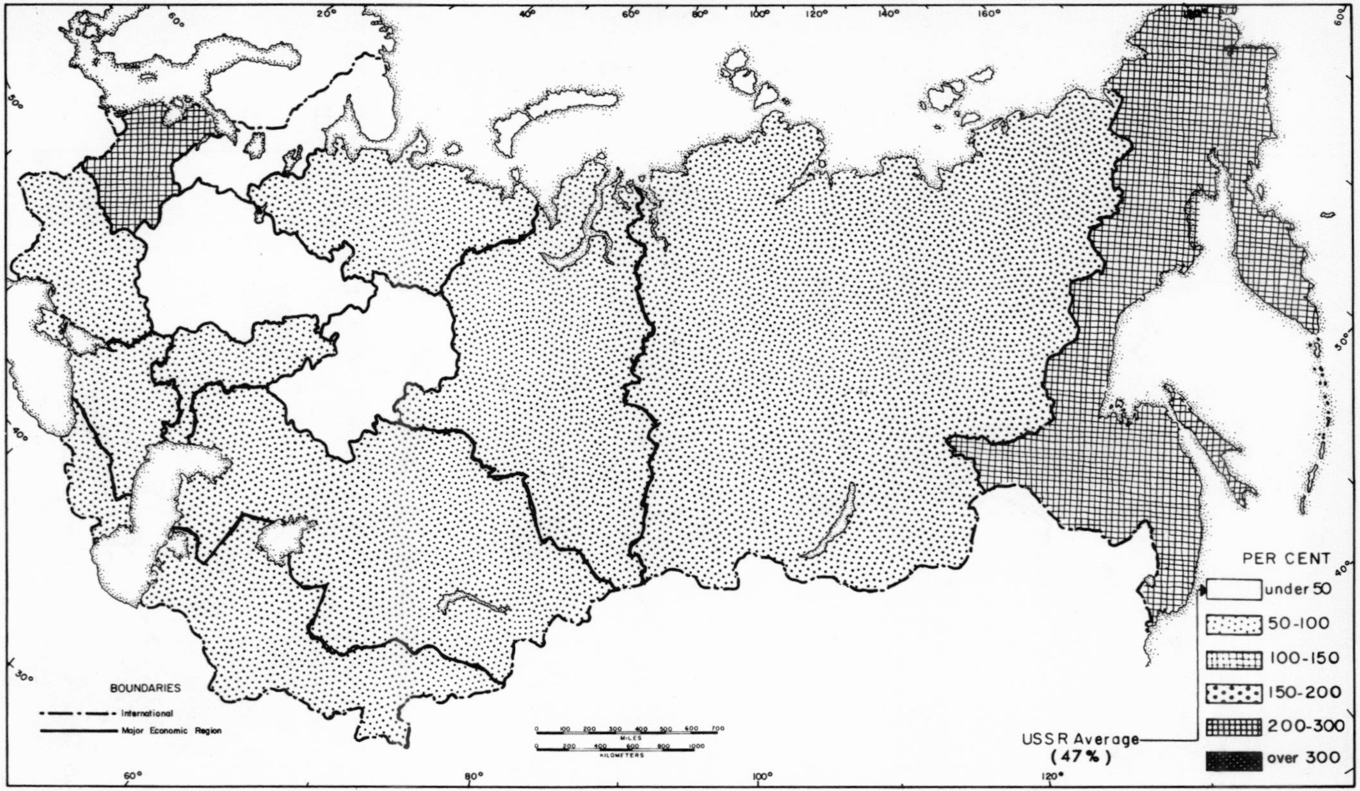

PER CENT INCREASE OF INDUSTRIAL WORKERS: FOOD INDUSTRY

(By Major Economic Regions, 1940 to 1960)

MAP 31

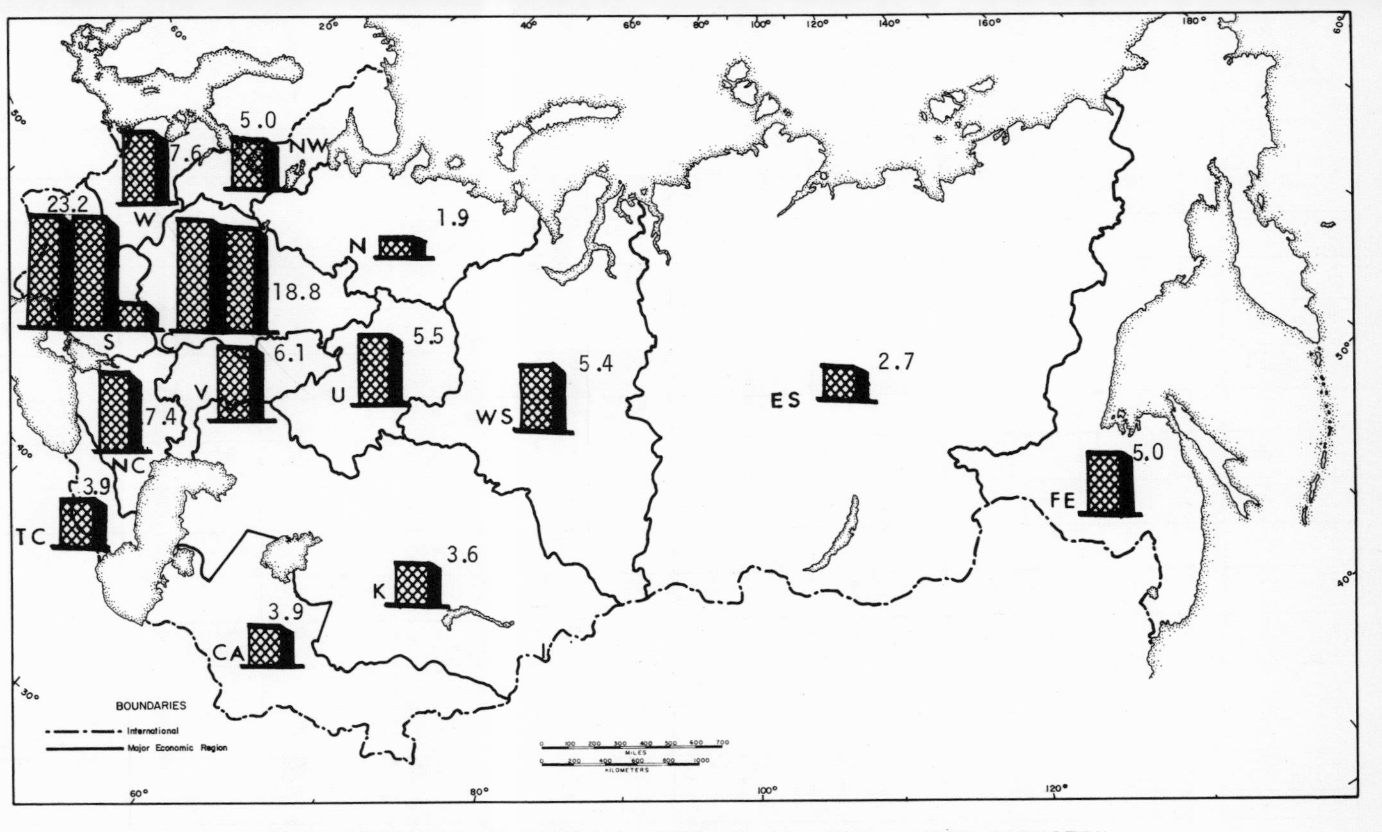

DISTRIBUTION OF INDUSTRIAL WORKERS IN 1960: FOOD INDUSTRY

(Major Economic Regions as Per Cent of U.S.S.R.)

MAP 32

TABLE 23

Ranking of Major Economic Regions, 1940-60; Workers as Per Cent of the U.S.S.R.

	Number of Industry																	
	0		1		2		3		4		5		6		7		8	
	1940	1960	1940	1960	1940	1960	1940	1960	1940	1960	1940	1960	1940	1960	1940	1960	1940	1960
Center	1	1	2	2	2	3	1	1	1	1	2	2	1	1	1	1	1	2
South	2	2	1	1	1	1	2	2	2	2	1	1	3	3	2	2	2	1
Northwest	3	4	6	14	4	5	3	5	3	4	5	9	4	8	3	4	4	8
Ural	4	3	3	4	3	2	4	3	4	3	4	3	2	2	5	6	5	6
West	5	7	5	6	13	11	8	8	5	6	3	4	5	6	4	3	6	3
Volga	6	5	11	8	6	7	5	4	6	5	8	6	8	9	6	7	7	5
North Caucasus	7	8	4	5	9	9	6	7	12	8	6	5	11	10	9	10	3	4
West Siberia	8	6	12	3	8	4	7	6	7	7	11	7	7	7	10	9	8	7
East Siberia	9	9	9	9	5	10	9	10	10	9	13	12	9	5	11	12	13	13
Trans-Causasus	10	10	7	10	12	6	10	11	8	10	9	11	12	13	8	8	11	10
Far East	11	14	8	11	11	12	14	13	14	13	10	13	10	11	14	14	9	9
Central Asia	12	11	13	13	14	13	11	9	9	11	7	10	14	14	7	5	10	11
North	13	12	14	12	10	14	12	14	11	14	14	14	6	4	12	13	14	14
Kazakhstan	14	13	10	7	7	8	13	12	13	12	12	8	13	12	13	11	12	12

Key to Industries:
0-All Industries
1-Energy and Fuel Industries
2-Heavy Industry
3-Machine Manufacturing
4-Chemical Industry
5-Building Materials Industry
6-Forest Industries
7-Light Industry
8-Food Industry

from the shift to the east induced by World War II. Another region, North, registered a substantial increase (667 per cent) caused mainly by the necessity of relying on the Pechora coal field during the war when Donbas was under German occupation.

Finally, the highest over-all increase was registered in the building materials industry. The number of workers in this industry more than quadrupled and the per cent increase was the highest among the eight major branches of industry. The need for a gigantic rebuilding of both industrial and residential structures that were destroyed during the war was obviously imperative. Map 25 demonstrates that the actual and effective increase was greatest in the western regions since their needs were acute due to the war devastation.

In summary, it may be noted that in all eight industrial branches the share of the eastern U. S. S. R. has increased. Also, a decrease in the block of western regions (Center-Northwest-South) was accompanied by a simultaneous increase in the share of the Ural-West Siberia block in the east. The significant changes occurred in the same industries where the share of the western regions as a whole declined substantially, namely in heavy industry, energy and fuel industries, and in machine manufacturing.

Notes to Chapter 7

1. Demitri B. Shimkin, *The Soviet Mineral-Fuels Industries, 1928-1958: A Statistical Survey,* U. S. Bureau of the Census, International Population Statistics Reports, Series P-90, No. 19 (Washington, D. C. : U. S. Government Printing Office, 1962), p. 30. See also *Gazovaya promyshlennost* [*Gas Industry*], No. 7 (1966).

2. Shimkin, *loc. cit.* Also U. S., Department of the Interior, *Minerals Yearbook 1960,* Vol. II (Washington, D. C. : Government Printing Office, 1960), pp. 4-5.

3. Shimkin, *op. cit.*, pp. 84 and 93.

4. J. P. Cole and F. C. German, *A Geography of the U. S. S. R.* (London: Butterworths, 1961), p. 146.

5. Shimkin, loc. cit. See also Gazovaya promyshlennost, op. cit.

6. Shimkin, loc. cit.

CHAPTER 8 STRUCTURE OF MAJOR ECONOMIC REGIONS, 1960

While Chapters 3 and 7 analyzed the distribution of industrial workers within each of the principal branches of industry, the focus in this chapter, as in Chapter 4, is on each of the fourteen major economic regions and their internal structure. The data are presented in three charts (Figures 5, 6, and 7) and sixteen tables.

Figure 5 shows the industrial workers in each industrial branch as a per cent of each region in 1960. To make easier the comparison between Figure 2 in Chapter 4 and Figure 5, which together show the changes in the industrial structure of the major economic regions between 1940 and 1960, two more charts combine the data from Figures 2 and 5. Figure 6 shows the comparison of the regional industrial structure in 1940 and in 1960 for the eight regions of the western U. S. S. R., while Figure 7 does the same for the six eastern regions. In each of the three charts (Figures 5, 6, and 7) a top bar has been added (two bars in Figures 6 and 7) showing the percentage breakdown of the eight industrial branches for the U. S. S. R.

In order to have a better and clearer view of the general trends in the U. S. S. R., a summary of all the information contained in the fourteen separate tables is given in several tables and charts. In each case the summary of Tables 26-39 is given for both 1940 and 1960: Table 22 (in Chapter 7) gives the summary of the information contained in the two rows marked (A)--"Workers as per cent of the U. S. S. R."; Table 23 (in Chapter 7) summarizes the information from the two rows marked (B)--"Rank among the major regions" (for workers as per cent of the U. S. S. R.); Figures 6 and 7 present a

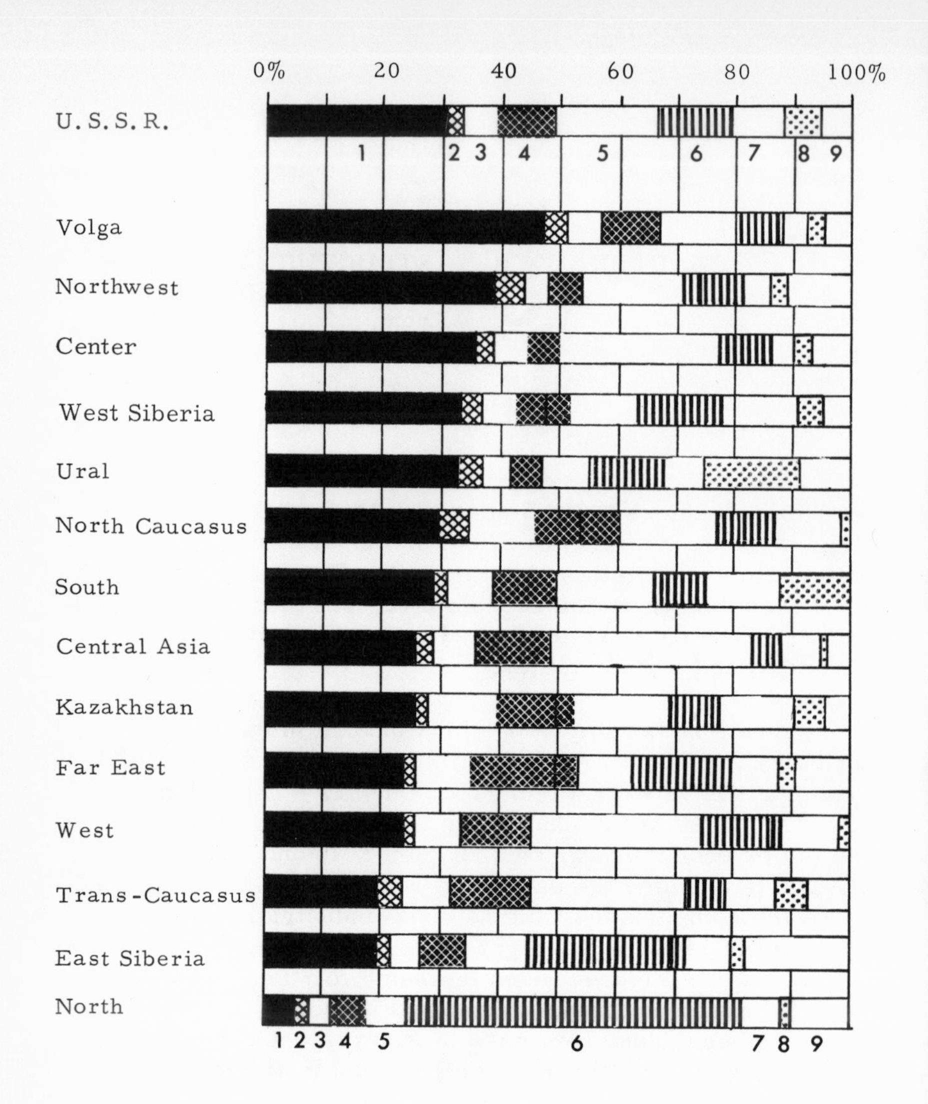

FIGURE 5

INDUSTRIAL WORKERS BY BRANCHES OF INDUSTRY AS A PER CENT OF THE MAJOR ECONOMIC REGIONS, 1960

Key: 1 = Machine Manufacturing
2 = Chemical Industry
3 = Building Materials Industry
4 = Food Industry
5 = Light Industry
6 = Forest Industries
7 = Energy and Fuel Industries
8 = Heavy Industry
9 = Other Industries

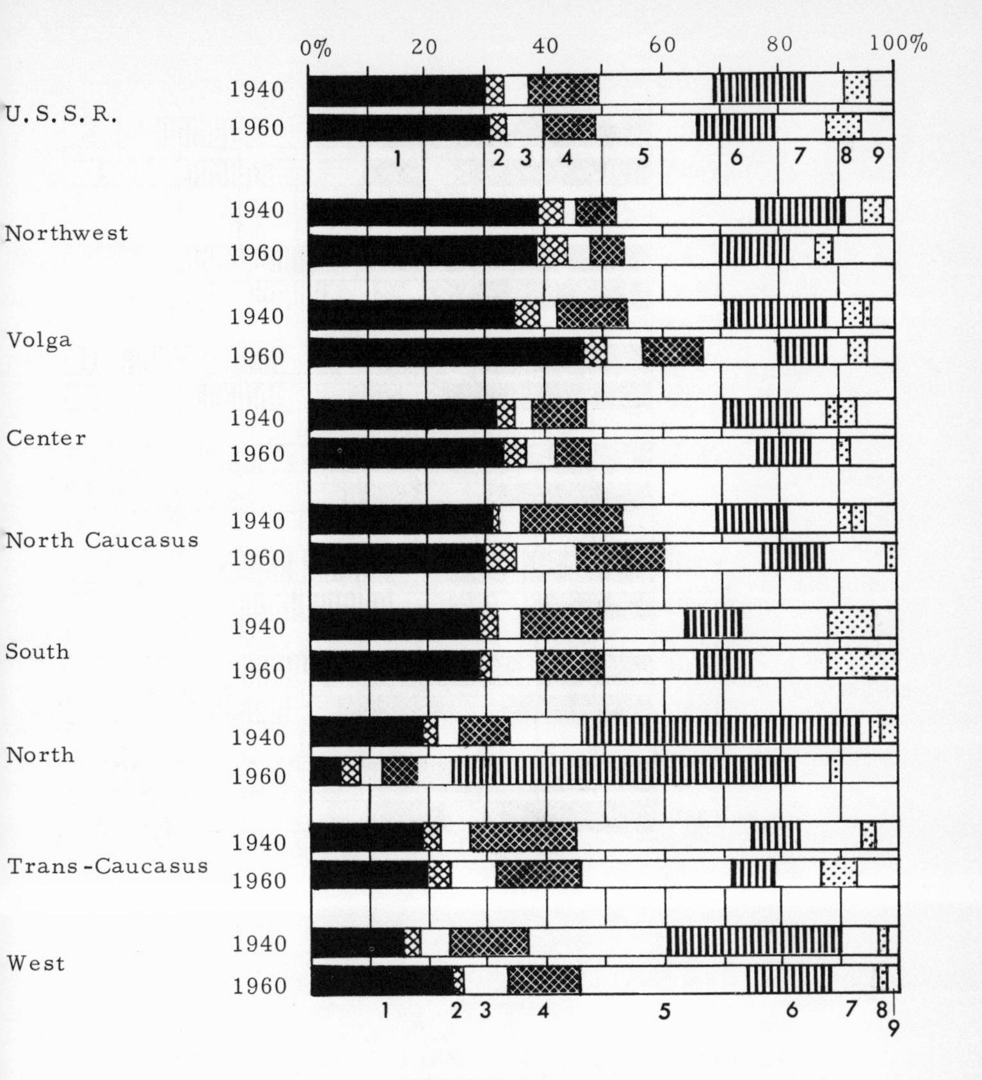

FIGURE 6

WESTERN U. S. S. R. : COMPARISON OF REGIONAL INDUSTRIAL STRUCTURE, 1940 AND 1960

Key: 1 = Machine Manufacturing
2 = Chemical Industry
3 = Building Materials Industry
4 = Food Industry
5 = Light Industry
6 = Forest Industries
7 = Energy and Fuel Industries
8 = Heavy Industry
9 = Other Industries

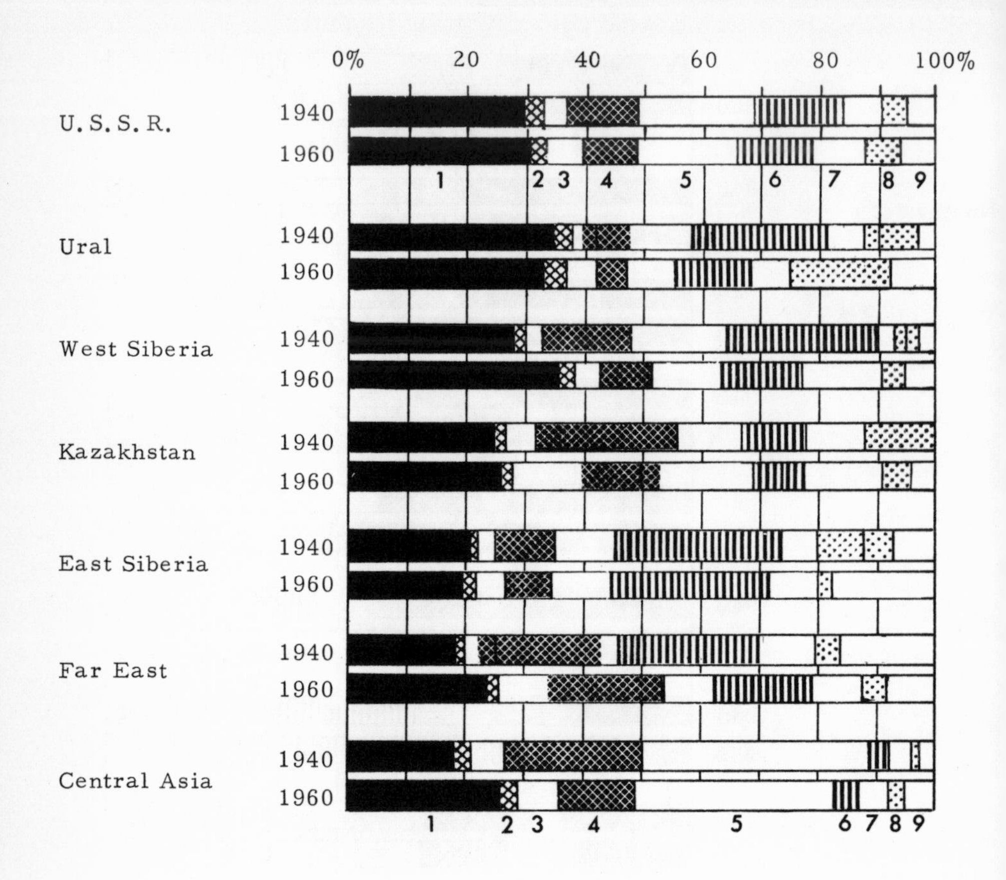

FIGURE 7

EASTERN U. S. S. R. : COMPARISON OF REGIONAL INDUSTRIAL STRUCTURE, 1940 AND 1960

Key: 1 = Machine Manufacturing
2 = Chemical Industry
3 = Building Materials Industry
4 = Food Industry
5 = Light Industry
6 = Forest Industries
7 = Energy and Fuel Industries
8 = Heavy Industry
9 = Other Industries

visual summary and comparison of the data in the two rows labeled (C)--"Workers as per cent of the region"; and finally, Table 25 in this chapter offers the summary of the information in the two rows marked (D)--"Rank among the major regions" (for workers as a per cent of the region). Since a location quotient, given in the two rows marked (E), has a meaning only when applied to one particular region, no regional comparison of the quotients is possible and thus no summary table is given.

Figures 6 and 7 show that the industrial structure of the three older and leading regions did not change significantly, despite the fact that in all three of them (Center, South, and Northwest) their shares of the U. S. S. R. were reduced between 1940 and 1960. On the other hand, all the eastern regions registered significant changes in the industrial structure (both increase and decrease of shares), and the same changes occurred also in the regions Volga, West and North.

A detailed discussion of the industrial structure, as presented in charts and tables in this chapter, is given for the chemical industry and comsumer goods industries. The discussion of machine manufacturing is presented as a case study in Chapter 9.

CHEMICAL INDUSTRY

If the industrial structure of major economic regions is considered during the period 1940-60, it becomes apparent that few regions registered a change in the share of the chemical industry.[1] The question of why this stability occurred and especially why almost no increases in share took place, could be answered by considering several possibilities. For example, a deliberate economic policy of the Soviet government in allocating the investments to other branches rather than to chemicals could have been responsible for this absence of change in the share. As a matter of fact, a serious lag of investments in the chemical industry existed prior to the Seven-year plan (1959-65) and only after 1959 did the Soviet government attempt to make up for the earlier neglect of this industry by making the increase in the capital investment in the chemical industry greater than in any other branch.[2] Another possible cause could lie in the damages

TABLE 24

Ranking of Major Economic Regions, 1960

A - Workers as Per Cent of the U.S.S.R. B - Workers as Per Cent of the Region

	Number of Industry																
	0	1		2		3		4		5		6		7		8	
	A	A	B	A	B	A	B	A	B	A	B	A	B	A	B	A	B
Center	1	2	13	3	7	1	3	1	12	2	12	1	9	1	2	2	13
South	2	1	1	1	2	2	7	2	7	1	5	3	12	2	9	1	7
Northwest	4	14	14	5	6	5	2	4	1	9	13	8	7	4	5	8	11
Ural	3	4	11	2	1	3	6	3	3	3	11	2	5	6	13	6	14
West	7	6	6	11	13	8	8	6	9	4	6	6	4	3	4	3	4
Volga	5	8	12	7	8	4	1	5	2	6	7	9	10	7	8	5	8
North Caucasus	8	5	4	9	9	7	5	8	6	5	2	10	8	10	7	4	2
West Siberia	6	3	3	4	4	6	4	7	13	7	10	7	6	9	10	7	9
East Siberia	9	9	9	10	10	10	13	9	5	12	8	5	2	12	11	13	10
Trans-Caucasus	10	10	7	6	3	11	12	10	11	11	4	13	13	8	3	10	6
Far East	14	11	5	12	11	13	10	13	4	13	9	11	3	14	14	9	1
Central Asia	11	13	10	13	12	9	9	11	8	10	3	14	14	5	1	11	3
North	12	12	8	14	14	14	14	14	14	14	14	4	1	13	12	14	12
Kazakhstan	13	7	2	8	5	12	11	12	10	8	1	12	11	11	6	12	5

Key to Industries: 0-All Industries
1-Energy and Fuel Industries
2-Heavy Industry
3-Machine Manufacturing
4-Chemical Industry
5-Building Materials Industry
6-Forest Industries
7-Light Industry
8-Food Industry

TABLE 25

Ranking of Major Economic Regions, 1940-60; Workers as Per Cent of the Region

	Number of Industry															
	1		2		3		4		5		6		7		8	
	1940	1960	1940	1960	1940	1960	1940	1960	1940	1960	1940	1960	1940	1960	1940	1960
Center	9	13	5	7	5	3	2	12	12	12	9	9	4	2	12	13
South	1	1	4	2	6	7	9	7	6	5	12	12	9	9	8	7
Northwest	14	14	6	6	1	2	1	1	13	13	8	7	5	5	14	11
Ural	8	11	2	1	3	6	3	3	9	11	6	5	12	13	13	14
West	6	6	14	13	14	8	5	9	2	6	2	4	3	4	9	4
Volga	12	12	8	8	2	1	7	2	10	7	7	10	6	8	7	8
North Caucasus	3	4	10	9	4	5	13	6	7	2	10	8	8	7	4	2
West Siberia	11	3	7	4	7	4	6	13	14	10	5	6	7	10	6	9
East Siberia	7	9	3	10	9	13	11	5	11	8	3	2	10	11	10	10
Trans-Caucasus	2	7	12	3	10	12	4	11	3	4	13	13	2	3	5	6
Far East	5	5	11	11	13	10	14	4	5	9	4	3	14	14	3	1
Central Asia	10	10	13	12	12	9	8	8	1	3	14	14	1	1	2	3
North	13	8	9	14	11	14	10	14	8	14	1	1	13	12	11	12
Kazakhstan	4	2	1	5	8	11	12	10	4	1	11	11	11	6	1	5

Key to Industries: 1-Energy and Fuel Industries 2-Heavy Industry 3-Machine Manufacturing 4-Chemical Industry 5-Building Materials Industry 6-Forest Industries 7-Light Industry 8-Food Industry

TABLE 26

Breakdown of Industrial Workers in the

Central Region in 1940 and 1960

	All Industries		Number of Industry							
			1	2	3	4	5	6	7	8
(A) Workers as Per Cent of the U.S.S.R.	1940 1960	33% 27%	22% 13%	26% 10%	35% 31%	41% 26%	23% 20%	27% 21%	40% 40%	27% 19%
(B) Rank among the Major Regions	1940 1960	1 1	2 2	2 3	1 1	1 1	2 2	1 1	1 1	1 2
(C) Workers as Per Cent of the Region	1940 1960	100% 100%	5% 4%	4% 2%	31% 35%	4% 3%	2% 5%	13% 9%	22% 27%	11% 7%
(D) Rank among the Major Regions[a]	1940 1960	---- ----	9 13	5 7	5 3	2 12	12 12	9 9	4 2	12 13
(E) Location Quotient (LQ)[b]	1940 1960	---- ----	.7 .5	.8 .4	1.1 1.2	1.3 1.0	.7 .7	.8 .8	1.2 1.5	.8 .7

Key to Industries:

1 - Energy and Fuel Industries
2 - Heavy Industry
3 - Machine Manufacturing
4 - Chemical Industry
5 - Building Materials Industry
6 - Forest Industries
7 - Light Industry
8 - Food Industry

Note: All per cent figures are rounded values (decimal points have been omitted).

[a]Row D: Rank (among the 14 major regions) of the share of a given industry as per cent of the region (Row C above). See also Fig. 5: e.g., Central Region ranks third in machine manufacturing.

[b]"The location quotient measures the degree to which a specific region has more or less than its share of any particular industry...." [John W. Alexander, Economic Geography (Englewood Cliffs, New Jersey: Prentice-Hall, 1963), p. 406]. See Appendix V for a more complete definition of this term.

TABLE 27

Breakdown of Industrial Workers in the

Region South in 1940 and 1960

	All Industries		Number of Industry							
			1	2	3	4	5	6	7	8
(A) Workers as Per Cent of the U.S.S.R.	1940 1960	20% 19%	42% 34%	29% 38%	20% 17%	15% 19%	28% 24%	11% 12%	15% 14%	23% 23%
(B) Rank among the Major Regions	1940 1960	2 2	1 1	1 1	2 2	2 2	1 1	3 3	2 2	2 1
(C) Workers as Per Cent of the Region	1940 1960	100% 100%	15% 15%	8% 12%	29% 28%	3% 3%	4% 9%	9% 8%	14% 14%	14% 12%
(D) Rank among the Major Regions[a]	1940 1960	---- ----	1 1	4 2	6 7	9 7	6 5	12 12	9 9	8 7
(E) Location Quotient (LQ)[b]	1940 1960	---- ----	2.1 1.8	1.4 2.0	1.1 1.0	.8 1.0	1.4 1.3	.6 .7	.8 .8	1.1 1.3

Key to Industries:

1 - Energy and Fuel Industries
2 - Heavy Industry
3 - Machine Manufacturing
4 - Chemical Industry
5 - Building Materials Industry
6 - Forest Industries
7 - Light Industry
8 - Food Industry

Note: All per cent figures are rounded values (decimal points have been omitted).

[a]Row D: Rank (among the 14 major regions) of the share of a given industry as per cent of the region (Row C above). See also Fig. 5: e.g., Central Region ranks third in machine manufacturing.

[b]"The location quotient measures the degree to which a specific region has more or less than its share of any particular industry...." (Alexander, loc. cit.). See Appendix V for a more complete definition of this term.

TABLE 28

Breakdown of Industrial Workers in the

Ural Region in 1940 and 1960

		All Industries	Number of Industry							
			1	2	3	4	5	6	7	8
(A) Workers as Per Cent of the U.S.S.R.	1940 1960	8% 11%	7% 8%	16% 34%	9% 11%	10% 12%	7% 9%	12% 14%	5% 5%	6% 6%
(B) Rank among the Major Regions	1940 1960	4 3	3 4	3 2	4 3	4 3	4 3	2 2	5 6	5 6
(C) Workers as Per Cent of the Region	1940 1960	100% 100%	6% 6%	11% 18%	32% 31%	4% 3%	3% 6%	23% 15%	10% 8%	9% 5%
(D) Rank among the Major Regions[a]	1940 1960	---- ----	8 11	2 1	3 6	3 3	9 11	6 5	12 13	13 14
(E) Location Quotient (LQ)[b]	1940 1960	---- ----	.8 .7	2.0 3.1	1.1 1.1	1.2 1.1	.9 .8	1.5 1.2	.6 .4	.7 .5

Key to Industries:

1 - Energy and Fuel Industries
2 - Heavy Industry
3 - Machine Manufacturing
4 - Chemical Industry
5 - Building Materials Industry
6 - Forest Industries
7 - Light Industry
8 - Food Industry

Note: All per cent figures are rounded values (decimal points have been omitted).

[a]Row D: Rank (among the 14 major regions) of the share of a given industry as per cent of the region (Row C above). See also Fig. 5: e.g., Central Region ranks third in machine manufacturing.

[b]"The location quotient measures the degree to which a specific region has more or less than its share of any particular industry...." (Alexander, loc. cit.). See Appendix V for a more complete definition of this term.

TABLE 29

Breakdown of Industrial Workers in the

Northwest Region in 1940 and 1960

		All Industries	Number of Industry							
			1	2	3	4	5	6	7	8
(A) Workers as per Cent of the U.S.S.R.	1940	10%	3%	7%	13%	14%	6%	10%	11%	6%
	1960	6%	2%	3%	7%	8%	5%	5%	6%	5%
(B) Rank among the Major Regions	1940	3	6	4	3	3	5	4	3	4
	1960	4	14	5	5	4	9	8	4	8
(C) Workers as Per Cent of the Region	1940	100%	3%	4%	39%	5%	2%	16%	21%	8%
	1960	100%	3%	3%	36%	4%	5%	10%	18%	8%
(D) Rank among the Major Regions[a]	1940	----	14	6	1	1	13	8	5	14
	1960	----	14	6	2	1	13	7	5	11
(E) Location Quotient (LQ)[b]	1940	----	.4	.8	1.3	1.4	.6	1.0	1.2	.6
	1960	----	.3	.5	1.2	1.3	.7	.8	1.0	.8

Key to Industries:

1 - Energy and Fuel Industries
2 - Heavy Industry
3 - Machine Manufacturing
4 - Chemical Industry
5 - Building Materials Industry
6 - Forest Industries
7 - Light Industry
8 - Food Industry

Note: All per cent figures are rounded values (decimal points have been omitted).

[a]Rows D: Rank (among the 14 major regions) of the share of a given industry as per cent of the region (Rows C above). See also Fig. 5: e.g., Central Region ranks third in machine manufacturing.

[b]"The location quotient measures the degree to which a specific region has more or less than its share of any particular industry...." (Alexander, <u>loc. cit.</u>). See Appendix V for a more complete definition of this term.

TABLE 30

Breakdown of Industrial Workers in the

Volga Region in 1940 and 1960

		All Industries	Number of Industry							
			1	2	3	4	5	6	7	8
(A) Workers as Per Cent of the U.S.S.R.	1940	5%	2%	4%	5%	4%	4%	5%	4%	5%
	1960	6%	3%	2%	8%	6%	6%	4%	4%	6%
(B) Rank among the Major Regions	1940	6	11	6	5	6	8	8	6	7
	1960	5	8	7	4	5	6	9	7	5
(C) Workers as Per Cent of the Region	1940	100%	3%	4%	34%	3%	2%	18%	17%	15%
	1960	100%	4%	2%	44%	4%	7%	9%	14%	10%
(D) Rank among the Major Regions[a]	1940	----	12	8	2	7	10	7	6	7
	1960	----	12	8	1	2	7	10	8	8
(E) Location Quotient (LQ)[b]	1940	----	.4	.8	1.2	.9	.8	1.1	.9	1.2
	1960	----	.5	.4	1.4	1.1	1.0	.7	.8	1.1

Key to Industries:

1 - Energy and Fuel Industries
2 - Heavy Industry
3 - Machine Manufacturing
4 - Chemical Industry
5 - Building Materials Industry
6 - Forest Industries
7 - Light Industry
8 - Food Industry

Note: All per cent figures are rounded values (decimal points have been omitted).

[a]Rows D: Rank (among the 14 major regions) of the share of a given industry as per cent of the region (Rows C above). See also Fig. 5: e.g., Central Region ranks third in machine manufacturing.

[b]"The location quotient measures the degree to which a specific region has more or less than its share of any particular industry...." (Alexander, loc. cit.). See Appendix V for a more complete definition of this term.

TABLE 31

Breakdown of Industrial Workers in the

Region West Siberia in 1940 and 1960

		All Industries	Number of Industry							
			1	2	3	4	5	6	7	8
(A) Workers as Per Cent of the U.S.S.R.	1940	4%	2%	3%	3%	3%	2%	6%	3%	5%
	1960	6%	9%	5%	6%	5%	5%	7%	4%	5%
(B) Rank among the Major Regions	1940	8	12	8	7	7	11	7	10	8
	1960	6	3	4	6	7	7	7	9	7
(C) Workers as Per Cent of the Region	1940	100%	4%	4%	25%	3%	2%	25%	15%	18%
	1960	100%	13%	5%	34%	3%	6%	14%	12%	9%
(D) Rank among the Major Regions[a]	1940	----	11	7	7	6	14	5	7	6
	1960	----	3	4	4	13	10	6	10	9
(E) Location Quotient (LQ)[b]	1940	----	.5	.8	.9	.9	.6	1.6	.9	1.4
	1960	----	1.6	.9	1.1	.9	.9	1.2	.7	1.0

Key to Industries:

1 - Energy and Fuel Industries
2 - Heavy Industry
3 - Machine Manufacturing
4 - Chemical Industry
5 - Building Materials Industry
6 - Forest Industries
7 - Light Industry
8 - Food Industry

Note: All per cent figures are rounded values (decimal points have been omitted).

[a]Rows D: Rank (among the 14 major regions) of the share of a given industry as per cent of the region (Rows C above). See also Fig. 5: e.g., Central Region ranks third in machine manufacturing.

[b]"The location quotient measures the degree to which a specific region has more or less than its share of any particular industry...." (Alexander, <u>loc. cit.</u>). See Appendix V for a more complete definition of this term.

TABLE 32

Breakdown of Industrial Workers in the

Region West in 1940 and 1960

		All Industries	Number of Industry							
			1	2	3	4	5	6	7	8
(A) Workers as Per Cent of the U.S.S.R.	1940	5%	5%	1%	3%	5%	8%	10%	7%	6%
	1960	5%	6%	1%	4%	5%	7%	8%	8%	8%
(B) Rank among the Major Regions	1940	5	5	13	8	5	3	5	4	6
	1960	7	6	11	8	6	4	6	3	3
(C) Workers as Per Cent of the Region	1940	100%	8%	1%	14%	3%	5%	30%	24%	14%
	1960	100%	10%	1%	24%	3%	8%	17%	26%	13%
(D) Rank among the Major Regions[a]	1940	----	6	14	14	5	2	2	3	9
	1960	----	6	13	8	9	6	4	4	4
(E) Location Quotient (LQ)[b]	1940	----	1.0	.2	.5	.9	1.6	1.9	1.4	1.1
	1960	----	1.2	.1	.8	1.0	1.2	1.4	1.4	1.4

Key to Industries:

1 - Energy and Fuel Industries
2 - Heavy Industry
3 - Machine Manufacturing
4 - Chemical Industry
5 - Building Materials Industry
6 - Forest Industries
7 - Light Industry
8 - Food Industry

Note: All per cent figures are rounded values (decimal points have been omitted).

[a] Rows D: Rank (among the 14 major regions) of the share of a given industry as per cent of the region (Rows C above). See also Fig. 5: e.g., Central Region ranks third in machine manufacturing.

[b] "The location quotient measures the degree to which a specific region has more or less than its share of any particular industry...." (Alexander, loc. cit.). See Appendix V for a more complete definition of this term.

TABLE 33

Breakdown of Industrial Workers in the

North Caucasus Region in 1940 and 1960

	All Industries		Number of Industry							
			1	2	3	4	5	6	7	8
(A) Workers as Per Cent of the U.S.S.R.	1940	4%	5%	3%	5%	1%	5%	3%	3%	6%
	1960	4%	7%	2%	5%	4%	6%	4%	4%	7%
(B) Rank among the Major Regions	1940	7	4	9	6	12	6	11	9	3
	1960	8	5	9	7	8	5	10	10	4
(C) Workers as Per Cent of the Region	1940	100%	10%	3%	32%	1%	4%	12%	14%	19%
	1960	100%	12%	2%	32%	3%	10%	10%	16%	16%
(D) Rank among the Major Regions[a]	1940	----	3	10	4	13	7	10	8	4
	1960	----	4	9	5	6	2	8	7	2
(E) Location Quotient (LQ)[b]	1940	----	1.3	.6	1.1	.3	1.2	.8	.8	1.5
	1960	----	1.5	.4	1.1	1.0	1.5	.8	.9	1.7

Key to Industries:

1 - Energy and Fuel Industries
2 - Heavy Industry
3 - Machine Manufacturing
4 - Chemical Industry
5 - Building Materials Industry
6 - Forest Industries
7 - Light Industry
8 - Food Industry

Note: All per cent figures are rounded values (decimal points have been omitted).

[a]Rows D: Rank (among the 14 major regions) of the share of a given industry as per cent of the region (Rows C above). See also Fig. 5: e.g., Central Region ranks third in machine manufacturing.

[b]"The location quotient measures the degree to which a specific region has more or less than its share of any particular industry...." (Alexander, *loc. cit.*). See Appendix V for a more complete definition of this term.

TABLE 34

Breakdown of Industrial Workers in the

Region East Siberia in 1940 and 1960

	All Industries		Number of Industry							
			1	2	3	4	5	6	7	8
(A) Workers as Per Cent of the U.S.S.R.	1940 1960	2% 3%	2% 3%	5% 1%	2% 2%	1% 3%	2% 3%	4% 8%	1% 2%	2% 3%
(B) Rank among the Major Regions	1940 1960	9 9	9 9	5 10	9 10	10 9	13 12	9 5	11 12	13 13
(C) Workers as Per Cent of the Region	1940 1960	100% 100%	7% 7%	11% 1%	19% 18%	2% 3%	2% 7%	28% 28%	11% 9%	12% 8%
(D) Rank among the Major Regions[a]	1940 1960	---- ----	7 9	3 10	9 13	11 5	11 8	3 2	10 11	10 10
(E) Location Quotient (LQ)[b]	1940 1960	---- ----	.9 .9	2.0 .2	.7 .6	.6 1.0	.8 1.0	1.7 2.3	.6 .5	1.0 .8

Key to Industries:

1 - Energy and Fuel Industries
2 - Heavy Industry
3 - Machine Manufacturing
4 - Chemical Industry
5 - Building Materials Industry
6 - Forest Industries
7 - Light Industry
8 - Food Industry

Note: All per cent figures are rounded values (decimal points have been omitted).

[a]Rows D: Rank (among the 14 major regions) of the share of a given industry as per cent of the region (Rows C above). See also Fig. 5: e.g., Central Region ranks third in machine manufacturing.

[b]"The location quotient measures the degree to which a specific region has more or less than its share of any particular industry...." (Alexander, loc. cit.). See Appendix V for a more complete definition of this term.

TABLE 35

Breakdown of Industrial Workers in the

Trans-Caucasus Region in 1940 and 1960

		All Industries	Number of Industry							
			1	2	3	4	5	6	7	8
(A) Workers as Per Cent of the U.S.S.R.	1940	2%	3%	1%	1%	2%	4%	1%	4%	3%
	1960	3%	3%	3%	2%	3%	4%	1%	4%	4%
(B) Rank among the Major Regions	1940	10	7	12	10	8	9	12	8	11
	1960	10	10	6	11	10	11	13	8	10
(C) Workers as Per Cent of the Region	1940	100%	11%	2%	19%	3%	5%	8%	30%	18%
	1960	100%	8%	6%	20%	3%	9%	6%	27%	13%
(D) Rank among the Major Regions[a]	1940	----	2	12	10	4	3	13	2	5
	1960	----	7	13	12	11	4	13	3	6
(E) Location Quotient (LQ)[b]	1940	----	1.5	.4	.6	1.0	1.6	.5	1.7	1.4
	1960	----	1.1	1.1	.7	1.0	1.3	.5	1.5	1.4

Key to Industries:

1 - Energy and Fuel Industries
2 - Heavy Industry
3 - Machine Manufacturing
4 - Chemical Industry
5 - Building Materials Industry
6 - Forest Industries
7 - Light Industry
8 - Food Industry

Note: All per cent figures are rounded values (decimal points have been omitted).

[a]Rows D: Rank (among the 14 major regions) of the share of a given industry as per cent of the region (Rows C above). See also Fig. 5: e.g., Central Region ranks third in machine manufacturing.

[b]"The location quotient measures the degree to which a specific region has more or less than its share of any particular industry...." (Alexander, loc. cit.). See Appendix V for a more complete definition of this term.

TABLE 36

Breakdown of Industrial Workers in the

Region Central Asia in 1940 and 1960

		All Industries	Number of Industry							
			1	2	3	4	5	6	7	8
(A) Workers as Per Cent of the U.S.S.R.	1940	2%	1%	1%	1%	2%	4%	1%	4%	4%
	1960	3%	2%	1%	2%	3%	4%	1%	5%	4%
(B) Rank among the Major Regions	1940	12	13	14	11	9	7	14	7	10
	1960	11	13	13	9	11	10	14	5	11
(C) Workers as Per Cent of the Region	1940	100%	4%	1%	18%	3%	6%	3%	38%	23%
	1960	100%	6%	1%	23%	3%	10%	5%	35%	13%
(D) Rank among the Major Regions[a]	1940	----	10	13	12	8	1	14	1	2
	1960	----	10	12	9	8	3	14	1	3
(E) Location Quotient (LQ)[b]	1940	----	.5	.3	.6	.8	2.1	.2	2.1	1.8
	1960	----	.8	.1	.8	1.0	1.4	.4	2.0	1.4

Key to Industries:

1 - Energy and Fuel Industries
2 - Heavy Industry
3 - Machine Manufacturing
4 - Chemical Industry
5 - Building Materials Industry
6 - Forest Industries
7 - Light Industry
8 - Food Industry

Note: All per cent figures are rounded values (decimal points have been omitted).

[a]Rows D: Rank (among the 14 major regions) of the share of a given industry as per cent of the region (Rows C above). See also Fig. 5: e.g., Central Region ranks third in machine manufacturing.

[b]"The location quotient measures the degree to which a specific region has more or less than its share of any particular industry...." (Alexander, loc. cit.). See Appendix V for a more complete definition of this term.

TABLE 37

Breakdown of Industrial Workers in the

Region North in 1940 and 1960

	All Industries		Number of Industry							
			1	2	3	4	5	6	7	8
(A) Workers as Per Cent of the U.S.S.R.	1940	2%	1%	1%	1%	1%	2%	6%	1%	2%
	1960	3%	3%	1%	1%	1%	1%	11%	1%	2%
(B) Rank among the Major Regions	1940	13	14	10	12	11	14	6	12	14
	1960	12	12	14	14	14	14	4	13	14
(C) Workers as Per Cent of the Region	1940	100%	3%	4%	18%	2%	3%	49%	10%	11%
	1960	100%	8%	1%	6%	1%	4%	54%	9%	7%
(D) Rank among the Major Regions[a]	1940	----	13	9	11	10	8	1	13	11
	1960	----	8	14	14	14	14	1	12	12
(E) Location Quotient (LQ)[b]	1940	----	.4	.7	.6	.7	.9	3.1	.6	.9
	1960	----	1.0	.1	.2	.2	.5	4.4	.5	.8

Key to Industries:

1 - Energy and Fuel Industries
2 - Heavy Industry
3 - Machine Manufacturing
4 - Chemical Industry
5 - Building Materials Industry
6 - Forest Industries
7 - Light Industry
8 - Food Industry

Note: All per cent figures are rounded values (decimal points have been omitted).

[a] Rows D: Rank (among the 14 major regions) of the share of a given industry as per cent of the region (Rows C above). See also Fig. 5: e.g., Central Region ranks third in machine manufacturing.

[b] "The location quotient measures the degree to which a specific region has more or less than its share of any particular industry...." (Alexander, loc. cit.). See Appendix V for a more complete definition of this term.

TABLE 38

Breakdown of Industrial Workers in the

Kazakhstan Region in 1940 and 1960

	All Industries		Number of Industry							
			1	2	3	4	5	6	7	8
(A) Workers as Per Cent of the U.S.S.R.	1940 1960	1% 3%	2% 5%	3% 2%	1% 2%	1% 3%	2% 5%	1% 2%	1% 2%	3% 4%
(B) Rank among the Major Regions	1940 1960	14 13	10 7	7 8	13 12	13 12	12 8	13 12	13 11	12 12
(C) Workers as Per Cent of the Region	1940 1960	100% 100%	10% 14%	13% 4%	25% 22%	2% 3%	4% 14%	11% 8%	11% 17%	24% 13%
(D) Rank among the Major Regions[a]	1940 1960	---- ----	4 2	1 5	8 11	12 10	4 1	11 11	11 6	1 5
(E) Location Quotient (LQ)[b]	1940 1960	---- ----	1.3 1.8	2.4 .7	.9 .7	.6 1.0	1.5 1.9	.7 .7	.6 1.0	1.9 1.4

Key to Industries:

1 - Energy and Fuel Industries
2 - Heavy Industry
3 - Machine Manufacturing
4 - Chemical Industry
5 - Building Materials Industry
6 - Forest Industries
7 - Light Industry
8 - Food Industry

Note: All per cent figures are rounded values (decimal points have been omitted).

[a]Rows D: Rank (among the 14 major regions) of the share of a given industry as per cent of the region (Rows C above). See also Fig. 5: e.g., Central Region ranks third in machine manufacturing.

[b]"The location quotient measures the degree to which a specific region has more or less than its share of any particular industry...." (Alexander, loc. cit.). See Appendix V for a more complete definition of this term.

TABLE 39

Breakdown of Industrial Workers in the

Region Far East in 1940 and 1960

	Year	All Industries	Number of Industry 1	2	3	4	5	6	7	8
(A) Workers as Per Cent of the U.S.S.R.	1940	2%	2%	1%	1%	1%	3%	4%	1%	4%
	1960	2%	3%	1%	2%	2%	2%	4%	1%	5%
(B) Rank among the Major Regions	1940	11	8	11	14	14	10	10	14	9
	1960	14	11	12	13	13	13	11	14	9
(C) Workers as Per Cent of the Region	1940	100%	9%	3%	15%	1%	4%	26%	2%	22%
	1960	100%	10%	1%	23%	3%	7%	18%	8%	20%
(D) Rank among the Major Regions[a]	1940	----	5	11	13	14	5	4	14	3
	1960	----	5	11	10	4	9	3	14	1
(E) Location Quotient (LQ)[b]	1940	----	1.1	.6	.5	.1	1.4	1.7	.2	1.7
	1960	----	1.2	.2	.8	1.0	1.0	1.5	.4	2.1

Key to Industries:

1 - Energy and Fuel Industries
2 - Heavy Industry
3 - Machine Manufacturing
4 - Chemical Industry
5 - Building Materials Industry
6 - Forest Industries
7 - Light Industry
8 - Food Industry

Note: All per cent figures are rounded values (decimal points have been omitted).

[a]Rows D: Rank (among the 14 major regions) of the share of a given industry as per cent of the region (Rows C above). See also Fig. 5: e.g., Central Region ranks third in machine manufacturing.

[b]"The location quotient measures the degree to which a specific region has more or less than its share of any particular industry...." (Alexander, loc. cit.). See Appendix V for a more complete definition of this term.

suffered by the chemical industry during World War II. As Miller points out, the chemical industry did indeed suffer greatly since "many of the plants were located in German-occupied territory and were seriously damaged or destroyed."[3]

In observing the share of the chemical industry in the United States (period 1947-54), a similar pattern emerges: Of the nine Census regions seven show no change in share and the median share of the chemical industry as a per cent of a region remains a stable 6 per cent.[4] Since the median share in the U. S. S. R. also was stable--2 per cent of a major economic region both in 1940 and 1960--it would be tempting to conclude that a similarity exists in the pattern of chemical industry in both countries. However, the chemical industry was much stronger in the United States even before World War II in terms of investments, numbers of workers, and higher technology. Even if the technological level in the Soviet Union were equal to that of the United States during the period 1940-60, the Soviet chemical industry, with a much smaller share of each region, would indicate a slower progress relative to the United States where chemicals continue to occupy a larger share in all Census regions.

Finally, as Fryer points out,

> Some industries, such as chemicals, appear to show little proportionate increase in employment with a higher level of economic development. This is because industrial expansion largely involves an increase on the capital-labor ratio; most chemical products necessitate the use of large, capital-intensive plants if they are to be produced at all. Modern chemical plants operate almost automatically and require only a very small labor force in relation to their floor space.[5]

Since the overall increase in the absolute numbers of Soviet workers in all industries was substantial in all regions, the small absolute increase of chemical workers resulted in almos no change in the share of chemical industry in most of the regions. It might be concluded therefore, that despite the apparent stability of the share of chemical industry, some progress in this industry did occur between 1940 and 1960.

CONSUMER GOODS INDUSTRIES

While the share of the chemical industry in most regions remained almost unchanged during the period 1940-60, the consumer goods industries--light industry and food industry--registered a decrease of their share of the major economic regions. The share of the food industry declined in all the fourteen major regions while in light industry eight of the regions showed a decrease. In the United States, a similar pattern could also be observed between 1947 and 1954 with seven of the nine Census regions showing a decrease of the share of light industry, while the share of the food industry declined in four regions.[6]

The reasons for the decline of the share of the consumer goods industries in both countries were quite different. One of the reasons in both countries was probably the technological innovation and mechanization, especially in the textile industry, permitting a much greater output through a relatively small absolute increase in the number of industrial workers. Incidentally, the food industry in the U. S. S. R. showed a very small over-all increase (50 per cent) in the number of industrial workers relative to a 99 per cent increase of the total industrial labor force. In the region South, for example, this industry decreased its share despite an absolute increase of more than 165, 000 workers.

An additional reason for the decrease of its share could be cited in the Soviet Union. As most students of the Soviet economy agree, the Soviet consumer goods industries are a nonpriority sector, neglected during the Stalin era, and, in addition, not being noted for either their quality or their productivity.[7] Since World War II resulted in a serious damage to the Soviet industrial capacity, with the emphasis even in normal times being overwhelmingly in favor of capital goods industries, it was logical for the Soviet planners to continue this course in the postwar decade of reconstruction. Thus the reduction of the share of the consumer goods industries in most of the major economic regions of the U. S. S. R. could be traced primarily to a continuing low priority attached to these industries and also, to a lesser extent, to the greater labor productivity as a result of improved mechanization.

A further comment regarding the decrease of the share of the consumer goods industries in the Soviet Union should be added. Fryer states that:

> In underdeveloped economies the greatest industrial employment is found in industries that have relatively simple technologies and modest capital requirements, utilize local raw materials, and produce goods for which there is a wide and stable local demand.[8]

The best examples of such industries are textiles (major component of Soviet light industry) and food. Fryer adds that:

> As economic development proceeds, textile industries become progressively less important . . . even though the output of textile industries continues to increase; technologically more complex and capital-intensive industries come to command a larger share of the labor force. The metal industries become of increasing importance . . . .[9]

In this sense, all of the Soviet Union was a developing industri country in the period 1940-60, while some of the major economic regions were clearly "underdeveloped" in 1940 and were beginning to become industrialized in the postwar period. For instance, between 1940 and 1960, the combined share of light and food industry declined in Central Asia from 61 to 48 per cent of the total industrial employment, in West Siberia it decreased from 33 to 21 per cent, and in Kazakhstan it was reduced from 35 to 31 per cent. The industries which increased their share of the region in the three examples above were either machine manufacturing or heavy industry. Thus another explanation of the reduced share of the consumer goods industries would be the suggestion that this also indicated a progress in industrialization, especially in the regions that were relatively backward and undeveloped before 1940.

OTHER INDUSTRIES

While the three industries previously discussed exhibited a relatively uniform pattern of change in their share of the major regions, the other five branches registered a mixed pattern. The pattern in the four industries is briefly commented upon but more attention is devoted to the discussion of machine manufacturing in the next chapter.

The share of the forest industries decreased in more than half of the major regions and only one region registered a significant increase. This decrease could be interpreted as a consequence of the reduction in use of firewood in the total fuel consumption (see Chapter 7) and also the reduction in use of wood in construction, and increased use of reinforced concrete. The increase of the share of forest industries in the North from 49 to 54 per cent of all industrial workers in that region might have been the result of an urgent temporary need for timber for postwar housing reconstruction in the neighboring regions, such as the Center and South, which had suffered great destruction during World War II.

Most regions registered an increase in the share of the building materials industry, especially in the western U. S. S. R. where the needs for the postwar reconstruction of both residential and industrial buildings were greatest. In most of the western regions the share of the workers in this industry as a per cent of the region more than doubled. In the South it increased from 4 to 9 per cent, in the Northwest from 2 to 5, in the Volga region from 2 to 7, and in North Caucasus from 4 to 10 per cent.

The shares of the heavy industry showed little change in most regions where this industry had an important position before 1940, as for example in the regions Center and South. This, of course, does not mean that there was no increase in the absolute numbers of workers in this industry. For example, the South increased the number from 174, 000 to 486, 000 between 1940 and 1960. In the Urals the share increased from 11 to 18 per cent, mostly due to the transfer of entire evacuated factories from the western regions, especially the South, after the German attack on the U. S. S. R. in 1941. After the war these factories were not dismantled and new ones were added so that by 1960 the Urals replaced the region Center as the second leading region in terms of the number of workers in heavy industry.

Despite the substantial absolute increase in the number of industrial workers in energy and fuel industries in the leading regions--Center, South, Ural, and Northwest added a total of over 390,000 workers in this branch--the share of this industry in these four regions remained unchanged. Two regions on the other hand, recorded a significant increase. In the North and in West Siberia this was due to the impetus given to these two regions during World War II when the Donbas coal fields were occupied by the Germans. The Kuzbas coal field in West Siberia became second most important in the U. S. S. R. accounting for about 16 per cent of all Soviet coal production in 1960. The Pechora fields in the North supplied the Moscow area during World War II and remained an important coal producer after the war as the major supplier of the Leningrad industrial complex.

Notes to Chapter 8

1. The term "share" of a given industry means that industry as a per cent of all industrial workers in a given region. "Share" is used in that sense throughout this chapter.

2. Paul E. Lydolph, Geography of the U. S. S. R. (New York: John Wiley and Sons, 1964), p. 364.

3. E. Willard Miller, A Geography of Manufacturing (Englewood Cliffs, New Jersey: Prentice-Hall, 1962), p. 194.

4. U. S., Bureau of the Census, United States Census of Manufactures, 1954, Vol. I: Summary Statistics (Washington, D. C.: U. S. Government Printing Office, 1957), p. 73.

5. D. W. Fryer, World Economic Development (New York: McGraw-Hill Book Company, 1965), p. 261.

6. U. S., Bureau of the Census, op. cit., pp. 72-76.

7. Paul K. Cook, "The Administration and Distribution of Soviet Industry," in Dimensions of Soviet Economic Power (Studies Prepared for the Joint Economic Committee, 87th Congress, 2nd Session; Washington, D. C.: U. S. Government Printing Office, 1962), pp. 206-7. Miller, op. cit., p. 196.

8. Fryer, op. cit., pp. 260-61.

9. Ibid.

CHAPTER 9 MACHINE MANUFACTURING: A CASE STUDY

The official Soviet view states that "machine building is the foundation of technical progress and development of the whole national economy."[1] Hoyt believes that this industry, which has been a high priority sector in the drive for industrialization throughout the era of the five-year plans (1928-1956), has been expected to serve three purposes:

> (1) the strengthening of the economic independence of the country (because of capitalist "encirclement"); (2) the growth of the defense potential of the country . . . ; and (3) the provision of capital equipment to be used for further forced development of heavy industry.[2]

A Soviet author states that "Soviet machine-building [machine manufacturing] is becoming the technical base necessary for the gradual transition from socialism to communism."[3] A further possible ideological and political reason for the heavy emphasis on machine manufacturing in the Soviet Union could be suggested: Increase in this sector would be a crowning achievement in the propaganda drive "to catch up and overtake the United States." If this slogan failed to materialize in the case of trying to overtake the 1956 levels of the U. S. per capita production of milk and meat, it should be recognized that after long years of hammering at the theme, "the U. S. S. R. must overtake the U. S. in production of machine tools," this finally became a reality about 1954.[4]

Before observing the locational patterns of machine manufacturing in the U. S. S. R., the Soviet locational doctrine should be examined. According to Livshits this doctrine consists of five principles:

> (1) ever more uniform distribution of industry throughout the country; (2) the proximity of industry to raw material and fuel sources and to consuming areas; (3) the accelerated development of national districts and formerly underdeveloped regions; (4) the complex development of individual economic regions; and (5) the strengthening of the defense potential of the Soviet Union.[5]

In considering how the five preceding principles were implemented in the machine manufacturing industry, the views of an American and a Soviet author are presented. The first principle of "even distribution," according to Hoyt,

> . . . appears to be receiving more explicit attention at the present time [1959], although the policy statements intended to show a recognition of the principle have considerably predated the evidence of actual practice designed to carry it out.[6]

Omarovskiy makes the following typical Soviet statement which proves Hoyt's contention:

> The concern of the party and government about speeding up the development and uniform distribution of the machine-building industry in many regions of the country . . . has led to a more rational distribution of the machine-building industry over the regions of the country.[7]

Later on, however, while repeating that machine manufacturing is distributed in all the economic regions, he admits that in some regions certain branches of this industry have not been sufficiently developed. As an example, he mentions automobile manufacturing with 80 per cent concentrated in the Central region, while almost all the Diesel and electric locomotives are produced in the regions Center and South.[8]

The second principle, of "the proximity of industry to raw material and fuel sources and to consuming areas," has been the primary factor in determining the locational pattern according to Hoyt.[9] Omarovskiy, while concluding that the general tendency in the distribution of machine manufacturing does follow this principle, states that "it cannot be restricted by this general definition because various industries [branches of machine manufacturing] depend to a greater or lesser degree on different factors."[10] He gives two examples, one of Siberia where he suggests that the production should be organized to build, primarily, machinery and equipment requiring large amounts of steel, while in Central Asia and the Trans-Caucasus industries requiring more labor and less metal should be favored.[11] Omarovskiy also mentions two benefits that result from bringing this industry closer to the sources of raw materials and to the market--reduction of transportation costs and the possibility of adapting machine design better to operating conditions.[12]

The third and the fifth principle are dismissed from serious consideration by Hoyt since he believes that the former is "a political plank rather than a serious consideration of policy and practice," while the latter did occur as a consequence of World War II which necessitated an eastward shift or a locational "push" rather than pull.[13] Omarovskiy, while not discussing the "defense potential" principle, states in favor of the third principle that "the creation of machine-building enterprises in formerly backward and remote regions of the country insures the raising of production technology" and also of the "general cultural level of the population."[14]

Finally, the fourth principle, of "the complex development of individual economic regions"--which would make each region economically independent--remains to be implemented in the future, even though plans for it were being made in the early 1960's. Hoyt explicitly states that little has been done to implement this principle "to date" (1959), while Omarovskiy, writing in the same year, describes what could be and should be done "in the next ten to fifteen years" to implement fully this principle.[15] Regarding the locational patterns of machine manufacturing, Hoyt concludes that:

> . . . [they] have been a function of the development of the iron and steel industry rather than of the conscious implementation of locational policies. The location of the industry has, however, consistently reflected a recognition of the [second] principle--location close to supply sources and to consuming regions.[16]

Hoyt believes that World War II had some effect on the locatio of this industry--a locational eastward "push"--but that this impact had been greatly altered ten years after the war throug the locational pull of the older industrialized regions of the western U. S. S. R.[17] This interpretation of the effects of World War II has been already suggested in Chapter 6.

Another indirect effect of the war should also be considered. While it is true that the damages to machine manufacturing were considerable in the western, German-occupied territories, in the postwar period the damaged or destroyed factories had to be reequipped with modern and up-to-date machinery. Some of this machinery was imported, some was received as part of war reparations, and some was simply seized from the countries that were occupied. (East Germany and Manchuria are the best examples.) Also many of the factories that were relocated to the eastern regions during the war were equipped with machinery imported from the United States.[18] Thus one beneficial result of the partial destruction of machine manufacturing has been the improvement and updating of its equipment and the possibility of greater automation in this industry. As Bulganin reported in 1956, speaking about the economic effect of automation in machine manufacturing, it was "possible to reduce the number of workers between approximately one-fifth and one-tenth of wha it was, and to curtail working time in processing to the same extent."[19] In the same year (1956) the total number of automatic and semi-automatic devices in the U. S. S. R. reached 100, 000--constituting 6. 5 per cent of the total number of machine-tools (against 10 per cent in the United States).[20]

Machine manufacturing--even more in 1960 than in 1940--was the most characteristic and most important industrial branch in most of the major regions: in nine regions it had the highest share of all the workers and in four it had the second-highest share. The leading regions, Center and Northwest, had over one-third of their workers in machine manufacturing and the rising newer regions (Ural, West Siberia, Volga) had also high share between 31 and 44 per cen On the other hand, the less industrialized regions had a much smaller share of their workers in machine manufacturing, ranging from less than 25 per cent down to only 6 per cent. This industry recorded the greatest increase: In five regions the increase was between four and ten percentage points, the highest being in the Volga and the West where the share increased from 34 to 44 per cent, and from 14 to 24 per cent, respectively. The reasons for the change of the share in some regions, as well as in selected *sovnarkhozy*, should be discussed in terms of the five principles of Soviet locational doctrine as presented in the previous paragraphs.

A general test of the effectiveness of the first principle of "more even distribution" could be made by considering the distribution of the workers in machine manufacturing among the groups of major economic regions. While the three leading regions--Center, South, and Northwest--represented 67 per cent of Soviet workers in this industry in 1940 and the other eleven regions together accounted for 33 per cent, a better balance was achieved by 1960 when the share of the three regions was reduced to 55 per cent and the share of all the other regions was brought up to 45 per cent of the total.

A more meaningful test could be obtained by measuring the tendency to bring the share of a *sovnarkhoz* in Soviet machine manufacturing into balance with its share of the total population of the U. S. S. R. In this example and throughout the rest of this chapter the data for fifty selected *sovnarkhozy* are used since their breakdowns by industries for both 1940 and 1955 are available. They could be considered as representative of the U. S. S. R. as a whole since together they contained 53 per cent of Soviet industrial workers in 1940, and 49 per cent in 1955. In the several examples that follow, the fifty *sovnarkhozy* will be considered both as a whole and in two groups: the twenty-one larger ones, each representing 1 per cent and more of Soviet industrial labor in all industries, and twenty-nine smaller ones, each with less than 1 per cent of the national total.

While the share of the fifty *sovnarkhozy* as a per cent of the total population was 52 in 1940 and 50 per cent in 1955, their share of Soviet machine manufacturing decreased from 57 to 52 per cent, thus bringing the two shares (population and machine manufacturing) almost into a balance. The total share of the twenty-one larger *sovnarkhozy* decreased from 48 to 41 per cent of the workers in machine manufacturing while their share of total population remained about the same: 32 in 1940 and 31 per cent in 1955. The twenty-nine smaller *sovnarkhozy* increased their total share of machine manufacturing from 9 to 11 per cent while their share of total population barely declined from 20 per cent in 1940 to 19 per cent in 1955. If individual cases are considered, then the pattern is even more apparent: Of the twenty-one larger sovnarkhozy, two-thirds begin to approach the balance between the share of population and of machine manufacturing.

The changes in the internal industrial structure of the fifty selected sovnarkhozy, showing increase or decrease of the share of machine manufacturing as a per cent of the sovnarkhoz, are used to test the second principle of "proximity to raw material and fuel sources and to consuming areas." Almost 75 per cent of the sovnarkhozy show an increase, while of the remainder half register no change and the rest a small decrease. Six sovnarkhozy with a significant increase are selected to illustrate several aspects of the second principle. These are Kirov (in the Central region, the share of machine manufacturing in the sovnarkhoz increasing from 14 per cent in 1940 to 24 per cent in 1955), Tatar and Saratov (both in the Volga region, the share increasing from 26 to 43, and from 38 to 52 per cent, respectively), Novosibirsk (West Siberia, from 38 to 59 per cent), and Belorussian and Latvian sovnarkhozy (both in the region West, the share increasing from 15 per cent in both in 1940 to 25 and 26 per cent in 1955, respectively). In each of the six cases, it must be determined which of the three factors (raw materials, fuel sources, or consumers) were most influential in causing the increase in machine manufacturing in these sovnarkhozy.

Five of the six sovnarkhozy are located in the western regions and this very likely reflects the concern with labor productivity, since the area east of the Urals is "expensive both in terms of labor and capital, as compared to such other areas . . . as Latvia."[21] All six sovnarkhozy contain large populations: in 1955 four had over 2 million people, one had almost three (Tatar), and one (Belorussian) had 8 million. Thus the first factor, "consuming areas," seems to be satisfied since these six sovnarkhozy had a total of almost 10 per cent of the Soviet population in 1955, and increasing machine manufacturing in them seems to be both realistic and rational. While in three of the sovnarkhozy by 1955 the share of the population is nearly balanced by the share of machine manufacturing, in the other three the share of machine manufacturing exceeds the share of the population. In Tatar sovnarkhoz these are respectively 1.8 and 1.4 per cent, in Saratov 1.5 and 1.0, and in Novosibirsk 2.1 and 1.1 per cent. This might lead to the consideration of other factors, since the "consuming area" factor has been not only satisfied but exceeded. In other words, in addition to a large population the favorable factors that influenced the concentration of machine manufacturing in these three sovnarkhozy should also be investigated.

After considering all six sovnarkhozy in terms of "proximity to raw materials and fuel sources," it is clear that while all six were relatively close to raw materials (iron and steel and other heavy industry), only three (Tatar, Saratov and Novosibirsk) had superior and varied fuel sources. While the Kirov sovnarkhoz is not far from the Volga scheme to profit from the hydro-electric stations that were being developed near Kuybishev and Volgograd, and while the Belorussian and Latvian sovnarkhozy had to rely for their thermal stations on the coal imported from other regions (mainly Donbas coal fields in the South), Novosibirsk had both hydro-electric power (dam on the Ob River, south of the city of Novosibirsk), and coal from the nearby Kuzbas coalfield. The Tatar and Saratov sovnarkhozy have hydro-electric power from the Volga scheme, as well as a new source of both natural gas and petroleum from the "Second Baku" field.[22]

The proximity to raw materials and the relative magnitude of the steel mills that supplied the machine manufacturing were reflected in the size of the increase of the share in the six sovnarkhozy. The greatest increase occurred in Novosibirsk sovnarkhoz and it is certainly no coincidence that it is the only one among the six to contain an important steel mill within its own boundaries. Since the steel mill is located in the city of Novosibirsk, where most of the machine manufacturing in the sovnarkhoz is also located, the distance from the factories to the raw materials has been literally reduced to zero. The next highest increases occurred in the Tatar and Saratov sovnarkhozy. While in both cases the steel mills were as important as in the previous case, the distances were much greater: about 150 miles by rail in Tatar sovnarkhoz (from Izhevsk steel mills in the Urals to the main center of machine manufacturing in the city of Kazan'), and about 200 miles by rail in Saratov (from the Volgograd steel mills to the city of Saratov, main center of machine manufacturing). In the other three sovnarkhozy the increases were smaller possibly since the steel mills were of lesser importance than in the three previous cases. The distances were about 150 miles by rail in both Kirov and Latvian sovnarkhozy (from the steel mills of Omutninsk and Liepaya to the main centers of machine manufacturing in the cities of Kirov and Riga, respectively). In Belorussia, the increase was small and the sovnarkhoz' share of U. S. S. R. population exceeds its share of Soviet machine manufacturing in 1955. In the other five sovnarkhozy the shar are either equal or the share of population is exceeded by the share of machine manufacturing. In Belorussia, the nearest steel mills are in Bezhitsa (in the Central region) and they are of small importance. Also the distance by rail to Minsk, the chief center of machine manufacturing in Belorussia, is about 300 miles, or about twice as much as in the other three sovnarkhozy.

If the six sovnarkhozy, containing a total of 9 per cent o: industrial workers in machine manufacturing in 1955, are use as an example which is applied to all of machine manufacturin it might be concluded that the second principle of Soviet locational doctrine seems to be operative in many regions of the U. S. S. R. The most important factor that is necessary for satisfactory implementation of the principle, seems to be "proximity to consuming areas" (satisfied in all the six cases discussed previously), followed by "proximity to raw material (satisfied in at least five cases), while the "proximity of fuel sources" when added to the other two factors, assures a significant progress.

The answer to whether the third principle of "accelerate development of formerly underdeveloped regions" is also operative in the Soviet Union is more difficult than the discussion of the second principle. However, assuming that Fryer's statement on the distribution in the industrial structure of a country (or a major region, or a sovnarkhoz) is a good indication of the measure of development or underdevelop ment, then some tentative answers are possible.[23] The third principle might mean that the "development of formerly under developed regions" will generally proceed when a reduction in the total share of industrial employment by the consumer good industries (especially textiles) is offset by an increase in the share of machine manufacturing. The fourth principle can be interpreted as reflecting this same change--increase in machi manufacturing and decrease in light and food industry. This helps to bring about both a more balanced and a more complex development in each region and *sovnarkhoz*, leading to a large degree of regional industrial self-sufficiency.

In the six *sovnarkhozy* already discussed, the decrease of the combined share of light and food industry was accompanied by an equivalent rise in the share of machine manufacturing. For example, in Saratov the share of the former declined by fifteen points while the share of the latter rose by fourteen points. In Kirov the figures were nine and ten points respectively, while in Tatar *sovnarkhoz* both figures were identical--seventeen points decline and seventeen points increase. Of the fifty selected *sovnarkhozy*, thirty-seven show an increase in the shares of machine manufacturing while forty-one show a decrease in the shares of food and light industry. While the median combined share of the workers in machine manufacturing and consumer goods industries as a per cent of a *sovnarkhoz* was about the same in 1940 and in 1955 (54 vs. 53 per cent), the division between them was almost balanced by 1955. The median share of machine manufacturing in a *sovnarkhoz* increased from 21 to 27 per cent while the median combined share of light and food industry decreased from 33 per cent in 1940 to 26 per cent in 1955.

By that year, as a measure of the progress in industrial development, there were very few *sovnarkhozy* with less than one-fifth of their workers in machine manufacturing. The few *sovnarkhozy*, especially those with an extremely low share in machine manufacturing, certainly are not examples of underdevelopment although the lack of complex development--meaning balance among industrial branches and some emphasis on machine manufacturing--is obvious. For example, Arkhangel'sk *sovnarkhoz* had only 10 and 14 per cent of its workers in machine manufacturing in 1940 and 1955, respectively. This is only the result of the extreme specialization in the timber industry: Forest industries accounted for 71 per cent of all workers in 1940 and 68 per cent in 1955. Another quite industrialized *sovnarkhoz* is an even better example: Ivanovo had the lowest share of its workers in machine manufacturing among all the fifty selected *sovnarkhozy*--6 per cent in 1940 and 7 per cent in 1955. This is because, as the largest center of the textile industry in the Soviet Union since before the Revolution, Ivanovo continues this extreme specialization with 72 per cent of its workers in light industry (mainly textiles) both in 1940 and in 1955.

The last principle, that of "defense potential," implying the need for strategic decentralization, might be involved in the increases in at least four of the six sovnarkhozy: Novosibirsk, Tatar, Saratov, and Kirov. However, it is more difficult to see this principle involved in the other two cases--the location and increases in the Belorussian and Latvian sovnarkhozy.

Notes to Chapter 9

1. A. G. Omarovskiy, "Changes in the Geography of Machine Building in the U. S. S. R.," Soviet Geography, Vol. I, No. 3 (March, 1960), p. 42.

2. John Stanley Hoyt, Jr., "An Investigation of the Economics of Soviet Locational Doctrine, Policy, and Practice--With Special Emphasis on Heavy Industry" (unpublished Ph. D. dissertation, Department of Economics, The America University, 1959), p. 111.

3. K. Klimenko, "The Development of Soviet Machine Building," Voprosy Ekonomiki (March, 1958). In translation in Problems of Economics, Vol. I, No. 5 (September, 1958), p. 56.

4. Anthony J. Daukas, "Machine Tool Production in the United States and U. S. S. R.," Dimensions of Soviet Economic Power (Studies Prepared for the Joint Economic Committee, 87th Congress, 2nd Session; Washington, D. C.: U. S. Government Printing Office, 1962), p. 165.

5. R. S. Livshits, Ocherki po razmeshcheniya promyshlennosti SSSR [Outline of the Distribution of U. S. S. R. Industry] (Moscow, 1954), pp. 13-16, quoted in Hoyt, op. cit., p. 31.

6. Hoyt, op. cit., p. 121.

7. Omarovskiy, op. cit., p. 48.

8. Ibid., p. 49.

9. Hoyt, op. cit., p. 120.

10. Omarovskiy, op. cit., p. 51.

11. Ibid.

12. Ibid., p. 48.

13. Hoyt, op. cit., pp. 121-22.

14. Omarovskiy, op. cit., p. 49.

15. Hoyt, op. cit., p. 119; Omarovskiy, op. cit., p. 52.

16. Hoyt, op. cit., pp. 154-55.

17. Ibid.

18. E. Willard Miller, A Geography of Manufacturing (Englewood Cliffs, New Jersey: Prentice-Hall, 1962), p. 193.

19. Ibid., p. 347.

20. Klimenko, op. cit., p. 52.

21. Paul K. Cook, "The Administration and Distribution of Soviet Industry," in Dimensions of Soviet Economic Power (Studies Prepared for the Joint Economic Committee, 87th Congress, 2nd Session; Washington, D. C.: U. S. Government Printing Office, 1962), pp. 198-99.

22. The "Second Baku" was later justly renamed Volga-Ural oil field, when its share in 1953 reached over one-half of the U. S. S. R. total while the original Baku field dropped to one-third.

23. D. W. Fryer, World Economic Development (New York: McGraw-Hill Book Company, 1965), pp. 260-61.

CHAPTER 10 COMMUNIST DOCTRINE AND ECONOMIC GEOGRAPHY

The discussion of the five principles of Soviet locational doctrine in the previous chapter has considered only the practical aspects of the actual implementation of that doctrine. However, a broader consideration of the locational doctrine might include some theoretical aspects. It would raise such questions as the impact of the Communist doctrine on economic geography and also whether the Soviet public policy in reality affects the industrial location to such an extent as to make the emerging locational patterns significantly different from any non-Communist developing economy.

In discussing the Soviet approach to industrial location and after listing the principles of the socialist distribution of production (almost identical to the five principles of the locational doctrine), Ian Matley, an American geographer, states that:

> . . . there is nothing very startling about them [the principles], and many planners in the Western world would present very similar ideas if asked to state an ideal policy. However, Soviet economists and geographers seem to feel that they have got something here that the rest of the world outside the socialist camp does not possess.[1]

After analyzing other aspects of the Soviet approach to economic geography,[2] Matley concludes that:

> . . . the basic differences in the Soviet and Western approaches to economic geography lie to a great extent in the conviction of Soviet geographers, supported by Marxist theories of the development of society, that the Soviet economy is superior in every way to the

> capitalist economy, if not in actual production at the moment then in future potential.[3]

It would be a very hopeful development if there were signs indicating the lessening of the rigidity in the attitude of Soviet economic geographers by ascribing their above-quoted conviction as belonging to the now discredited era of Stalinism. However, one of the leading scholars of the more liberal school among economic geographers, Yu. G. Saushkin, in a most recent history of economic geography in the U. S. S. R. gives little hope that a basic change in their thinking has occurred in the post-Stalin era. After briefly attacking leftist trends in Soviet economic geography in the 1930's--especially the thesis of a uniform distribution of industry throughout the country, as having caused "great practical harm" since it replaced "a rational location of industry, advocated by Lenin"[4]--Saushkin ends on a very rigid and dogmatic note when he discusses the prospects of Soviet economic geography.

> The most important task of Soviet economic geography has been, remains, and will be in the years and decades to come . . . the economically most effective territorial organization of labor in the socialist countries.
>
> More and more countries are taking the socialist course of development in the world. The future belongs to socialism . . . .
>
> Soviet economic geography should now already, and in the future even more, pose and solve problems on a global scale, based on the inevitability of the victory of socialism on all continents and on a sensible division of labor among countries of all geographic zones of the earth . . . .[5]

To American geographers who might tend to dismiss the above statements as political pronouncements addressed to the general public, and who might also believe in a rational discussion on a higher intellectual level between American and Soviet geographers, Saushkin shatters this hope. He leaves no doubt what he considers to be the only choice that American geographers must make if they are to be addressed as "honorable foreign geographers" instead of as "bourgeois reactionaries."

> It should be recalled that Lenin said scholars would advance toward the ideas of socialism both through the material and through the logic of their own disciplines. Now many geographers of the capitalist countries have been convinced by the logic of the facts of geography that an economically effective territorial organization of productive forces is incompatible with capitalism, and that only socialism can solve these problems. The differentiation among scholars of the capitalist countries is one of the characteristic features of the present time; some of them are looking to socialist theories, others are in helpless rage siding with the forces of reaction, neo-Malthusianism and preaching of atomic war, and many are vacillating trying to remain on the sidelines, avoiding the solution of theoretical problems and following the course of empiricism. The struggle against bourgeois reactionary theories and on behalf of honorable foreign geographers is a major aspect of the elaboration of global problems in economic geography. Soviet economic geography should be much broader than in the past; it should look ahead and cover the entire world.[6]

Since this study has presented an objective reality of the "territorial organization of productive forces" in the Soviet Union without accepting the socialist theories that allegedly govern this organization, after the words of Saushkin it is doubtful that this objective presentation would be acceptable to the Soviet economic geographers even if the comments and criticism are made with the best intentions in mind.

According to Soviet economists, "capitalist production is characterized by an extremely uneven development and increasing contradictions between developed and underdeveloped regions."[7] Also since only "under capitalism territorial-production complexes arise in haphazard fashion," one would expect that this could not (certainly, should not) occur under socialism.[8] Therefore, the comparison of the 1960 data with those already presented for 1940 in Chapter 4, is quite instructive. While the combined total share of the seven less developed regions (East Siberia, Far East, Central Asia, Kazakhstan, North, Trans-Caucasus, and West) represented close to 30 per cent of the Soviet population in both years, their combined share of the gross industrial output rose from 13 per cent in 1940 to about 20 per cent in 1960, their share of the electric power increased from 14 to about 22 per cent, and their share of the coal production increased in the same period from 17 to 23 per cent.[9] However, the other four key categories showed very little change: In 1960 the seven less industrialized regions still represented only a fraction of the Soviet crude steel production (their combined share increased from 2 to about 5 per cent), and their combined share was less than 4 per cent of pig iron, and about 5 per cent of coke and iron ore production.[10] With figures such as these, one begins to wonder what "tremendous advantages . . . socialism offers in the rational territorial organization of production . . ., rationally distributed through the country,"[11] and whether there might be some "contradictions between developed and underdeveloped regions" even in the Soviet Union.

Of course, there is some evidence that the planning must be more rational and thus, for example, a leading Soviet economist, Ya. Feigin demands an "investigation of the distribution and most rational use of labor resources, the principal productive force, by large economic areas."[12] Feigin suggests that "the problem of labor resources will be solved differently in the west [U. S. S. R.] than in the east [U. S. S. R.], the latter having a shortage of labor at present."[13] However, while "increasing theoretical recognition has been given to the traditional role of skilled labour," two British geographers believe that "little real financial incentive has been given to workers in remote areas" and this could be one of the reasons for the labor shortage in the eastern regions.[14] Cole and German conclude on a hopeful note that "the principles and practice of Soviet locational theory have . . . been increasingly empirical, although retaining their flavour of theoretical origin, and consequent infallibility."[15]

A recent study by an Australian geographer goes beyond the theoretical considerations of Soviet locational doctrine or dogmatic expressions of the superiority of socialism in solving all the problems in the Soviet economy, and raises some fundamental geographic questions based on the reality of the physical environment of the Soviet Union. Hutchings first asks the question:

> Could the Soviet economy be effectively decentralized, in the sense that while public ownership of means of production and overall state economic planning are retained, much larger shares of authority over economic matters are devolved to the regions?[16]

And his answer is that:

> . . . whatever other reasons can be invoked, certain of the reasons why decentralization is apparently so difficult to effect lie deeply within the geography of the Soviet Union--the physical environment which, even if not formally a part of the economy, constitutes the framework within which it has to function.[17]

Hutchings distinguishes between geographic, geopolitical and political influences, and also between primary, sub-primary, secondary and tertiary characteristics.[18] For example, under geographic influences he lists two primary characteristics: large size of the country and its high latitude. In considering how a combination of geographic and geopolitical influences work together, Hutchings gives several examples which he regards as general propositions. For instance, under the heading "There is a wide diversity of nationality, language and religion; Relationships between federal and other territorial authorities are inevitably complex," he states that:

> The size and diversity of the USSR in turn necessitates a federal system . . . Typically, federal multinational societies, if they undertake "economic planning," must consider not only welfare or growth rates of the whole economy but those of particular regions. As a result certain regions are likely to be particularly favoured; for example, Macedonia receives a larger share of investments than would be warranted if one neglected its backwardness as compared with other provinces of Yugoslavia. The requirement can slow down the economic development of a country, perhaps for example Malaysia. One cannot ascertain whether Soviet development may have been retarded for similar reasons, for we lack statistical data, e.g., concerning the percentage shares in industrial output of the various republics. It _is_ clear that any diversion of resources in response to regional

> pressures implied the existence of a central investment authority [italics in the original].[19]

In summing up his study Hutchings states that "the physical circumstances of the Soviet economy impose certain limits on the type of economic organization which can be effective."[20] He concludes that "it is likely that the permanent geographic factors will continue to obstruct any more fundamental move towards decentralizing the Soviet economy."[21] Comparing Soviet data for 1960 with those for 1955, it becomes apparent that a slowdown has occurred since the share of the eastern regions remained at 28 per cent of all Soviet industrial workers in this five-year period. Thus, Hutchings might be correct about no more fundamental move towards decentralization, at least as of 1960, but it is quite possible that the future might indicate the potential for a different pattern in the U. S. S. R. on a more limited scale and over a much longer period of time.

David Hooson, a Canadian geographer, seems to share this opinion in his study in which he develops two general regional categories, the established European Core, and the expanding Volga-Baykal zone (including the Ural and Volga regions, with parts of West and East Siberia and Northern Kazakhstan). After describing the Volga-Baykal Zone, Hooson concludes that:

> . . . the question would remain, perhaps even more acutely, of whether to intensify the concentration of industry in the European area and the Urals (which would virtually abandon Central Siberia except as a reservoir of power) or to step up the transfer of population and industry to the east to make use of the resources (not only energy) on the spot . . . It is unlikely that the phenomenal scale and speed of transfer from west to east witnessed since 1939 will be maintained, let alone exceeded. Instead, a balanced industrial development, combined with a steady, but not hectic, easterly drift will probably become the long-term policy.[22]

In support of Hooson's view, a Soviet economist, commenting on the continued population outflow from the eastern regions, stated that "in 1956-60, over 700,000 persons . . .

moved into Siberia. Nevertheless, . . . the number of people who left Siberia in those years exceed the number who moved in."[23] Finally, Hooson suggests in looking at the future that there is yet "another consideration favoring the easterly industrial dispersion which would undoubtedly still override much greater economic deterrents than actually exist: national security."[24] The creation of a new Soviet heartland in the Volga-Baykal zone is resulting not so much in the reduction of military vulnerability from the west--which certainly has been reduced since 1945--but even more in the reduced strategic vulnerability from the east--"in relation to an emergent, expansionist, and hostile China."[25] Hooson believes that "it would not be surprising if the Soviet reaction to Chinese provocation was to try to fill up its open spaces and develop its resources."[26] A very far-sighted observation which might have appeared somewhat problematic and academic in 1964 but is quite within the realm of possibility in 1968.

Notes to Chapter 10

1. Ian Murray Matley, "The Soviet Approach to Geography" (unpublished Ph. D. dissertation, Department of Geography, The University of Michigan, 1961), p. 131.

2. _Ibid._, p. 138: "Econometrics . . . is seen as another bourgeois attempt to save capitalism from its present crisis."

3. _Ibid._, p. 150.

4. Yu. G. Saushkin, "A History of Soviet Economic Geography," _Ekonomicheskaya Geografiya v SSSR_ [_Economic Geography in the USSR_], edited by N. N. Baransky, N. P. Nikitin, V. V. Pokshishevsky, Yu. G. Saushkin (Moscow: Prosveshcheniye, 1965), pp. 54-172. In translation in _Soviet Geography_, Vol. VII, No. 8 (October, 1966), p. 31.

5. _Ibid._, pp. 95-96.

6. _Ibid._, pp. 96-97.

7. N. T. Agafonov and S. B. Lavrov, "On the Fundamental Differences Between Capitalist and Socialist Regional Territorial-Production Complexes," Vestnik Leningradskogo Univerziteta, No. 6 (1966), pp. 80-87. In translation in Soviet Geography, Vol. VII, No. 7 (September, 1966), p. 61.

8. A. Ye. Probst, "Territorial-Production Complexes in the U. S. S. R.," Geografiya v Shkole, No. 6 (1965), pp. 6-12. In translation in Soviet Geography, Vol. VII, No. 7 (September, 1966), p. 56.

9. Data for 1960 from Paul K. Cook, "The Administration and Distribution of Soviet Industry," in Dimensions of Soviet Economic Power (Studies Prepared for the Joint Economic Committee, 87th Congress, 2nd Session; Washington, D. C.: U. S. Government Printing Office, 1962), pp. 701-33.

10. Ibid.

11. Probst, loc. cit.

12. Ya. Feigin, "On the Study of the Current Problems of Territorial Distribution of Productive Forces," Voprosy Ekonomiki, No. 1 (January, 1960). In translation in Problems of Economics, Vol. III (May, 1960), p. 46.

13. Ibid.

14. J. P. Cole, and F. C. German, A Geography of the U. S. S. R. (London: Butterworths, 1961), pp. 30 and 36.

15. Ibid., p. 30.

16. Raymond Hutchings, "Geographic Influences on Centralization in the Soviet Economy," Soviet Studies, Vol. XVII (January, 1966), p. 286.

17. Ibid.

18. Ibid., p. 287.

19. Ibid., pp. 293-94.

20. *Ibid.*, p. 302.

21. *Ibid.*

22. David J. M. Hooson, *A New Soviet Heartland?* (Princeton, New Jersey: D. Van Nostrand Company, 1964), pp. 124-25.

23. E. Manevich, "The Problem of Rational Utilization of Manpower in the Soviet Union," *Voprosy ekonomiki*, No. 6, 1965. In translation in *Studies on the Soviet Union* (New Series), Vol. V, No. 2 (1965), pp. 90-98.

24. Hooson, *op. cit.*, p. 125.

25. *Ibid.*

26. *Ibid.*

CHAPTER 11 SUMMARY AND CONCLUSION

The purpose of this study has been to describe and analyze the spatial distribution of the industrial workers in the Soviet Union. The change in the regional distribution has been investigated over a period of twenty years in order to discover any patterns exhibited during this time. As a result, this study has graphically presented the regional distribution of Soviet industrial manpower from 1940 to 1960.

Considering the data that have been presented in this study in maps, charts, and tables, it is apparent that only one question has been answered in detail: "Where are the industrial workers located in the Soviet Union?" The next obvious question is "Why are the industrial workers located where they are?" However, some limitations are imposed through the lack of pertinent data. Unfortunately, much of the data needed to make meaningful comparisons are lacking due to the Soviet policy of revealing only selective statistical data on their industrial progress. In addition to industrial employment, other data are needed such as gross industrial output, capital investment in industry, and wages of industrial workers. Also, it would be preferable to have a breakdown for these data by major economic regions and sovnarkhozy, and a breakdown by major industrial branches, and to have all data available for several selected years (1940 and 1960 for the purpose of this study). Since the need for such detailed data remains an unfulfilled wish--expressed not only by this author but by many leading Soviet scholars--it must be regretfully concluded that a complete analysis is impossible at this time. Therefore, the observations and limited conclusions that are given must be accepted as tentative. Nevertheless, this study fills a gap in our knowledge of the Soviet industry and it provides one set of data, until now not readily available, that might prove of value in further studies that will be undertaken when the additional detailed data become available for all the major economic regions and their subdivisions.

By analyzing maps, charts, and tables in Chapters 6 and 7, several observations can be made. During the period 1940-60, the eastern regions marked a relative gain in the number of industrial workers in comparison with the western regions, partly because of war destruction suffered in the western U. S. S. R. during the first three years of conflict. Afterwards, the recovery in the west was much more vigorous than in the eastern regions, and thus the western U. S. S. R. still remains the most important industrial area in the country. On the other hand, the large percentage gains experienced in the eastern U. S. S. R. reflect the smaller industrial base in this area at the beginning of the period in 1940.

The discussion of the five principles of the Soviet locational doctrine indicates that some measure of the "more uniform distribution" of industrial workers has been achieved, especially in machine manufacturing. In addition to a planned implementation of this principle, it must be emphasized that World War II gave the Soviet Union an added impetus to this long-desired industrial shift to the eastern regions. While this shift would have occurred even without a war, it is possible to argue that without the war-induced industrial relocation, the increase in the eastern regions would have been slower and would not have reached the actual 1960 levels until some years later. Also, it should be noted that this shift was in effect less significant as of 1960 than the previous assertions by Soviet geographers and economists claimed it to be.

Finally, the discussion of the industrial structure of the major economic regions and of the fifty selected sovnarkhozy points to the effectiveness of the other three principles of the Soviet locational doctrine: location of industry close to supply sources and consumers, development of underdeveloped areas, and the achievement of regional industrial self-sufficiency. Thus, in addition to the first major conclusion (the actual eastward shift of the Soviet industry as a planned effort, but also partly stimulated by the war), a second major conclusion should be added: The implementation of several principles of the Soviet locational doctrine has resulted in a redistribution of the industrial labor force among the major branches of industry, demonstrating a rising level of economic development in the Soviet Union--both on the national and the regional level.

APPENDIXES

APPENDIX I

LIMITATIONS ON THE STATISTICAL DATA AVAILABLE

Among the gaps in the statistical data for some sovnarkhozy were the figures for the number of industrial-production personnel. These figures were estimated from the available data for the total labor employment in a given sovnarkhoz. Other omissions in the statistical data were the breakdowns of industrial workers by the eight major branches of industry as a per cent of the total number of workers. Several solutions were possible. For all the sovnarkhozy that did not have the breakdowns by industries,[1] the per cent breakdowns for the R. S. F. S. R. as a whole were inserted for both 1940 and 1955. The danger of estimating the probable breakdown for each sovnarkhoz was avoided, and although the resulting figures are far from an ideal solution, the errors are probably more or less uniformly distributed. One consequence of this solution is that the results for individual sovnarkhozy, where the breakdowns were missing, could not be regarded as highly reliable, and therefore the discussion of the pattern of distribution and changes by the eight principal branches of industry is restricted to the level of major economic regions only.

The basic data were compiled for the seventy-nine sovnarkhozy (all the sixty-eight sovnarkhozy of the R. S. F. S. R. plus eleven S. S. R. 's representing one sovnarkhoz each) and the three S. S. R. 's (Ukraine, Kazakh, Uzbek) for which only partial data exist on the sovnarkhoz level. The actual problem of computing and preparing statistical tables to be used as direct sources from which the maps, figures, and tables in this study are prepared, was assigned to an IBM 1620 Data Processing computer. Data cards were punched for each sovnarkhoz and the three S. S. R. 's containing the following information: (a) the number of the *sovnarkhoz* (1-104) for identification purposes; (b) the number of industrial-production personnel (for 1940 and 1955); and (c) the breakdown of workers by industrial branches as per cent figures (1940 and 1955). A computer program was prepared resulting in the following output: industrial workers by *sovnarkhozy* and major economic regions, and industrial workers by eight major branches of industry (1940-55). The output consists of a ten-column table for each *sovnarkhoz* and major economic region (see Table 40): the first column indicates totals, columns 2-9 represent the eight major branches of industry, and column 10 gives the balance (other industries). The first three rows (A) give the actual numbers of industrial workers (1940, 1955, per cent increase or decrease 1940-55); the next two rows (B) give the breakdown of workers as a per cent of the *sovnarkhoz* or region; and the last two rows (C) give the figures for industrial workers as a per cent of the U. S. S. R. total (industrial workers in the *sovnarkhoz* or region as a per cent of all industrial workers in the U. S. S. R.; *sovnarkhoz* workers in a branch of industry as a per cent of all Soviet workers in that industry).

The data for 1960 were obtained from Table 5 in the study of major economic regions by L. N. Telepko.[2] This table required some further calculations and modifications to fill certain gaps. First, the table did not include the regional breakdown for the chemical industry. This was obtained from a table in a study by A. M. Korneyev.[3] Second, the 1963 division into seventeen major economic regions used both in Telepko and Korneyev tables, had to be changed to the fourteen-region scheme as used in this study and the figures had to be adjusted accordingly. For example, Penza *oblast* was part of the Central region during the period 1940-60 but was transferred to the Volga region after 1960. Thus the figures in Telepko and Korneyev tables had to be reduced in the Volga region and correspondingly increased in the Central region to correct for this administrative change. A similar adjustment had to be made in the regions Ural and West Siberia because two *oblasts* (Kurgan and Tyumen) were transferred from West Siberia to the Ural after 1960. The data for the Belorussian and Moldavian S. S. R. 's had to be calculated since they were not given directly in the Telepko table.

TABLE 40

Sample Computer Output: Industrial Workers by Sovnarkhozy--Moscow (City)

		1	2	3	4	5	6	7	8	9	10	
	I	693.8	6.2	26.3	326.8	26.3	6.9	21.5	175.5	49.2	54.8	1940
A	II	910.0	13.6	50.0	423.1	37.3	22.7	28.2	214.7	56.4	63.7	1955
	III	31.1	118.5	89.8	29.4	41.4	227.8	31.1	22.3	14.5	16.2	1940/1955
B	IV	100.0	.9	3.8	47.1	3.8	1.0	3.1	25.3	7.1	7.9	1940
	V	100.0	1.5	5.5	46.5	4.1	2.5	3.1	23.6	6.2	7.0	1955
C	VI	8.1	.9	6.8	13.4	9.9	2.3	1.5	10.1	5.0	14.5	1940
	VII	6.2	1.0	5.9	9.2	7.8	2.6	1.3	8.6	4.2	10.6	1955

Notes: A = the number of industrial workers in thousands: I - in 1940, II - in 1955, III - per cent increase or decrease (indicated by minus sign) 1940-55.

B = breakdown of workers as a per cent of the sovnarkhoz (sovnarkhoz = 100): IV - in 1940, V - in 1955.

C = industrial workers as a per cent of U. S. S. R. total: column 1 = workers in the sovnarkhoz as a per cent of all industrial workers in the U. S. S. R.; columns 2-10 = sovnarkhoz workers in a branch of industry as a per cent of all Soviet workers in that branch, VI - in 1940, VII - in 1955.

Column 1 = totals for the sovnarkhoz (in rows I, II, IV and V only = totals of columns 2-10).

Columns 2-9 = eight major branches of industry:

2 - Energy and Fuel Industries
3 - Heavy Industry
4 - Machine Manufacturing
5 - Chemical Industry
6 - Building Materials Industry
7 - Forest Industries
8 - Light Industry
9 - Food Industry

Column 10 = the balance (other industries) = column 1 less the total of columns 2-9 (in rows I, II, IV, and V only).

Notes to Appendix I

1. *Sovnarkhozy* with missing breakdowns are identified in Appendix II.

2. L. N. Telepko, *Krupnyye ekonomicheskiye raiony SSSR* [*Major Economic Regions of the U. S. S. R.*] (Moscow: Academy of Sciences of the U. S. S. R., Institute of Economics, 1963), p. 97.

3. A. M. Korneyev *et al.* (eds.), *Promyshlennost' v khozyaystvennom komplekse ekonomicheskikh raionov SSSR* [*Industry in the Economic Complex of the Economic Regions of the U. S. S. R.*] (Moscow: Academy of Sciences of the U. S. S. R. Institute of Economics, 1964), p. 142.

APPENDIX II

NUMERICAL LIST OF 104 SOVNARKHOZY (AS OF SEPTEMBER 1, 1958) GROUPED BY MAJOR ECONOMIC REGIONS

Sovnarkhoz Number on Map 33 in Appendix IV	Name of the Sovnarkhoz
	CENTER
1	Moscow City
2	*Moscow Oblast
3	Kalinin
4	Smolensk
5	*Bryansk
6	**Kaluga
7	Tula
8	*Ryazan'
9	*Vladimir
10	Ivanovo
11	Yaroslavl'
12	*Kostroma
13	Kirov
14	**Gor'kiy
15	Tambov
16	Penza
17	Voronezh
18	**Lipetsk
19	Belgorod
20	Kursk
21	Orel
22	Mordva
23	Mari
24	Chuvash
	NORTHWEST
25	Leningrad
26	**Karelian
27	**Murmansk
28	**Kaliningrad

Sovnarkhoz Number on Map 33 in Appendix IV	Name of the Sovnarkhoz
	NORTH
29	Arkhangel'sk
30	Vologda
31	*Komi
	URAL
32	*Sverdlovsk
33	Chelyabinsk
34	*Orenburg (formerly Chkalov)
35	Perm' (formerly Molotov)
36	**Bashkir
37	Udmurt
	VOLGA
38	Tatar
39	*Ul'yanovsk
40	*Kuybyshev
41	Saratov
42	Stalingrad (now Volgograd)
43	*Astrakhan'
	NORTH CAUCASUS
44	Stavropol'
45	Krasnodar
46	*Dagestan
47	North-Ossetian
48	Kabardino-Balkar
49	*Checheno-Ingush
50	Rostov
	WEST SIBERIA
51	Tyumen'
52	*Kurgan

Sovnarkhoz Number on Map 33 in Appendix IV	Name of the Sovnarkhoz
WEST SIBERIA (continued)	
53	*Omsk
54	Novosibirsk
55	Tomsk
56	*Kemerovo
57	Altay
EAST SIBERIA	
58	Krasnoyarsk
59	*Irkutsk
60	**Chita
61	Buryat
62	**Yakut
FAR EAST	
63	Khabarovsk
64	Primorskiy
65	Amur
66	*Sakhalin (Island)
67	**Kamchatka
68	Magadan
SOUTH	
69	Kiyev
70	Khar'kov
71	Stalino (now Donetsk)
72	Lugansk (formerly Voroshilovgrad)
73	Zaporozh'ye
74	Dnepropetrovsk
75	Kherson
76	Odessa
77	Vinnitsa
78	L'vov

Sovnarkhoz Number on Map 33 in Appendix IV	Name of the Sovnarkhoz
SOUTH (continued)	
79	Stanislav (now Ivano-Frankovsk)
80	Moldavian
KAZAKHSTAN	
81	Alma-Ata
82	Southern Kazakhstan
83	Eastern Kazakhstan
84	Semipalatinsk
85	Karaganda
86	Northern Kazakhstan
87	Kustanay
88	Aktyubinsk
89	Gur'yev
CENTRAL ASIA	
90	Tashkent
91	Fergana
92	Samarkand
93	Kara-Kalpak
94	Bukhara
95	Kirgiz
96	Tadzhik
97	Turkmen
TRANS-CAUCASUS	
98	Georgian
99	Azerbaydzhan
100	Armenian
WEST	
101	Belorussian
102	Lithuanian
103	Latvian
104	Estonian

Notes: The R. S. F. S. R. sovnarkhozy with missing breakdowns by industries for 1940 are marked with an asterisk (*) preceding each name. If the breakdowns were missing for both 1940 and 1955 then a double asterisk (**) precedes the name.

The underlined sovnarkhozy have gone through territorial changes between 1955 and 1958 and thus their statistical data for 1940 and 1955 had to be modified and recalculated to conform to their 1958 boundaries as shown on Map 33.

The following territorial shifts of internal administrative boundaries should be noted especially:

1. Former Velikolukskaya (Velikiye Luki) oblast has been divided between two oblasts: c. 52 per cent of the population and employment to Leningrad sovnarkhoz (that part of Velikiye Luki oblast incorporated into Pskov oblast, which is part of Leningrad sovnarkhoz); and c. 48 per cent of the population and employment to Kalinin oblast.

2. Gor'kiy oblast incorporates the former Arzamas oblast.

3. Former Balashov oblast has been divided between three oblasts: c. 40 per cent of the population and employment to Saratov oblast, c. 30 per cent of the population and employment to Stalingrad (now Volgograd) oblast, and c. 30 per cent of the population and employment to Voronezh oblast.

4. Rostov oblast incorporates the former Kamenskaya (Kamensk) oblast.

5. Tuva A. S. S. R., although officially outside the sovnarkhoz system, is included as part of Krasnoyarsk kray.

APPENDIX III

ALPHABETICAL LIST OF 104 SOVNARKHOZY (AS OF SEPTEMBER 1, 1958)

Sovnarkhoz Number on Map 33 in Appendix IV	Name of the Sovnarkhoz
88	Aktyubinsk
81	Alma-Ata
57	Altay
65	Amur
29	Arkhangel'sk
100	Armenian
43	Astrakhan'
99	Azerbaydzhan
36	Bashkir
19	Belgorod
101	Belorussian
5	Bryansk
94	Bukhara
61	Buryat
49	Checheno-Ingush
33	Chelyabinsk
60	Chita
24	Chuvash
46	Dagestan
74	Dnepropetrovsk
83	Eastern Kazakhstan
104	Estonian
91	Fergana
98	Georgian
14	Gor'kiy
89	Gur'yev
59	Irkutsk
10	Ivanovo
48	Kabardino-Balkar
3	Kalinin
28	Kaliningrad
6	Kaluga
67	Kamchatka
85	Karaganda
93	Kara-Kalpak

Sovnarkhoz Number on Map 33 in Appendix IV	Name of the Sovnarkhoz
26	Karelian
56	Kemerovo
63	Khabarovsk
70	Khar'kov
75	Kherson
95	Kirgiz
13	Kirov
69	Kiyev
31	Komi
12	Kostroma
45	Krasnodar
58	Krasnoyarsk
52	Kurgan
20	Kursk
87	Kustanay
40	Kuybyshev
103	Latvian
25	Leningrad
18	Lipetsk
102	Lithuanian
72	Lugansk (formerly Voroshilovgrad)
78	L'vov
68	Magadan
23	Mari
80	Moldavian
22	Mordva
1	Moscow City
2	Moscow *Oblast*
27	Murmansk
86	Northern Kazakhstan
47	North-Ossetian
54	Novosibirsk
76	Odessa
53	Omsk
21	Orel
34	Orenburg (formerly Chkalov)
16	Penza
35	Perm' (formerly Molotov)

Sovnarkhoz Number on Map 33 in Appendix IV	Name of the Sovnarkhoz
64	Primorskiy
50	Rostov
8	Ryazan'
66	Sakhalin (Island)
92	Samarkand
41	Saratov
84	Semipalatinsk
4	Smolensk
82	Southern Kazakhstan
42	Stalingrad (now Volgograd)
71	Stalino (now Donetsk)
79	Stanislav (now Ivano-Frankovsk)
44	Stavropol'
32	Sverdlovsk
96	Tadzhik
15	Tambov
90	Tashkent
38	Tatar
55	Tomsk
7	Tula
97	Turkmen
51	Tyumen'
37	Udmurt
39	Ul'yanovsk
77	Vinnitsa
9	Vladimir
30	Vologda
17	Voronezh
62	Yakut
11	Yaroslavl'
73	Zaporozh'ye

APPENDIX IV

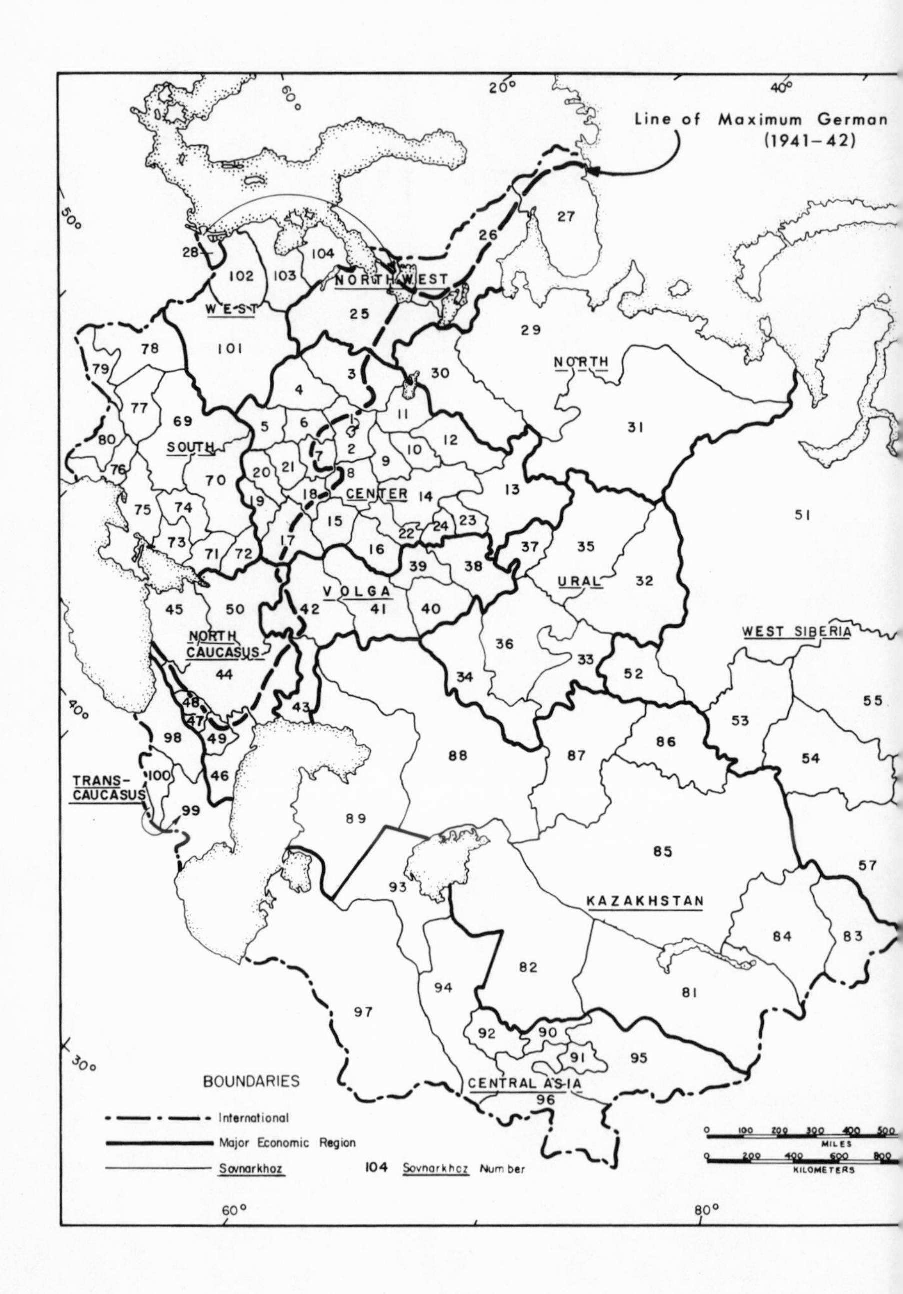

Line of Maximum German
(1941–42)
NORTH WEST
WEST
NORTH
SOUTH
CENTER
URAL
VOLGA
NORTH CAUCASUS
WEST SIBERIA
TRANS-CAUCASUS
KAZAKHSTAN
CENTRAL ASIA
BOUNDARIES
International
Major Economic Region
Sovnarkhoz
104 Sovnarkhoz Number
MILES
KILOMETERS

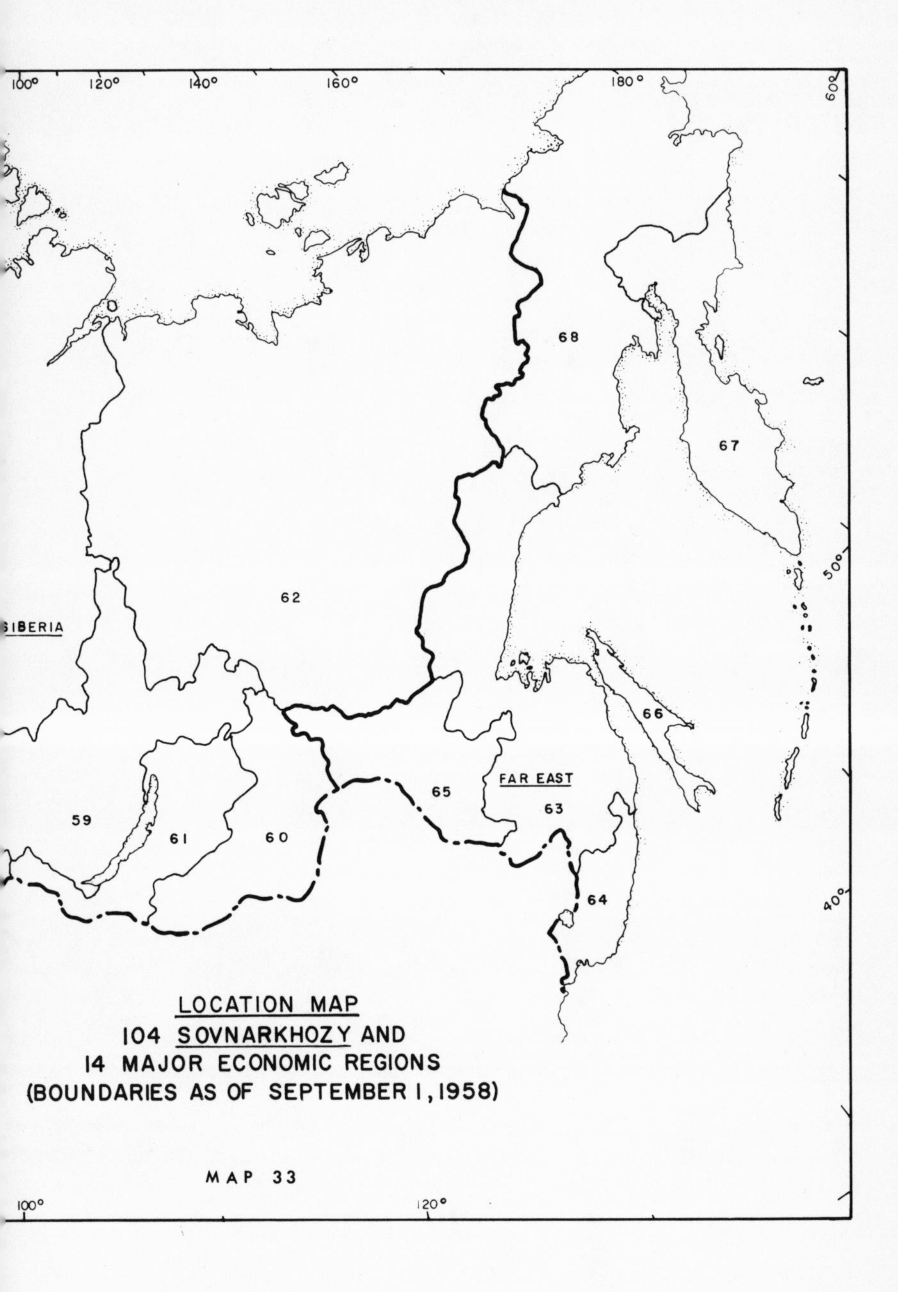
100°
120°
140°
160°
180°
60°
50°
40°
100°
120°
SIBERIA
FAR EAST
59
60
61
62
63
64
65
66
67
68
LOCATION MAP
104 SOVNARKHOZY AND
14 MAJOR ECONOMIC REGIONS
(BOUNDARIES AS OF SEPTEMBER 1, 1958)
MAP 33

APPENDIX V

EXPLANATION OF THE LOCATION QUOTIENT

According to John Alexander:

> The location quotient measures the degree to which a specific region has more or less than its share of any particular industry.
>
> . . . .
>
> A location quotient of 1. 0 means that a region has neither more nor less of the national industry than its overall volume of manufacturing would suggest. A quotient over 1. 0 indicates a high particular concentration in that locality, relative to local industrial development. A quotient less than 1. 0 suggests that an industry is less developed in that region than is manufacturing in general.[1]

Note to Appendix V

1. John W. Alexander, Economic Geography (Englewood Cliffs, New Jersey: Prentice-Hall, 1963), pp. 406-7 and 594-95. It should be also noted that the location quotient can never be less than zero.

BIBLIOGRAPHY

BIBLIOGRAPHY

Books and Periodicals

Agafonov, N. T., and Lavrov, S. B. "On the Fundamental Differences Between Capitalist and Socialist Regional Territorial-Production Complexes," Vestnik Leningradskogo Univerziteta, No. 6 (1966), pp. 80-87. In translation in Soviet Geography, Vol. VII, No. 7 (September, 1966), pp. 56-65.

Alexander, John W. Economic Geography. Englewood Cliffs, New Jersey: Prentice-Hall, 1963.

Ballis, William B. "Political Implications of Recent Soviet Economic Reorganizations," The Review of Politics, Vol. XXIII, No. 2 (April, 1961), pp. 153-71.

Balzak, S. S., Vasyutin, V. F., and Feigin, Ya. G. Economic Geography of the U. S. S. R. Translated by Robert M. Hanklin and Olga Adler Titelbaum. New York: Macmillan, 1952.

Baransky, N. N. Economic Geography of the U. S. S. R. Moscow: Foreign Languages Publishing House, 1956.

Campbell, Robert W. "Research on the Soviet Economy--Achievements and Prospects," in Study of the Soviet Economy ("Indiana University Publications: Russian and East European Series," Volume 25; Bloomington, Indiana: Indiana University, 1961), pp. 129-43.

Cole, J. P., and German, F. C. A Geography of the U. S. S. R. London: Butterworths, 1961.

Cook, Paul K. "The Administration and Distribution of Soviet Industry," in Dimensions of Soviet Economic Power (Studies Prepared for the Joint Economic Committee, 87th Congress, 2nd Session; Washington, D. C.: U. S. Government Printing Office, 1962), pp. 181-210.

Daukas, Anthony J. "Machine Tool Production in the United States and U. S. S. R.," in Dimensions of Soviet Economic Power (Studies Prepared for the Joint Economic Committee, 87th Congress, 2nd Session; Washington, D. C.: U. S. Government Printing Office, 1962), pp. 163-80.

Esposito, Colonel Vincent J. (ed.). The West Point Atlas of American Wars. Vol. II: 1900-1953. New York: Frederick A. Praeger, 1959.

Feigin, Ya. (ed.). Osobennosti i faktory razmeshcheniya otrasley narodnogo khozyaystva SSSR [Aspects and Factors of the Distribution of the Branches of the National Economy of the U. S. S. R.]. Moscow: Academy of Sciences of the U. S. S. R., Institute of Economics, 1960.

Feigin, Ya. "On the Study of the Current Problems of Territorial Distribution of Productive Forces," Voprosy Ekonomiki, No. 1 (January, 1960). In translation in Problems of Economics, Vol. III (May, 1960), pp. 43-47, and 62.

Fryer, D. W. World Economic Development. New York: McGraw-Hill Book Company, 1965.

Hooson, David J. M. A New Soviet Heartland? Princeton, New Jersey: D. Van Nostrand Company, 1964.

Hoyt, John Stanley, Jr. "An Investigation of the Economics of Soviet Locational Doctrine, Policy, and Practice--With Special Emphasis on Heavy Industry." Unpublished Ph. D. dissertation, Department of Economics, The American University, 1959.

Hutchings, Raymond. "Geographic Influences on Centralization in the Soviet Economy," Soviet Studies, Vol. XVII (January, 1966), pp. 286-302.

Klimenko, K. "The Development of Soviet Machine Building," Voprosy Ekonomiki (March, 1958). In translation in Problems of Economics, Vol. I, No. 5 (September, 1958), pp. 50-56.

Korneyev, A. M., et al. (eds.). Promyshlennost' v khozyaystvennom komplekse ekonomicheskikh raionov SSSR [Industry in the Economic Complex of the Economic Regions of the U. S. S. R.]. Moscow: Academy of Sciences of the U. S. S. R., Institute of Economics, 1964.

Livshits, R. S. Ocherki po razmeshcheniya promyshlennosti SSSR [Outline of the Distribution of U. S. S. R. Industry]. Moscow, 1954.

Lonsdale, Richard E., and Thompson, John H. "A Map of the U. S. S. R.'s Manufacturing," Economic Geography, Vol. 36, No. 1 (January, 1960), pp. 36-52.

Lorimer, Frank. The Population of the Soviet Union: History and Prospects. "Series of League of Nations Publications," Vol. II: Economic and Financial (1946: II. A. 3). Geneva: League of Nations, 1946.

Lydolph, Paul E. Geography of the U. S. S. R. New York: John Wiley and Sons, 1964.

Manevich, E. "The Problem of Rational Utilization of Manpower in the Soviet Union," Voprosy ekonomiki, No. 6, 1965. In translation in Studies on the Soviet Union (New Series), Vol. V, No. 2 (1965), pp. 90-98.

Matley, Ian Murray. "The Soviet Approach to Geography." Unpublished Ph. D. dissertation, Department of Geography, The University of Michigan, 1961.

Miller, E. Willard. A Geography of Manufacturing. Englewood Cliffs, New Jersey: Prentice Hall, 1962.

Nove, Alec. The Soviet Economy. New York: Frederick A. Praeger, 1961.

Nutter, G. Warren. Growth of Industrial Production in the Soviet Union. Princeton, New Jersey: Princeton University Press, 1962.

Omarovskiy, A. G. "Changes in the Geography of Machine Building in the U. S. S. R.," Soviet Geography, Vol. I, No. 3 (March, 1960), pp. 42-56.

Probst, A. Ye. "Territorial-Production Complexes in the U. S. S. R.," Geografiya v Shkole, No. 6 (1965), pp. 6-12. In translation in Soviet Geography, Vol. VII, No. 7 (September, 1966), pp. 47-56.

Saushkin, Yu. G. "A History of Soviet Economic Geography," in Ekonomicheskaya Geografiya v SSSR [Economic Geography in the U. S. S. R.], edited by N. N. Baransky, N. P. Nikitin, V. V. Pokshishevsky, and Yu. G. Saushkin Moscow: Prosveshcheniye, 1965, pp. 54-172. In translation in Soviet Geography, Vol. VII, No. 8 (October, 1966), pp. 3-104.

Shimkin, Demitri B. The Soviet Mineral-Fuels Industries, 1928-1958: A Statistical Survey. U. S. Bureau of the Census, International Population Statistics Reports, Series P-90, No. 19. Washington, D. C.: U. S. Government Printing Office, 1962.

Telepko, L. N. Krupnyye ekonomicheskiye raiony SSSR [Major Economic Regions of the U. S. S. R.]. Moscow: Academy of Sciences of the U. S. S. R., Institute of Economics, 1963.

Voznesensky, Nikolai A. The Economy of the U. S. S. R. During World War II. Washington, D. C.: Public Affairs Press, 1948.

Werth, Alexander. Russia at War 1941-1945. New York: E. P. Dutton and Company, 1964.

U. S. Bureau of the Census. United States Census of Manufactures, 1954. Vol. I: Summary Statistics. Washington, D. C.: U. S. Government Printing Office, 1957.

Soviet Statistical Handbooks

(A)--U. S. S. R. as a Whole

U. S. S. R. Tsentral'noye statisticheskoye upravleniye SSSR [Central Statistical Board of the U. S. S. R.]. Narodnoye khozyaystvo SSSR [National Economy of the U. S. S. R.]. Moscow, 1956.

________. Narodnoye khozyaystvo SSSR v 1956 godu [National Economy of the U. S. S. R. in 1956]. Moscow, 1957.

________. Narodnoye khozyaystvo SSSR v 1958 godu. Moscow, 1959.

________. Narodnoye khozyaystvo SSSR v 1959 godu. Moscow, 1960.

________. Narodnoye khozyaystvo SSSR v 1960 godu. Moscow, 1961.

________. Itogi vsesoyuznoy perepisi naseleniya 1959 goda--SSSR (Svodniy tom) [Results of All-Union Census of 1959--U. S. S. R. (Summary Volume)]. Moscow, 1962.

________. Narodnoye khozyaystvo SSSR v 1961 godu. Moscow, 1962.

________. Narodnoye khozyaystvo SSSR v 1962 godu. Moscow, 1963.

________. Narodnoye khozyaystvo SSSR v 1963 godu. Moscow, 1965.

________. Narodnoye khozyaystvo SSSR v 1964 godu. Moscow, 1965.

________. Promyshlennost' SSSR [U. S. S. R. Industry]. Moscow, 1957.

(B)--R. S. F. S. R. as a Whole

U. S. S. R. Tsentral'noye statisticheskoye upravleniye RSFSR. Narodnoye khozyaystvo RSFSR. Moscow, 1957.

________. Narodnoye khozyaystvo RSFSR v 1958 godu. Moscow, 1959.

________. Narodnoye khozyaystvo RSFSR v 1959 godu. Moscow, 1960.

________. Narodnoye khozyaystvo RSFSR v 1960 godu. Moscow, 1961.

________. Narodnoye khozyaystvo RSFSR v 1961 godu. Moscow, 1962.

________. Narodnoye khozyaystvo RSFSR v 1962 godu. Moscow, 1963.

________. Narodnoye khozyaystvo RSFSR v 1963 godu. Moscow, 1965.

________. Narodnoye khozyaystvo RSFSR v 1964 godu. Moscow, 1965.

(C)--Regional Handbooks and R. S. F. S. R. Administrative Divisions

CENTER

U. S. S. R. Tsentral'noye statisticheskoye upravleniye SSSR. Narodnoye khozyaystvo Belgorodskoy oblasti [National Economy of the Belgorod oblast]. 1957.

________. Narodnoye khozyaystvo Bryanskoy oblasti. 1957.

________. Narodnoye khozyaystvo Chuvashskoy oblasti. 1960.

________. Narodnoye khozyaystvo Gorkovskoy oblasti. 1960.

________. Narodnoye khozyaystvo Ivanovskoy oblasti. 1957.

________. Narodnoye khozyaystvo Kalininskoy oblasti. 1961.

________. Narodnoye khozyaystvo Kaluzhskoy oblasti. 1957.

________. Narodnoye khozyaystvo Kirovskoy oblasti. 1960.

________. Narodnoye khozyaystvo Kostromskoy oblasti. 1956.

________. Narodnoye khozyaystvo Kurskoy oblasti. 1958.

________. Narodnoye khozyaystvo Lipetskoy oblasti. 1959.

________. Narodnoye khozyaystvo Mariiskoy ASSR. 1960.

________. Narodnoye khozyaystvo Mordovskoy ASSR. 1958.

________. Narodnoye khozyaystvo Moskovskoy oblasti. 1958.

________. Narodnoye khozyaystvo Orlovskoy oblasti. 1960.

________. Narodnoye khozyaystvo Penzenskoy oblasti. 1958.

________. Narodnoye khozyaystvo Ryazanskoy oblasti. 1958.

________. Narodnoye khozyaystvo Smolenskoy oblasti. 1958.

________. Narodnoye khozyaystvo Tambovskoy oblasti. 1957.

________. Narodnoye khozyaystvo Tulskoy oblasti. 1958.

________. Narodnoye khozyaystvo Vladimirskoy oblasti. 1958.

________. Narodnoye khozyaystvo Voronezhskoy oblasti. 1957.

________. Narodnoye khozyaystvo Yaroslavskoy oblasti. 1957.

NORTHWEST

________. Narodnoye khozyaystvo goroda Leningrada. 1957.

________. Narodnoye khozyaystvo Karelskoy ASSR. 1957.

________. Narodnoye khozyaystvo Leningradskoy oblasti. 1957.

________. *Narodnoye khozyaystvo Murmanskoy oblasti.* 1957.

________. *Narodnoye khozyaystvo Novgorodskoy oblasti.* 1958.

________. *Narodnoye khozyaystvo Pskovskoy oblasti.* 1960.

________. *Narodnoye khozyaystvo Velikolukskoy oblasti.* 1957.

NORTH

________. *Narodnoye khozyaystvo Arkhangelskoy oblasti.* 1962.

________. *Narodnoye khozyaystvo Komi ASSR.* 1961.

________. *Narodnoye khozyaystvo Vologodskoy oblasti.* 1961.

URAL

________. *Narodnoye khozyaystvo Bashkirskoy ASSR.* 1959.

________. *Narodnoye khozyaystvo Chelyabinskoy oblasti.* 1961.

________. *Narodnoye khozyaystvo Chkalovskoy oblasti.* 1957.

________. *Narodnoye khozyaystvo Molotovskoy oblasti.* 1957.

________. *Narodnoye khozyaystvo Permskoy oblasti.* 1961.

________. *Narodnoye khozyaystvo Sverdlovskoy oblasti i goroda Sverdlovska.* 1956.

________. *Narodnoye khozyaystvo Udmurtskoy ASSR.* 1960.

________. *Orenburgskaya oblast za 25 let.* 1960.

VOLGA

________. *Narodnoye khozyaystvo Astrakhanskoy oblasti.* 1958.

________. *Narodnoye khozyaystvo Kuybyshevskoy oblasti i goroda Kuybysheva.* 1960.

________. *Narodnoye khozyaystvo Saratovskoy oblasti.* 1962.

________. Narodnoye khozyaystvo Stalingradskoy oblasti. 1957.

________. Narodnoye khozyaystvo Tatarskoy ASSR. 1960.

________. Narodnoye khozyaystvo Ulyanovskoy oblasti. 1957.

________. Narodnoye khozyaystvo Volgogradskoy oblasti. 1962.

NORTH CAUCASUS

________. Narodnoye khozyaystvo Adygeyskoy avtonomnoy oblasti. 1957.

________. Narodnoye khozyaystvo Checheno-Ingushskoy ASSR. 1960.

________. Narodnoye khozyaystvo Dagestanskoy ASSR. 1960.

________. Narodnoye khozyaystvo Kabardino-Balkarskoy ASSR. 1957.

________. Narodnoye khozyaystvo Kalmytskoy ASSR. 1960.

________. Narodnoye khozyaystvo Krasnodarskovo kraya. 1958.

________. Narodnoye khozyaystvo Rostovskoy oblasti. 1961.

________. Narodnoye khozyaystvo Severo-Osetinskoy ASSR. 1958.

________. Narodnoye khozyaystvo Stavropolskova kraya. 1959.

WEST SIBERIA

________. Narodnoye khozyaystvo Altayskovo kraya. 1957.

________. Narodnoye khozyaystvo Kemerovskoy oblasti. 1958.

________. Narodnoye khozyaystvo Kurganskoy oblasti. 1957.

________. Narodnoye khozyaystvo Novosibirskoy oblasti. 1957.

________. Narodnoye khozyaystvo Omskoy oblasti i goroda Omska. 1957.

________. *Narodnoye khozyaystvo Tomskoy oblasti*. 1957.

________. *Narodnoye khozyaystvo Tyumenskoy oblasti*. 1958.

EAST SIBERIA

________. *Narodnoye khozyaystvo Buryat-Mongolskoy ASSR*. 1957.

________. *Narodnoye khozyaystvo Chitinskoy oblasti*. 1960.

________. *Narodnoye khozyaystvo Irkutskoy oblasti*. 1962.

________. *Narodnoye khozyaystvo Krasnoyarskovo kraya*. 1958.

________. *Narodnoye khozyaystvo Tuvinskoy ASSR*. 1962.

________. *Razvitiye otrasley narodnovo khozyaystva Irkutskoy oblasti*. 1957.

FAR EAST

________. *Narodnoye khozyaystvo Amurskoy oblasti*. 1957.

________. *Narodnoye khozyaystvo Khabarovskovo kraya*. 1957.

________. *Narodnoye khozyaystvo Magadanskoy oblasti*. 1960.

________. *Narodnoye khozyaystvo Primorskovo kraya*. 1958.

________. *Narodnoye khozyaystvo Sakhalinskoy oblasti*. 1960.

(D)--Union Republics

ARMENIAN S. S. R.

________. *Narodnoye khozyaystvo Armyanskoy SSR*. 1957.

AZERBAYDZHAN S. S. R.

________. *Narodnoye khozyaystvo Azerbaydzhanskoy SSR*. 195

BELORUSSIAN S. S. R.

________. Narodnoye khozyaystvo Belorusskoy SSR. 1957.

ESTONIAN S. S. R.

________. Narodnoye khozyaystvo Estonskoy SSR. 1957.

GEORGIAN S. S. R.

________. Narodnoye khozyaystvo Gruzinskoy SSR. 1957.

KAZAKH S. S. R.

________. Narodnoye khozyaystvo Kazakhskoy SSR. 1957.

KIRGIZ S. S. R.

________. Narodnoye khozyaystvo Kirgizskoy SSR. 1957.

LATVIAN S. S. R.

________. Narodnoye khozyaystvo Latviyskoy SSR. 1957.

LITHUANIAN S. S. R.

________. Narodnoye khozyaystvo Litovskoy SSR. 1957.

MOLDAVIAN S. S. R.

________. Narodnoye khozyaystvo Moldavskoy SSR. 1957.

TADZHIK S. S. R.

________. Narodnoye khozyaystvo Tadzhikskoy SSR. 1957.

TURKMEN S. S. R.

________. Narodnoye khozyaystvo Turkmenskoy SSR. 1957.

UKRAINIAN S. S. R.

________. Narodnoye khozyaystvo Ukrainskoy SSR. 1957.

________. *Narodnoye khozyaystvo Ukrainskoy SSR v 1959 godu.* 1960.

________. *Narodnoye khozyaystvo Ukrainskoy SSR v 1960 godu.* 1961.

________. *Narodnoye khozyaystvo Ukrainskoy SSR v 1961 godu.* 1962.

UZBEK S. S. R.

________. *Narodnoye khozyaystvo Uzbekskoy SSR.* 1957.

Note: Most handbooks for the S. S. R. 's are published by the Central Statistical Board of the respective union republic, although some are published by the U. S. S. R. Central Statistical Board.

Almost all regional handbooks (*oblast*, *kray*, A. S. S. R.) in the R. S. F. S. R. are published in Moscow.

ABOUT THE AUTHOR

Emilo J. Stanley was graduated from the University of Michigan where he also received his M. A. and Ph. D. in Geography. He was Assistant Professor of Geography at Beloit College, Pitzer College, and Claremont Graduate School. After completing extensive research on the economic geography of the Soviet Union, he served as a consultant to the Bureau of the Census, Foreign Demographic Analysis Division, in Washington, D. C., advising the U. S. Government on improving the methods of estimating the geographical distribution of Soviet gross industrial output.

At present Dr. Stanley is Project Director of the Computer-Assisted Education Curriculum Program being developed at the University of California, Irvine, for the National Center for Air Pollution Control in Washington, D. C.